Critical Issues
in
Electronic Media

SUNY Series in Film History and Theory
Maureen Turim, editor

Critical Issues
in
Electronic Media

edited by
Simon Penny

Breaut

STATE UNIVERSITY OF NEW YORK PRESS

Published by
State University of New York Press

© 1995 State University of New York

For information, address the State University of New York Press,
State University Plaza, Albany, NY 12246

Production by Bernadine Dawes
Marketing by Theresa Abad Swierzowski

Library of Congress Cataloging-in-Publication Data

Critical issues in electonic media / edited by Simon Penny.
        p.   cm. — (SUNY series in film history and theory)
    Includes bibliographical references and index.
    ISBN 0-7914-2317-4 (hc). — ISBN 0-7914-2318-2 (pb : acid-free paper).
        1. Video art. 2. Computer art. 3. Interactive media. I. Penny, Simon. II. Series.
    N6494.V53C75   1995
    306.4'7—dc20

                                                94-30826
                                                CIP

1 2 3 4 5 6 7 8 9 10

CONTENTS

INTRODUCTION

It would be difficult to refute the suggestion that technological change has been *the* major force for cultural change for at least a century. As we move out of the first technological era, that of industrial production, into the era of the digital, a profound warping and rifting occurs across the cultural surface. This collection seeks to sketch the changing topology of culture as it enters electronic space, and to specifically addresses questions of art practice in that space.

Electronic technology mediates our relation to the world. Although this book is outwardly a traditional object, it, like virtually all others produced in the last decade, was electronically designed, electronically typeset, and printed by computer-controlled machinery. The text was been formulated and edited on digital word processors and the contributors communicated through fax and e-mail networks. None of this technology existed a generation ago.

Since Sputnik, the planet has become wrapped in a blanket of electronic communications, the "datasphere," facilitated by satellite and fiber-optic links between computer "nodes." International satellite data communications and TV broadcast networks have completely re-organized the flow of information, inter- and intrastate. As long ago as the L.A. Olympics, press photographs were shot on still-video cameras, beamed via satellite to Japan, and distributed back over international press networks for appearance in L.A. newspapers. This transformation has been so rapid and so total that few areas of Western life are untouched by it.

The electronic mediascape is about to go through another resounding change of state. Telephone, computer networks, television, and interactive gaming will be digital, and thus connectable. The exponential growth of digital network communications has sent computer companies, cable TV companies, networks and telephone companies all scrambling for a piece of the interactive TV action.

The "information superhighway" looks poised to become a gargantuan virtual mall.

The pace of these changes is itself causing cultural dislocation. Between the time this anthology was conceived and the time of publication, some technologies that were major have become obsolete and others that two years ago were high end research tools have become consumer commodities. In 1990 at the SIGGRAPH conference and elsewhere, virtual reality came out of the research closet. Four years later, Sega released its domestic computer game VR interface. Cultural changes follow these technological changes. Who, in 1990, could have predicted that, under the influence of the rapid growth of the videogame industry, Hollywood would be imploding in 1994.

We have heard for twenty years that the electronic revolution will be as resounding as the industrial one. But we are only now moving beyond the techno-utopian rhetoric to understand the nature of this revolution. We can begin to assess who benefits and who suffers. The entire global economic structure is going through a change of state. The state we have occupied for 150 years is the system of centralized industrial production that consumes raw materials supplied by (economic) colonies. The new and quite unfamiliar state is transnational commodity capitalism, enabled by instantaneous, space-collapsing communication of electronic data, especially financial data. The goods which are produced in this system, and the channels by which the goods are marketed and controlled, are made possible by precisely the technologies that also make possible the practice of electronic media arts. Thus, a condition of esthetic distantiation is untenable for practitioners in electronic media arts. The advent of consumer electronics and software complicates both the esthetics and the politics of art production, by implicating artists as both producers and consumers of technological commodities.

Systems of communication and structures of power have changed; yet the worldviews and critical systems that operate in many of our institutions are pre-electronic, and often pre-industrial; the traditional art-historical methodologies are a case in point. Prior to the infiltration of postmodern theory and media theory, art history was without the tools to cope with multiplicity. How could such critical systems have any application to an aesthetic product that is created untouched by human hands, distributed at light speed as electromagnetic fields or bounced off satellites outside the earth's atmosphere, and decoded by electronic receiver units in a million homes simultaneously, only to evaporate one thirtieth of a second later?

Scientistic critical systems seem also to have played out their usefulness in the cultural arena. Many aspects of twentieth-century culture have come under the influence of scientific fashion. In art, modernism followed a trajectory of reductivism. It has been argued that computer graphics is the last refuge of modernism, and certainly the "art and technology movement" of the late 60s and 70s subscribed to a scientistic approach. But the wave of new critical theory of the 80s, particularly feminist and deconstructive theory, and the acceptance of computer-based 'inductive' proofs and simulations have weakened the claims of science to be objective and true, to be a "master discourse."

Neither the traditionally "artistic" nor the "technological" critical systems, nor a counterposing of the two, are adequate for our present historical moment. Critical systems that have evolved to deal with disciplines immersed in older technologies will not be adequate to the new task. Art practice with electronic tools must necessarily be interdisciplinary, and from this interdisciplinary approach will emerge a variety of relevant and useful critical tools.

This anthology is a response to these conditions. The new digital media promise new territories for artistic practice. But they demand a reconsideration of art production and consumption. The new dimensions and capabilities of the new forms (interactivity, instantaneous multiple distribution, ephemerality) demand the generation of new aesthetic models, new ethical models, new institutions . . . and new conventions of consumption.

In an electronic environment immersed in new versions and appropriations of cultural icons and images, the entire question of intellectual property must be reconsidered. Pre-electronic cultural ideas like "plagiarism" and "fakes," and the value systems attached to them, conflict with media designed specifically for precise rapid copying: videotape, photocopying, and, par excellance, computer media. Digital technology, applied to texts, images, and music, has spawned new genres of appropriative creative practice and has simultaneously thrown the copyright/intellectual property law into paroxysms of confusion.

Desert Storm was a cultural/technological threshold, throwing into high relief many of the aspects of this new electronic terrrain. At this moment art, dataspace, mass media, and politics are sandwiched together into a new complex; its site is neither the Middle East, the living rooms of America, nor deep in electronic space, but a combination of the three. This was not simply because the consumer media was full of synthetic imagery, nor just because geography was fully collapsed, but because the techno-utopian rhetoric of the previous generation was collapsed. Desert Storm demonstrated that greater (electronic) connectivity does not neccessarily result in greater world harmony, democracy and liberty.

It has been my goal in this collection to include authors of diverse training and experience. Represented are Australian, British, Canadian, Finnish, and German authors, as well as several from the USA. Professionally, they come from varied backgrounds, including computer graphics, video, sound, drama, and the visual arts; they are involved with media, cultural and literary theory, and the social sciences. But all share a common concern with the cultural implications of current technological change and have strong interests in interdisciplinary creative practice. Each author in this collection takes a different focus. Some essays are specialized, some are wide-ranging, some are pragmatic, some are more theoretical. Some consider the contemporary condition in its historical context, while others look to the future from the vantage point of the present.

These papers do not form a theoretically coherent group. The authors bring various theoretical systems to bear upon the issues they address. This divergence serves to indicate the breadth of interdisciplinary approaches that are informing the interpretation and use of these new media. Those writers who are artists grapple directly with these issues as they negotiate the use of new technologies in their work. I believe that this immediate connection of theory and practice affords these writings special relevance, and not simply to readers who may be practitioners. These papers are "reports from the front"; they come long before the possibility and security of historical distance.

Critical Issues in Electronic Media is an attempt to discuss the techno-cultural context that makes electronic media artwork both possible and necessary. The original impetus for this volume was the recognition that theoretical writings in the field of electronic media art practice were sparse, while neighboring territories such as video, film, media theory, and cultural studies were replete with such texts.

It is hoped this collection offers, if not a guide, at least a network of markers for practitioners, theoreticians, and students in this new territory. It is with pleasure and pride that I recommend each of these essays to the reader. As an added service to the researcher, I have compiled, with the assistance of the contributors, a selected bibliography of important texts in the field. This bibliography does not claim to be exhaustive, but each entry is regarded by at least one of the contributors as a valuable text.

I would like to thank Clay Morgan and Maureen Turim for guidance in the preparation of this anthology, and I would like to thank the contributors to the volume for going through this process with me. I would like to thank my wife, Mariá Fernández, for endlessly challenging conversation on these topics. Some of my best ideas are hers. Finally, I would like to dedicate this publication to the memories of two thinkers who, each in his own way, have profoundly influenced my development in these areas: Brian O'Nolan (Flann O'Brien) and Felix Guattari.

1

Suck on This, Planet of Noise!

McKenzie Wark

> We are no-one.
> Just whites,
> marooned in the East
> by history.
>
> —David Ireland

> Hell is truth seen too late.
>
> —G. W. F. Hegel

What do I know?

There is quite a particular view of culture and the world that comes with growing up by the sea. Since this is an essay about how media technologies have remade the surface of the world in general and about how we can grasp this from a particular vantage point, it seems appropriate to start by the sea.

In the house I grew up in, a model ship took pride of place on the mantel. It was a model of the Cutty Sark, one of the greatest of the clipper ships. To most people, the name means nothing but a brand of whiskey now.

I went to China once. I went to the Shanghai museum to look at the classical paintings. There's not much to see there, but there is a model of the Cutty Sark. Its famous record-breaking run was from my hometown of Newcastle, on the east coast of Australia, to Shanghai, China.

I still live by the sea, in Ultimo in Sydney, just behind all of the old abandoned wool stores that keep mysteriously burning down before artists can get their hands on them. They are relics of a lost economy and a fading culture, but even more they are the residues of a regime of power now surpassed. A new regime of power has taken hold of the byways of the planet—a regime not of sea-lanes and ship lore, but of comsats and data flows. We live now, as Manuel Castells says, not in a space of places but in a space of flows.[1]

Electronic art is potentially a medium for critical reflection on this new space, but is more often merely symptomatic of it. We need to know what regimes of power it partakes of, so we can consider it critically useful as art rather than merely decorative, interesting, or career enhancing for those concerned. This is a task for a kind of critical framing that, in this case, tries to find some resonance still in the idea of the local. We are not a "global village" yet, and may never be, so for the time being I prefer to consider how the new relations of media globalization can be thought from Ultimo in Sydney, Australia, rather than continue to traffic in received ideas approved in New York and Los Angeles.

You see some strange things from Ultimo—like a great flock of sailing ships, gliding through the bays. Ultimo was a good place from which to watch the symbolic passing, on 26 January 1988, from the naval regime of power to a new matrix of vectors. It was a strange experience, watching those sailing ships simultaneously entering Sydney harbor and entering my living room—and many thousands of others via the live TV broadcast. It was a reenactment of the white invasion of the Australian continent, performed two hundred years later for the cameras. As with the arrival of the first fleet, on this second coming the invaders parked their boats and thanked their sponsors.

Paul Virilio asks: "When we can go to the antipodes and back in an instant, what will become of us?"[2] This question fruitfully combines a temporal and a spatial problem about our experience of everyday life. The temporal dimension is: What are these times we are living in? The spatial dimension is: What space is this that makes us what we are? I think the answer on both counts must come from the antipodes. Australia is only one of the antipodes in the regime of spatial relations, but an interesting one. In his video work *Night's High Noon: An Anti-Terrain* (1988), Peter Callas shows an image of an Aboriginal standing on the beach, watching the first fleet arrive. Cut to an image of the same headland, some time later. A white figure stands on the beach, watching a mushroom cloud rise on the horizon. Callas manages to portray a place that is always in a relation to an elsewhere, that is always defined by its relation to a powerful other. First the British came and colonized. Then the Americans came and coca-colonized. This is that place. We are no one, whoever we are, always oscillating in antipodality with elsewheres. This is one of the necessary conditions, for most of us, of making art or criticism in Australia. That is a condition that even electronic art can only transcend by acknowledging it.

To talk about antipodes is to talk very centrally about the regimes of technology via which the West created its relation to its antipodes. These relations now have a life of their own. This is why I want to talk about what Raymond Williams called emergent, as opposed to dominant and residual, cultural technologies.[3] To do that means to talk about the vectors of relation between places and people rather than to talk about the identities of the people themselves. This essay is not one of those ethical statements about intersubjective relations of class, race, gender, or ethnicity. These things are very important, but so too are the social relations that subordinate the people of one place to another, or that organize the exploitation of nature as space itself, through the extraction and movement of value. This is an essay about people's connections to sailing ships and comsats. It is about what Donna Haraway calls our cyborg rather than our humanist selves.[4]

Arguably, the last thing a critical theory of culture ought to have anything to do with is electronic art. It is not popular. It is not cheap. It is not influential. No matter how much well-meaning people talk about how new technologies can empower people, it is still mostly American white boys who have their finger on the power stud. And yet there is something critically useful about electronic art, even if it does not always recognize this itself. Electronic artists negotiate between the dead hand of traditional, institutionalized aesthetic discourses and the organic, emergent forms of social communication.[5] Electronic art is an experimental laboratory, not so much for new technologies as for new social relations of communication. This is why electronic art matters to critical theories of culture, be they of the Frankfurt school or, in my case, the Birmingham school of cultural studies.[6]

Moreover, a confrontation with electronic art might have some salutary effects on criticism, which sometimes lapses into moral and conservative homilies. When confronted by technologies—the tools of rapid change—criticism gives in to Burkean urges to conserve

"cultural difference" from what it imagines to be the entirely negative and homogenizing effects of change. This moral reaction forecloses debate on the necessity and desirability of change. Some
dynamics in culture cannot be halted. Some may be positively beneficial. A dialogue with experimental electronic media may help
keep these questions open for a criticism that all too often forgets its
own history—and forgets how to think historically. This Burkean
criticism imagines that it is this technology, this epoch of change,
that ushers in "the fall" from grace, from an organic and unified culture. Everything from the newspaper and the illustrated magazine to
cinema and television, and now Nintendo and CNN, are imagined
to be the last straw that hurls us out of Eden. As Simon Penny notes,
"This all creeps up on us while we're asleep anyway: who worries
about our dependence on the global computerised telephone network, or that because of pocket calculators nobody can do mental
arithmetic anymore?"[7] While uncritical faith in the liberatory potential of technology may in the main be the principal ideology to com-
bat, uncritical fear of it is also debilitating. The convergence of the
critical tradition with new technology seems to me to be a dialectic
with potential to raise both to a new level of cultural and political
salience.[8]

Given a will to think historically about cultural change and to
use electronic art as a foil, two problems arise in thinking about the
emergent, global forms of culture. One is the problem of access to
knowledge about new techniques. The other is the problem of gen-
eralizing from specific experiences. In other words, we confront a
limit to what we know of time and of space. We know least about
what is nearest in time—the emergent present—and what is most
distant in space, namely, the forms of culture of our antipodean others. What compounds the issue is that the things we want to critically examine—new media—are precisely what appear to overcome
these problems for us. This is a problem that calls, in short, for art
and for theory: for intuitive visualization and speculative conceptu-
alization.

No matter how global and how abstract the analysis wants to
be, it can never extract itself from its quite specific cultural origins.
Hence this writing takes the form of an essay and asks the essay's
classic question: "What do I know?" I want to begin with my own
experience of this planet of noise we now live on. The result is a very
abstract essay, but also a very self-consciously partial one, tied to
particular experiences of sailing ships and television. In it I rephrase

Montaigne's self-questioning from "What do I know?" to the more suitably antipodean "From where am I interpolated?"[9]

To the vector the spoils

For a long time Australian culture has manifested a desperate attempt to fix a few things in consciousness between two great abstract terrains of movement. The first is the sea. The sea, as Hegel says, "gives us the idea of the indefinite, the unlimited, and infinite: and in feeling his own infinite in that Infinite, man is stimulated and emboldened to stretch beyond the limited: the sea invites man to conquest and to piratical plunder, but also to honest gain and to commerce."[10] Thus, ambivalently, did this first regime of the vector traverse the globe.

The cultures that invaded Australia did so using a naval technology. This technology turned the space of nautical dangers into an abstract space of movement, migration, trade, and, above all, strategy. This history was a history of the transformation of the space of the oceans into a universal space of movement. The project of transforming the antipodes through invasion and settlement presupposes a world of material flows. The "conquest" of nature and the creation of the second nature of built environments presupposes this abstract space of flows. From the first fleet to the fast clippers, its development is central to the project of modernity.

Yet overlaid on this second nature of material flows there is now another abstract space that produces another feeling of the unlimited—the terrain of the media vector. The passage from modernity to postmodernity seems to me to involve the passage from one form of abstraction to another—from the second nature of abstract social spaces created by sea and rail transport to the abstract communicational spaces created by the telegraph, telephone, television, and telecommunications. These are the techniques of telesthesia, of perception at a distance. Since the telegraph, the time of communications has been less than the time of transport, and indeed these two synonymous terms begin to diverge in meaning as they diverge as terrains of abstraction.[11]

Put somewhat more theoretically, second nature emerges out of the struggle to wrest freedom from necessity. It is an overcoming of the tyranny of nature, achieved through the social organization of labor. As we know only too well, the process of creating second nature creates new tyrannies as well. Freedom from nature becomes the elimination of nature. The social organization of second nature is, among other things, a class relation. The division of labor makes every function—including art—partial and fetishized.[12]

An artist who I think quite graphically maps most of the predicament of second nature is Stelarc, who makes of the surfaces of his body a theater of second nature. In his performances, his skin becomes the point of interface for relations to the technical. He appears strapped and wired to any and every device. Some are devices he controls through the movement of his muscles. Some are devices that control him, triggering involuntary parabolas and disconcerting jerks. Here is the body as second nature made it and maintains it: in a state of permanent dependence and symbiosis with what Peter Callas calls technology as territory.[13]

The decline of modernity is in many respects a loss of faith in second nature. The division of labor brings with it fragmentation, anomie—the compulsions of discipline and the anarchy of the market. The redemptive vision of second nature withered in both its Marxist and bourgeois forms. Yet this does not stop the projection of the fantasy of redemption onto third nature. In both the cool and the nerdy techno literature in *Mondo 2000* and *PC Monthly*, redemption is always around the corner in virtual reality, hypertext, cyberspace. Although the terrain is different, the projection of a vectoral field of total communication extends and completes the projection of a vectoral field of extraction and production. With an extra ten megabytes I can finally RAM down the doors of data heaven! Such is the new fantasy of wresting freedom from necessity—for those at least who are at the very heart of the relations of power that constitute third nature.

Representation and power

Sitting on the dock of the bay, the question concerning technology looks a little different. Viewed from the antipodes, the fundamental thing about modernity is the creation of the globe as an abstract space of movement, exploitation, and strategy. It is not what happened in Europe that is fundamental to modernity; it is Europe's relation to its many antipodes. It is not what is happening in the United States (or Japan) that is fundamental to postmodernity, but what is happening in its relations to its antipodes.[14] In both cases, that relation is only secondarily intersubjective. It is primarily the encounter of techniques of power premised on a radical abstracting of space overcoming prior modes of dwelling on the earth.

From the perspective of the antipodes, or at least from a harborside flat in Ultimo, one can contrast Foucault's notion of disciplinary technologies with a genealogy of what one might call vectoral technologies. It is not the *Panopticon* but the British navy that in this latter view emerges as a key technological regime of power in the early modern period. Let's not forget that Bentham's famous pamphlet was called *The Panopticon, or New South Wales?* Vectoral power was not based on close disciplining and inspection of the social body, but purging of the social body. The vector vents its spleen on an other that is partly mapped but still mostly imagined.[15]

Yet there is a link between the panoptic strategy and the vectoral strategy of transporting surplus, criminalized people to the antipodes. Both are regimes that combine a field of visibility, a technology for enclosing or traversing it, and a discourse and its executors. While the panoptic strategy is one of intensive techniques, subdividing, scrutinizing, and enclosing space within the city, transportation is an extensive vector, based on a technology that can project, plan, and traverse the globe. The world becomes the object of the vector, of the potentiality of movement. Bodies, cargoes, weapons, information: this principally naval technology produced, almost as an afterthought, Botany Bay and Sydney.

The antipodes are not the other of the west but the project of the West. While the idealized mythologies of the exotic still haunt global media exchanges (and the arts), they are subsidiary to the management of the antipodean other via techniques of appraisal that see in the antipodes not the noble savage or the evil demon, but a resource to be managed and mobilized along the lines opened up by the vector. The sublime antipodean other becomes enmeshed in an abstract grid capable of more mundane valuations of economic and strategic advantage. The other becomes a project, not a double for the West.[16]

In the development of the vectoral regime of power, everything depended on the development of technologies of perception.[17] In the naval regime, techniques for finding a ship's longitudinal position were decisive.[18] This made possible a much more productive relation between the abstract space of maps, charts, and solar calculations and the places through which ships passed on their travels. Gradually, every movement becomes equivalent and interchangeable with any other movement. Gradually, any destination becomes equivalent and interchangeable with any other place. As with physical movement, so too with information. Information no longer knows its destination.

In his remarkable book *European Vision and the South Pacific*, Bernard Smith shows how the rise of British naval imperialism precipitates the fall of neoclassical representation.[19] The neoclassical style pictured landscapes in terms of the ideal, and this aesthetic was institutionally enshrined in the Royal Academy. The Royal Society itself favored an aesthetic based on the representation of the typical. Through its connection with scientific naval expeditions to the Pacific, the Royal Society saw to it that the typical became the technique of representing what explorers like Cook and Banks found. The new mode of art became an organic part of the most advanced edge of modern social relations. The old form of representation was preserved—as if in aspic—as a traditional but no longer living form. This split has troubled modern art ever since.

It was alive and well in the tension between photography conceived as a fine art practice and the photography that was dependent on techniques developed from and organically connected to the practices of military reconnaissance. It is alive and well again in video practice dependent on cameras powered by CCDs developed for spy satellites and designed to track the telltale flare of Russian missile launches. Since the triumph of the model of the typical in pictorial representation, a certain type of art frames the world as picture and presents it to power as an image of its potential sites for the project of transforming nature into second nature.

Today we appear to have gone beyond technologies that frame the world, in Heidegger's sense. We live not with the discrete framing of the continuous space of the world but with the temporal editing of its multiple and continuous times into a singular rhythm of cuts and ruptures. The edit becomes the device for regulating, not static pictures or singular texts, but constant flows of information. Information about markets, products, consumers, events, forces and resources—above all, information about other information—now has to be organized in the exercise of far more extensive powers. The naval vectoral regime created a new role for the artist in framing and inscribing the typical. The typical became the mode of assessing the relative worth of projects designed to exploit what the typical pictured. This process could result in miscalculation, as it did notoriously in the decision to colonize Botany Bay, Australia. The land itself did not live up to its representation.[20] Nevertheless, the pursuit of the vector has also been the endless process of refining and verifying information about the world and hence increasing its openness to development and transformation into second nature.

Today, sophisticated techniques are gathering to make ever more complex projects instantly and constantly comparable and assessable—from refinancing News Corp. to selling Benetton jumpers. The development of vectoral flows of information is what makes possible the space of flows, in which jobs, troops, money—anything—can be redirected from one interchangeable site to another. Art, whether it likes it or not, is part of this emergent terrain of third nature, as Mike Davis shows in his book *City of Quartz*.[21] When Los Angeles sells itself as a destination for footloose global capital, it sells not only as a sound business investment but as a prestigious storehouse of cultural capital. The art gallery becomes an investment in attracting attention in the global space of flows. Art is not innocent, but that is why it still has critical value. It is art's relative organic proximity to the emergent vectoral relations that makes art interesting, not its relative detachment.

From second nature to third nature

But I have wandered across the Pacific again. To return to our question: "When we can go to the antipodes and back in an instant, what will become of us?" Perhaps, among other things, we will start making and appreciating art like the Photoshop collages of Robyn Stacey.[22] Stacey's work keys into this expanded terrain that the media vector creates. Stacey has grasped and exploited the radically new protocols of third nature as a space of perception and relation—a space that is not void of rules and conventions of historicity, appropriateness, genre, and scale, but a space where such rules are in a constant state of evolution. Unanchored from the space of places and cast into the space of flows, images become polyvalent, revealing a visual poetics that the surrealists could only imagine but that the vector has now rendered as a philosophy made concrete. While art can map and display an image of this new space of vectoral relations, it cannot theorize it. Both art and theory need to look into the experience of everyday life—that elusive reservoir of tactics and ethics—for the practical foundations of a critique of this new terrain, our third nature. So let us return, for a moment, to everyday life.

When I was a kid growing in suburban Newcastle, in a little weatherboard house perched between the railway line and the

Pacific highway, I loved to look at the atlas and draw maps with colored pencils. First I would draw the contours of nature. In green and blue and brown I projected an image of the ocean, the land, and the mountains. This was a jaggy mass of impassable terrains, each unique and torturous.

Then I filled those contours with dots of various sizes, all enclosed with jagged lines that divided the land mass up into a patchwork of spaces. Unknowingly, I drew the geography of places, of our second nature. The dots marked out cities and towns of various sizes; the borders marked out the territories these towns were able to bring under their control in the modern period. The railways and the newspapers between them defined spaces that were integrated economically, politically, and culturally. Regionalism gave way to nationalism.[23] This tendency breaks down the separation of places and aggregates them into bigger, more abstract units. Thus the natural barriers and contours of the land were overcome with a second nature of productive flows.

Next, I took out a big red magic marker and started to join up all of the dots. Big fat lines between the big towns, smaller ones between the regional centers. From the telegraph to telecommunications, a new geography has been overlaid on top of nature and second nature. This, it seems to me, is one way of reading what most Australians were and probably still are taught in school.

The development of third nature overlaps with the development of second nature—hence the difficulties of periodizing the modern and postmodern. The salient point for me is the development of the telegraph. What is distinctive about the telegraph is that it begins a regime of communication whereby information can travel faster than people or things. The telegraph, telephone, television, telecommunications—telesthesia. When information can move faster and more freely than people or things, its relation to those other movements and to space itself changes. From a space of places, we move on to a space of flows.

If there is a qualitative change in the social relations of culture that deserves the name of postmodern, perhaps this is it. Or perhaps we could call this state of affairs third nature. Second nature, which appears to us as the geography of cities and roads and harbors and wool stores, is progressively overlaid with a third nature of information flows, creating an information landscape that almost entirely covers the old territories. While this process has been going on since the telegraph, it reaches critical mass in the late 70s. The "postmodern" is thus a catalog of its symptoms. "Cyberspace" is a description of its subjective effects. Both postmodernism in theory and cyberspace in literature are explorations of the landscape of third nature.

We can see now, very clearly, what the terminal state of third nature would be. Deleuze and Guattari ask provocatively and more than once: "Perhaps we have not become abstract enough?"[24] What would it mean to become more abstract, ever more abstracted from the boundedness of territory and subjectivity? One can imagine a delirious future, beyond cyberspace. Not the future of Marx's communism: from each according to his abilities, to each according to his needs. Rather the future of the rhizome made concrete: where every trajectory is potentially connected to every other trajectory, and there all trajectories are equal and equally rootless. Where we no longer have roots, we have aerials. Where we no longer have origins, we have terminals.

This fantasy appears in different guises, also, among the Californian techofreaks, the postmodern wing of the Green movement, in the corporate improvisations of Rupert Murdoch, and among the high-frontier hegemonists in the Pentagon.[25] The struggle over the relations of communication and the making of third nature is every bit as intense as the struggles over the relations of production and the shaping of third nature—but many of the old rules no longer apply.

Autonomy versus antipodality

The perception of postmodernism, cyberspace, third nature—call it what you will—differs from place to place, and it is high time to start breaking down these rather ethnocentric concepts. One way to do so is to try to discover the relations of antipodality lurking within them. Antipodality is the feeling of being neither here nor there. It is an experience of identity in relation to the other in which the relation always appears more strongly to consciousness than either the identity it founds or the other it projects.

Experiencing antipodality is always very unsettling, sometimes a little schizophrenic. There is nothing uniquely Australian about it, although it is a very common anxiety in Australian culture.[26] This is a place that is always in a relation to an elsewhere, that is always defined by its relation to a powerful other. First the British came and colonized. Then the Americans came and coca-colonized. We are no one, whoever we are, always oscillating in antipodality with else-wheres.

I think that these days the anxiety of antipodality is growing ever more common. The globalization of trade flows and cultural flows made possible by information technology reopens the old wounds of identity, breaking the skin at unexpected places. The volume and velocity of cultural product in circulation on the planet of noise keeps rising. Popular music, cinema, and television, the raw materials of popular culture, are increasingly sold into global markets in accordance with transnational financing and marketing plans. Suddenly cultural identity looks like it is in flux. The relations and the flows are more clearly in view than the sources or destinations. Cultural differences are no longer so tied to the experience of the particularities of place. These "vertical" differences of locality, ethnicity, and nation are doubled by "'horizontal" differences, determined not by being rooted in a particular place but by being plugged into a particular circuit. We vainly try to preserve forms of difference that are rapidly reorganizing themselves along another axis.[27]

This new experience of difference is an experience of an active trajectory between places, identities, and formations, rather than a drawing of borders, be they of the self or place. This is antipodality. Antipodality is the cultural difference created by the vector. The acceleration of the vectors of transnational communication will make the antipodean experience more common. With CNN beaming into every part of the globe that can afford it, many people are experiencing "antipodality," the feeling of being caught in a network of cultural trajectories beyond their control.[28] In the overdeveloped world, both the culture of everyday life and the culture of scholarly thinking about the present seem to me to betray traces of unease, if not downright paranoia, about antipodality. Yet it is undoubtably the emergent axis of technocultural struggle.

At present, antipodality exists in the politics of third nature in two forms. On the one hand, it leads to attempts to shore up identity against the flux. Black nationalism and born-again Christianity seem to me to have elements of this reactive return to an imagined core of immutable identity and community. On the other hand, the kind of coalition building involved in queer politics and the politics of affinity Haraway speaks about in contemporary feminism seem to me to treat antipodality more as a fact of life than as a threat to identity.[29]

Now, the point about this is that any attempt to create communities of resistance of necessity exclude something or someone.

Community only exists dialectically, as a struggle against something other, be it nature, other communities, or the vector. While struggles still, of course, take place in relation to nature and second nature, they now have an added dimension: the struggle, not for natural space, not for social space, but for information space. Every community de-informates certain spaces within itself and creates certain barriers to the flow of information from without. Every community, by definition, requires some degree of "correctness" from would-be members. There is, then, a certain moral ambiguity about the concept of community and identity. They are necessary, perhaps, but as intellectuals we need to keep a critical distance.

The work of VNS Matrix plays on antipodality to the extent that this group of women artists continually draws a connecting line between phallocentric and technological culture. They play off, play on, and play up to the antipodal position women are supposed to occupy in relation to the male *techne*. "We are the virus of the new world disorder," they casually announce.[30] VNS is not afraid to take on board the threat to traditional notions of female identity posed by the relentless development of the masculinist technology of second nature and the phallocentric image repertoire of third nature. Their project, as in the work *All New Gen* (1992) is to create new and open relations of subjectivity. There is a sense of closure in the process of creating these works: VNS Matrix is an all-women collective. That closure makes possible a radical openness to the flow. VNS takes the most incorrigibly gendered imaginary of Nintendo and imagines it otherwise: literally, as a feminized space.[31]

The virtues of moral ambivalence

For every set of oppositions within a given culture, there is always a trajectory along which one can bypass the fixed speaking positions that identities prescribe.[32] One must try not to occupy either the position of domination in an antipodal relation, nor reactively take up the minor position. As petit-bourgeois intellectuals, we are always shuttling in-between.[33] I'm reminded here of the use video artist Peter Callas has made of the images from a Japanese card game, a game that is like the Western children's game of scissors, paper, stone. Each of the three terms is superior to one of the other terms and inferior to the other. There is no fixed hierarchy, and while every relation involves a difference, each is contingent on which cards turn up. That seems to me to be a diagram of antipodality.[34]

When one knows what it is like to always be both the major and the minor pole of these ambivalent relationships of flow—to be scissors one minute relative to paper but stone the next—then one can begin to think with some subtlety about the problem of cultural diversity and the information vector. This moral ambivalence to antipodality is, I think, very common in Australia, and something to be capitalized on methodologically rather than deplored or ignored. In relation to American culture and economic power, Australia is always on the receiving end of antipodality. As the tyranny of distance gives way to the vector, new defensive mechanisms have been required at the level of the nation. On the terrain of cultural flows, a twofold process has occurred. The integration of the space of the continent into one media market has only taken place quite recently, via satellite technology. At one and the same time broadcasters have integrated the national broadcasting space and hooked it up to the global satellite feeds.[35]

Until recently, this tendency towards antipodality was countered by local content rules in television broadcasting. As with local content rules in radio, these were successful in promoting the production of high-quality, popular media products, which in turn were successfully marketed overseas. Australian TV programming now has a global audience, and Australia is a successful supplier of recorded music to the world market. Overall, these policies balanced some degree of autonomy with a cosmopolitan media flow. The combined effect of lunatic "free market" policies and pressure from American program producers to have services, including cultural ones, included under GATT agreements are steadily leading to an erosion of autonomous Australian cultural intervention.[36]

On the other hand, there is very little room for moralizing or playing the "victim" in mainstream Australian culture. "We" may be no one, but "we" were also colonizers, enslavers. The imposition of second nature on this continent, as on continental America, was at the expense of indigenous people. The imposition of third nature, via satellite-distributed TV, has only just begun.[3]

Becoming abstract

It has taken a long time for white Australians to wake up to the extraordinary cultural forms Aboriginal people have relied upon to survive the two hundred years since invasion. Putting side by side the mechanisms of cultural autonomy deployed by traditional

Aboriginal Australians confronted by white Australians and that of white Australians confronted with global cultural flows illustrates the problem of sustaining autonomy and cultural diversity on the cultural landscape of third nature. It is a problem that involves diverse solutions and quite a number of different scales, from that of the individual and community to that of the nation. In thinking about new media tools and the new vectoral trajectories they may open up, we can do worse than look at historical examples of strategies of survival. We need to think tactically about every form of communication, new and old. Like rocks, paper, and scissors, media are never simply good or evil; they are always contingent.

The growth of an abstract space of third nature, covering the whole globe, is in no sense an unambiguously good thing. The enlightenment mythology of the unalloyed good of knowledge and information can mask a very damaging antipodality, in which powerful centers create and control vectors of information. Anglo-Celtic Australians know only too well what it is like to live in the shadow of the powerful flow of the American media. Unlike Europeans, we have neither a strong tradition nor an autonomous language with which to maintain a communion of identity. The historical trajectory of the vector puts white Australia in an ironically similar predicament to Aboriginal communities, which have great cultural resources for resistance but have been systematically denied the material resources for cultural survival. These situations are, however, quite different, and have to be approached tactically through their particularities.

To return to Deleuze's question: "What if we have not become abstract enough?" Out of the course of this analysis, some answers begin to suggest themselves. Whether we like it or not, cultural differences cannot be preserved from the impact of media vectors. New forms of difference are emerging out of the struggle with the vector; others succumb and become extinct. The abstraction of social relations from identity and place is not something that technologies achieve of their own accord. It results from the dialectic between communities and the technical regime of the media vector. Innovative forms of autonomous communication give the planet of noise something to suck on, so to speak. We no longer have roots, we have aerials. The dialectic of autonomy and antipodality structures an emerging politics of relationality and flow rather than of identity and locality. Our communicational interventions (for that is what both art and criticism are) have to be rethought for this world of third nature we have made, which is very rapidly remaking us.

New technology cannot be used to preserve cultural differences. Traditional culture reified as museum interactives—even if they are VR—does not constitute preservation so much as mummification. New technology can be used to create new differences and new forms of autonomy and community, but it cannot be used to "preserve" old differences in any meaningful sense. Traditional forms of cultural difference are not independent of the techniques used to maintain them. The work of Eric Michaels and Francis Jupurrurla in the Warlpiri Aboriginal community is interesting precisely because Michaels thought video could be used to create a viable community that would grow organically out of traditional information practices.[38] As Tim Rowse points out, Warlpiri social organization does not traditionally take the form of anything remotely like "community" at all.[39] This was, therefore, not preservation—it was a creative process. It was not ethnography—it was art. Naturally, it was a far more morally ambivalent project than simply preserving a form of communication assumed to have always already been there. Michaels thought that only by becoming abstract—by incorporating the information managing relations of third nature—could the constraints on knowledge so vital to the oral information economy of the Warlpiri be developed and sustained. Such is the order of problems for a critical practice of electronic media art.

The ends of art

This is, of course, a rather sweeping and world-historical way of framing criticism. I see no reason to relinquish the point of view of the totality to conservative interpreters of Hegel and Kojève such as Francis Fukuyama.[40] While we may be inclined to agree with Deleuze that the "only universal history is the history of contingency,"[41] there is something heuristically useful and perhaps even tactically necessary in framing the critical or creative act in such a way that it appears as an instant within a much wider and intelligible process. If anything, such a perspective makes us more humble about the possibilities of art and criticism, yet none the less cognizant of the significance of what is at stake. The point of this particular rewriting of the trajectory of cultural history is to insist that there is considerably more to struggle for and to struggle against than Fukuyama's rather smug picture of the completion of liberal democracy as the completion of universal history would suggest. When viewed from the antipodes rather than from the center, things appear otherwise. Both art and criticism can make a claim to imagine a particular vision of the totality. This seems to me entirely preferable to the folly, which begins with Hegel, of imagining a total vision that encompasses all particulars. As Adorno warns, "The whole is the false."[42] Our imaginings of what is at stake in the transformation of the space of the globe by third nature are still only that: imaginings.

Nevertheless, electronic art is a practice that cannot help but raise issues of the totality, for it works with the tools that are themselves transforming the totality of social relations into the domain of third nature. Electronic artists cannot help but use the material of transformation itself, although they do not always choose to work critically on the issues involved in this transformation itself. The artists mentioned in this essay—Peter Callas, Robyn Stacey, Stelarc, VNS Matrix, Eric Michaels, and Francis Jupurrurla—do, in my opinion. They have made use of the interzone of antipodal relations, of their status as "no one" marooned between the channels of third nature, to produce critical work in Australia that is also of a wider provenance.

Notes

1. Manuel Castells, *The Informational City* (Cambridge: Basil Blackwell, 1989).

2. On Virilio, see McKenzie Wark, "On Technological Time: Cruising Virilio's Overexposed City," *Arena* 83 (1988).

3. Raymond Williams, "Base and Superstructure in Marxist Cultural Theory," in *Problems in Materialism and Culture* (London: Verso, 1980).

4. Donna J. Haraway, "A Cyborg Manifesto," in *Simians, Cyborgs, and Women: The Reinvention of Nature* (New York: Routledge, 1991).

5. This distinction draws on Antonio Gramsci's contrast betwen traditional and organic intellectuals in *Selections from the Prison Notebooks* (New York: International Publishers, 1973).

6. On Birmingham school cultural studies, see Stuart Hall, "Cultural Studies and its Theoretical Legacies," in Lawrence Grossberg et al., *Cultural Studies* (New York: Routledge, 1992), and other essays in that volume.

7. Simon Penny, "Kinetics, Cybernetics, Art Practice in the Age of the Thinking Machine," in *Irrelevant Ethics: Notes on Art Practice in a Technological Context* (Sydney: Virtual Object, 1988).

8. Two useful works of political and cultural criticism of technology, respectively, are Langdon Winner, *Autonomous Technology: Technics-Out-of-Control as a Theme in Political Thought* (Cambridge: MIT Press, 1978); and Andrew Ross, *Strange Weather: Culture, Science and Technology in the Age of Limits* (London: Verso, 1991).

9. On the everyday, see Michel de Certeau, "Montaigne's 'Of Cannibals': The Savage 'I'" in *Heterologies: Discourse on the Other* (Minneapolis: University of Minnesota Press, 1986).

10. G. W. F. Hegel, *The Philosophy of History* (Buffalo, N.Y.: Prometheus Books, 1991), 90.

11. James Carey, "Technology and Ideology: The Case of the Telegraph," in *Communication as Culture* (Boston: Unwin & Hyman, 1989).

12. Charles Taylor, *Hegel* (Cambridge: Cambridge University Press, 1991), 535ff.; see also Guy Debord, *The Society of the Spectacle* (N. p. Black & Red, 1983), epigrams 186–88.

13. For documentation on Stelarc, see Allessio Cavalaro et al., *Cultural Diversity in the Global Village: The Third International Symposium on Electronic Art* (Adelaide: Australian Network for Art & Technology, 1992).

14. McKenzie Wark, "From Fordism to Sonyism: Perverse Readings of the New World Order," *New Formations* 16 (1992).

15. Compare Bernard Smith's neglected masterpiece *European Vision and the South Pacific* with Michel Foucault's *Discipline and Punish* (Harmondsworth: Penguin Books, 1977).

16. Paul Foss, "Theatrum Nondum Cogitorum," in *The Foreign Bodies Papers* (Sydney),Local Consumption Series 1 (N. p. 1981).

17. McKenzie Wark, "The Logistics of Perception," *Meanjin* 49, no. 1 (Autumn 1990).

18. Geoffrey Blainey, *The Tyranny of Distance: How Distance Shaped Australia's History* (Melbourne: Macmillan, 1986).

19. Bernard Smith, *European Vision and the South Pacific* (Oxford: Oxford University Press, 1989).

20. See Paul Carter, *The Road to Botany Bay* (New York: Knopf, 1988).

21. Mike Davis, *City of Quartz* (London: Verso, 1991).

22. On Stacey's work, see Ray Edgar & Ashley Crawford, "Point Blank,"*Tension* 24 (December 1990).

23. Benedict Anderson, *Imagined Communities*, (London: Verso, 1983).

24. Gilles Deleuze and Felix Guattari, *Anti-Oedipus: Capitalism and Schizophrenia* (London: Athlone Press, 1984), 321.

25. William Shawcross, *Murdoch* (Sydney: Random House Australia, 1992); Manuel De Landa, *War in the Age of Intelligent Machines* (New York: Zone Books, 1991)

26. See Ross Gibson's essays, especially his reading of Mad Max in *South of the West* (Bloomington: Indiana University Press, 1992).

27. Roland Robertson, *Globalisation: Social Theory and Global Culture* (London: Sage, 1992).

28. McKenzie Wark, *Virtual Geography: Living with Global Media Events.* (Bloomington: Indiana University Press, 1990).

29. Donna Haraway, "A Cyborg Manifesto" (see note 4). On black nationalism and its exclusions (particularly of women), see Michele Wallace, *Black Macho and the Myth of the Superwoman* (London: Verso, 1990).

30. VNS Manifesto, *Art & Text* 42 (May 1992), 66.

31. For documentation, see A. Cavellaro, R. Harley, L. Wallace and M. Wark eds., *Cultural Diversity in the Global Village: The Third International Symposium on Electronic Art* (Adelaide: Australian Network for Art & Technology, 1992).

32. McKenzie Wark, "Speaking Trajectories: Meaghan Morris, Antipodean Theory and Australian Cultural Studies,"*Cultural Studies* 6, no. 3 (October 1992), 433–48.

33. Meaghan Morris, "Politics Now (Anxieties of a Petit-Bourgeois Intellectual)," in *The Pirate's Fiancée* (London: Verso, 1988).

34. On Callas, cf. Ross Harley, "Alphabyte Cities," *Art & Text* 28 (1988); McKenzie Wark, "Japan, Postmodernism and Beyond,"*Tension* 22 (August 1990).

35. Tom O'Regan, "Towards a High Communications Policy," *Continuum* 2, no. 1 (1988).

36. Stuart Cunningham, *Framing Culture: Criticism and Policy in Australia* (Sydney: Allen & Uniwn, 1992).

37. See McKenzie Wark, "Autonomy and Antipodality in the Global Village," in A. Cavellaro et al., *Cultural Diversity* (see note 13).

38. Eric Michaels, *For a Cultural Future: Francis Jupurrurla Makes TV at Yuendumu*, Artspace Art & Criticism Monograph Series (Sydney, 1987).

39. Tim Rowse, "Enlisting the Warlpiri," *Continuum* 3, no. 2 (1990).

40. Francis Fukuyama, *The End of History and the Last Man* (London: Hamish Hamilton, 1992).

41. Deleuze and Guattari, *Anti-Oedipus*, 224.

42. Theodor Adorno, *Minima Moralia* (London: New Left Books, 1973), 50.

2

In/Quest of Presence: Virtuality, Aurality, and Television's Gulf War

Frances Dyson

The term "virtuality" emphasizes the indebtness that the development of artificial environments such as "virtual reality" (VR), or the simulation of experience via robotics, such as telepresence,[1] owes to the rich popular and theoretical discursive arena in which such technologies are located. The cultural imaginary propelling virtuality inhabits a curiously sophisticated rhetorical landscape, shaped by the endless permutations of futuristic, libertarian, psychedelic, cybernetic, anarchistic, subcultural, utopian, mystical and science-fiction mythologies permeating late-twentieth-century culture. The tropology thus formed has astonishing breadth, given the relatively short span of VR or "cyber-tech's" existence and its comparatively low level of development. It also engages audacious declarations that, for instance, cyber-tech represents not only a new electronic medium, but a radically different, autonomous, and authentic "reality."[2] This is quite a claim for what is still within the realm of media, and illuminates the intense networks of desire currently constructing the present state of virtual affairs, where, it seems, the actual technologies deployed are overshadowed by the glorious promises they hold: a revolution in modes of sociality, access to an electronic sublime, and new forms of thought arising from a redefined subjectivity and refigured ontology. The compulsion to fulfill such promises, or prophecies, is so great that enthusiasts will, for instance, debate the value of certain systems that do not actually exist; hence their term "vaporware."

Although the postmodern metaphor par excellence, virtuality cannot be thought of apart from modernist institutions of mass media and the mechanisms of desire they have promulgated.[3] Thus

27

when cyber-tech made its public "debut" during the Persian Gulf War to one of the largest audiences in television history, the media/public reaction to the "Nintendo"-like weaponry revealed a desire for virtuality that was and is intense but deeply conflicted. This "hi-tech war" seemed to concentrate a plethora of critiques already associated with media and technology into the paradox of a "bloodless war," and it is this kind of paradox, structured within the term "virtual reality" itself, that imbues visions of virtuality with a kind of ambivalent, anxious glee. When VR is described as a "reality" equivalent to, or "as real as," the earthbound, materially circumscribed reality most people endure, it diminishes the electro/spiritual mission that the "virtual" and the vaporlike are supposed to inaugurate.[4] Yet eulogizing the immaterial over the mundane worldliness of present 'reality' is highly problematic, not only because it entails the derogation of the body, the "meat" that has thus far defined twentieth-century humanism, but also because disembodiment has historically constituted the *lack* associated with mass media. As media theorists have argued, it is this lack that surrounded the acceptance of the telephone, radio, cinema, and television with hushed expressions of loss and a growing nostalgia for the "real" that media represents, and in representing, supplants. Advocates of virtuality have attributed such "loss" simply to the artifactual and two-dimensional nature of the image, which can only be viewed and never "entered," which produces phantoms rather than the real thing. The dream of virtual reality has developed along with and often in response to this hiatus between the real and the visual representation, and it is within this context that the spatiotemporal and participatory attributes of VR technology seem to provide a solution. Through an odd kind of disembodied "embodiment," activating an "unmediated" media, the virtual subject is thought to recoup the "there" absent in other media, although that "there" belongs as much to the future as to the past, as much to a radical posthumanism as to a nostalgic yearning for the environments, communities, and lifestyles lost to twentieth-century "progress."

The kind of envelopment that virtuality offers as a solution to the limits of screen-based media is, however, not without precedent. Historically, it is through *sound* that visual media and media industries have recuperated the "presence" lost in imagistic representation, and the conceptual strategies behind this recuperation are just as operational in the rhetoric of virtuality. This is not say say that virtual media offer presence through sound (although certainly this occurred in the representation of VR during the Gulf War), but rather to point to the phenomenal, ontological, and symbolic status that aurality has and that virtuality simulates, if only in theory. While the image has suffered a loss of credibility throughout the twentieth century, audiophony has maintained its claim to presence and truth, and thus presents a protovirtuality, equipped with an uncontested mythology and supplying a ready-made range of metaphors and technological precedents (Lanier, for instance, first likened VR to the telephone). However, audiophonic innovations continue to generate the same ambivalence towards technology and new media that virtuality is experiencing. The major concern of what follows will be to situate aspects of aurality—its "presence," its utopian histories, and its corporate deployment—within the rhetorical, mediumistic and militaristic emergence of virtuality.

Virtual metaphysics

"Aurality" refers to the phenomenal and discursive terrain of sound, and it is interesting that this terrain is formed by concepts and metaphors that also appear within virtuality. Like virtuality, the phenomenal invisibility, intangibility, multiplicity, and existential flux of sound challenges an understanding of the real based upon the visible, material, and enduring object. Sound cannot be held for close examination, nor can it be separated from the aural continuum and given a singular identity. In a constant state of becoming, sound comes into and goes out of existence in a manner that confounds ontological representation. Similarly, being both heard outside and felt within, sound blurs the distinction between the interior and exterior of the body, annihilating the distance between subject and object, self and other. This immersive quality, together with the physiology of the ear, destabilizes the subjectivity of the subject; unlike the eye, the ear cannot be closed. Unlike the gaze that is always *in front of* the subject and projected onto the world, listening involves an awareness of the unseen and possibly unwelcome spaces on the periphery of one's being. In short, aurality presages a reexamination of how the real is constituted, how knowledge is grounded, and the metaphorical and biological sense apparatus by which the "I" and the "world" coincide.

Within the opposition constructed between the sensible and the intelligible, the body and mind, sound emerges as an agent of destabilization, indicating the extreme fragility of dualistic structures. It is these structures that virtuality also disrupts. A virtual space exists only in the flicker of a simulation and can be "entered" only via a prosthetic body—a body that hovers between human and machine, animate and inanimate. The virtual body acting in cyberspace severely punctures the notion of the individual—the legacy of what Derrida terms "onto-theology"—since its multiple selves cannot be contained within the notion of the singular unified subject, that is, a subject in possession of a stable identity and grounded in an authentic origin. Refusing the primacy of One, of "I," it refuses the opposition between self and other, and by implication, all the oppositional boundaries upon which Western epistemology and metaphysics rely. As a result, it is difficult to say whether or not this virtual "I" exists, let alone to ascribe to it properties like "rational" or "masculine." According to Alberto Moreiras:

> Virtual reality, as analogy of analogy, opens the abyss of ontotheology by radically soliciting the essence of ground. . . . Virtual reality threatens the stability of the highest Principle of technological being, the Principle of sufficient reason, according to which there is nothing without a reason, there is nothing without a ground.[5]

Through its very immateriality, its lack of literal and metaphorical "ground," virtuality has the potential to generate a way of thinking that is philosophically "groundless" and in that sense radical. As Moreiras points out however, the key question here is whether "Virtual reality can be experienced as a possibility for a thinking of the Outside,"[6] whether virtuality is so determined by current Cartesian-based technological paradigms that it already forecloses the possibility of an epistemic rupture.

Thinking of the Outside involves looking past the body that Cartesian metaphysics grafted from a single organ, the eye, onto its homonymic counterpart, the "I"; the subject. And this means thinking outside of not only bodies and subjects, but also of visions and sights—the stuff of western thought itself. As the basis of knowledge, for instance, "contemplation" is already inscribed with an atomistic and ocularcentric ontology. Influenced by the Latin *templum*, meaning both a sacred edifice (cf. temple) and the "temple" of the head, "contemplation" is associated with L. *tempus* —time divided into periods—as well as the idea of a delimited space partitioned off into a separate sector in order to be viewed more closely. Thus knowl-

edge is reduced to the *visible* and the *divisible*, producing an ontology of Being dedicated to objects and units. Combined with a theology grounded in the intellect and founded in the *prima causa* of an
omniscient and incorporeal Creator, *ontotheology* develops as a conceptual machine of such power and magnitude that it is able to
incorporate and resolve often stunning contradictions, contradictions which virtual reality reiterates rather than resolves.[7]

Indeed, insofar as virtuality presents images in the context of an
agency that is disembodied and also omniscient, virtuality reproduces theology. Insofar as it maintains *the* foundational structure of
ontotheology—the logic of ocularcentrism—virtuality reproduces
Western ontology. For while the material world may not be relevant
in a virtual ontology, that other guarantor of the real—sight—is
hyperpresent, not just literally in terms of the images seen but
"behind" the virtual scenes, within the virtual structure, a priori.

Virtual media: Between loss and presence

If the ocularcentric basis of virtuality necessarily keeps ontotheology
in place, the rhetorical tropes that VR enthusiasts draw upon connote
an entirely "other" knowledge. Metaphors such as "immersive,"
"fluid," "simultaneous," and "spiritual" evoke the possibility of a
transcendent space in which "communion" knows no bounds
between human, machine, animal, object, or cosmic force. In contrast to the frankly nerdish associations of computer "contemplation," the cybernaut's experience is described in terms that apply,
coincidentally, to vision's historic other: aurality. The word "aural," it
is worth noting, comes from the Latin *auris*; pertaining to the ear. It
derives from "aura," originally Greek for "air" and adopted by Latin
as "a subtle, usually invisible exhalation or emanation."[8] Aurality
flows within and between bodies as an "aura" with all the spiritual
connotations the term implies. Through the aural, one is immersed in
here-and-now becoming, and this immersion is only possible within
a sphere outside of Western notions of subjectivity and objectivity.

However, while aurality beckons a radical metaphysics or
antimetaphysics, the mesmeric lull of the alterity it represents is
difficult to hear in late-twentieth-century technoculture. Within the
context of electronic media, sound cannot be conceived of apart
from the technological processes through which it is both channeled
and transformed. Like ontotheology, these processes organize
sonic material within a framework of ever increasing division and

reduction. Through recording, sound becomes dislocated and fragmented; it can be heard at any time, in any place, by any listener. Audio is no longer a temporal phenomenon bound to the here-and-now of lived experience, but a pseudo-object that can be collected and stored, transported and transmitted and infinitely repeated. With digital technology these possibilities are enhanced: by replacing the inscribed surface with the encoded signal, the indexical associations of phonography and magnetic tape are superseded by the arbitrariness of digital signs: zero and one. The computer simulations found in VR systems are no different—aural, visual, and tactile material simply becomes "information," data, signals within an electronic network, ready to be assembled and reassembled in any manner whatsoever in order to create an infinite array of audiophonic, imagistic, and even perhaps tactile simulations.

This movement towards objectification, delineation, and fragmentation subverts the "liberatory" space virtuality seems to offer—that is, the freedom to be anyone and anything anywhere. As if to deny this techno-metaphysical enclosure, the metaphors of virtuality—of cyborgs, cyberspaces and virtual realities—suggest the possibility of entering an inhabitable *space*. Yet the parameters of this "space" are ultimately defined by the binary yes/no, on/off commands of digital systems, designed to receive and process information according to set codes that are themselves not neutral. Rather than entering a "free-space," subjectivity is recontextualized within the programmatic grid of technology, and embedded in this grid are all those elements that drive the fixed and rigid reality, the prescribed subjectivity one might, through VR, be trying to escape. Causality , linearity, hierarchy, the discrete unit, the "one," the individual—all are situated within a teleology geared towards increasing control over systems of representation. As Michael Heim writes:

> Computerized reality synthesizes everything through calculation, and nothing exists in the synthetic world that is not literally numbered and counted. . . . [As a result] organic life energy ceases to initiate our mental gestures. . . . The more we mistake the cyberbodies for ourselves, the more the machine twists our selves into the prostheses we are wearing.[9]

As mentioned in the introduction to this chapter, the ambivalence towards virtuality that Heim expresses can be seen as a continuation of culture's ambivalence towards technology and media. Throughout the twentieth century a certain dread has accompanied technological development, as if with each new invention a portion of the body, corporeality, and here-and-now presence has been whittled away. Sound's role in media has traditionally been to recuperate, by simulation, the "presence" that media and mass communications, and in a general sense modern technology itself, has destroyed. For instance, the introduction of cinema sound was felt to breathe "life" into the mute images on the two-dimensional screen, giving them an aura of three-dimensionality. Early sound theorists were so keen on the introduction of the living here-and-now into what might otherwise appear as a dead medium, that they refused to acknowledge the difference between the original and the reproduced sound, arguing that because reproduced sound maintained its three-dimensionality it was *ontologically* the same sound.[10] In virtuality, presence is also "restored" via the simulation of a three-dimensional "space," and virtuality itself is referred to as a "reality" able to be "entered," rather than a mediated representation. Just as the introduction of lip sync in cinema made it almost impossible for the viewer to conceive of sound and image, voice and body as separate, the involvement of the participant in negotiating the virtual world via physically manipulated equipment makes it almost impossible to conceive of virtual space as anything other than real. In both screen-based media and VR, the actuality of the viewer's or participant's body becomes the map upon which the "embodiment" of virtuality is verified. Together with the simulation of space, simultaneity, and involvement, the appropriation of the body of the viewer/participant makes invisible and irrelevant the facts of technological mediation—the objectifying, decorporealizing logic of vested technology is repressed.

The history of radio offers another example of presence recuperated via the often spiritualized notion of embodiment, a notion that now appears in the rhetoric of virtuality. Michael Benedikt writes:

> Cyberspace: The realm of pure information, filling like a lake, siphoning the jangle of messages transfiguring the physical world, decontaminating the natural and urban landscapes, saving them . . . [from all the] corruptions attendant to the process of moving information attached to *things* —from paper to brains—across, over, and under the vast and bumpy surface of the earth rather than letting it fly free in the soft hail of electrons that is cyberspace.[11]

This smooth, frictionless surface is the same metaphorical surface that led early media theorists like Walter Ong to envision a "supra" subjectivity, created through the instantaneousness of radiophonic transmission, or artists like John Cage to celebrate the omnipresence that technology has bequeathed to our now "electronic souls."[12] It is a surface of fantasy, woven from the desire for immortality and omnipotence and articulated through the rhetorics of technophilia. Referring to the protovirtuality that the radio offered, Michael Benedikt remarks:

> What poured forth from every radio was the very sound of life itself. . . . Here are McLuhan's acoustically structured global villages . . . and support for the notion that the electronic media . . . provide a medium not unlike the air itself—surrounding permeating, cycling, invisible, without memory or the demand of it, conciliating otherwise disparate and perhaps antagonistic individuals and regional cultures.[13]

Rhetorically, the characteristics of aurality—that it is immersive, invisible, temporal, fluxlike and a force for social "harmony"—are superimposed upon the institution of radio. Radio reterritorializes the "airwaves," integrating the abstract and intellectual connotations of "air" with the sensuality and sociality of the "wave": fluid, aural, and coded as feminine. This integration is given a literalness in VR. Allucquere Stone mentions the artists and engineers working at Lucasfilm, who

> wanted to be able to get inside their own fantasies, to experientially inhabit the worlds they designed and built but could never enter. VR touched the same nerve that Star Wars had, the englobing specular fantasy made real.[14]

However, the very same corporate interests that transformed radio into a one-way transmission, that domesticated and commodified the ethereal spectrum and that gave democratic communication over to consumption are glued to the project of virtuality. In reference to on-line bulletin board services that developed in the mid-70s, Stone notes that, within a few years, their "visionary ethic" encompassing shared software ("shareware") and open access, was replaced by the monitoring of messages and the surveillance of participants.[15] The rationale for such regulations were remarkably similar to those that prohibited early-twentieth-century ham radio operators from tinkering with the ether.[16] Yet surrounded by the same rhetoric and corporate/social structures, why would anyone imagine VR to be different?

Virtual bodies in virtual wars

Questions of access, control, surveillance, and censorship have resurfaced with virtuality; most forcefully during the Gulf War, in which virtuality became the object of both televisual representation and mass public attention and debate. The Gulf War initiated entirely new relationships between the military, the media, and virtuality, all of which were concerned with the problem of annihilating, concealing, or disembodying actual bodies and images of bodies. Negotiating the appearance or nonappearance of the body became a matter of great dispute, and the conflicting interests of the Pentagon and the television networks ultimately made it necessary for the generic body (representing presence and truth, signifying the ultimate arbiter of the real) to appear without appearing.

One way out of this dilemma was to represent the war-body not through its *image*, but through its *sound*. Traditionally the sounds of the body—from its voice to its death rattle—have accomplished far more than mere "appearance" in authorizing a belief in the reality of what is being presented. Attached to the idea of reality is one of the most powerful rhetorical tools available, the idea of *truth*. In the age of electronic mediation, "truth" is often represented by nature, by common wisdom, lived experience, opinion polls, etc., and by "live" coverage of events, which is thought to recuperate the here-and-now, the "aura," lost in reproduction. Indeed, "liveness" is often seen as synonymous with the phenomenal world transmitted direct to the viewer, without the embellishments of media representation. During the war, the construction of "liveness" in the absence of corporeality occurred on a number of planes, and within each the phenomenality of aurality together with the broadcast of actual sound contributed to the overall effect. Television devoted an enormous amount of time to live coverage of the war, not because such coverage was particularly informational, but to create a sense of ambient viewing. The viewer has a sense not of receiving information, but of being there, with the reporter, in a war zone. The "being-thereness" of ambient viewing was partly authenticated by the soundtrack. As the term suggests, ambience is a fluid, atmospheric state not unlike aurality; and in many instances the images of the war that television was prohibited from showing were nonetheless "present" through sound. For example, on Friday, 25 January 1991, CBS broadcast the familiar sight of the wind-swept reporter (Scott Pelly) standing in front of the by now famous blue domes, saying next to nothing for some minutes and then "moving on" to some recently shot video footage. Most of the visuals were of the night sky, with the shaky, handheld camera inserting momentary shots of unrecognizable blurs (probably buildings) until finally settling on a group of reporters, one of whom was loudly exclaiming, "Where is it? I don't see it!" That perhaps was the point—for during this lengthy excerpt, all the information was presented through the sound. In contrast to the images, it was both very explicit and richly ambient, containing the sounds of sirens, Islamic singing, gunfire, shuffling feet, etc., and culminating in the voice of the reporter loudly lamenting his, and television's, inability to *see*.[17] In general, had it not been for the sound of sirens, explosions, and cries of anguish, the reporter, in whose physical presence the "being-there" of the viewer was invested, would hardly have seemed "there" at all. Thus the aural served a dual function: both to carry the signs of war censored from the image and to create a sense of presence that concealed the mediation of that censorship.

Ironically, the "liveness" of the reporting had to battle with the strategic guarding of actual, live bodies. Massive restrictions were placed on the physical mobility of the reporters, and the cameras had no way to film the dead and injured. The "body gap" that this created again threatened to suggest that this was *not* a war. To maintain credibility, television substituted images of surrogate bodies (such as those of an oil-soaked cormorant or of the POWs) that could be repeated ad nauseam. Any occasion, no matter how brief, to reveal the true state of the war-body was seized; as Walter Goodman wrote, "It was like an animal that had been denied red meat."[18] While the construction of surrogate bodies was fairly predictable in terms of television strategy, the inauguration of a mode of viewing that dispensed with the presence of bodies altogether was ingenious. The images of the smart bombs' "telepresence" allowed television to substitute the ethereal domain of technology, the domain where the body cannot go, for the world it was prohibited from showing. The first such image, which appeared early on in the coverage, was of a laser-guided "smart bomb" viewing its target through the "cross hairs" of its camera. The image was accompanied by the very distorted and "electronic" voice of an observer, who seemed to come from nowhere and whose speech was almost indecipherable. As Bruce Cumings writes of the smart bomb:

> The advance of American technology allowed us to sit in our living rooms and watch missiles homing onto their Baghdad targets, relayed via nosecone cameras that had the good taste to cease transmitting just as they obliterated their quarry, thus vetting a cool, bloodless war through a cool medium. Here was "a kind of video press release," said a pioneer of the use of images to manipulate public opinion [David Gergen, *New York Times*, 6 May 1991]: a bomb that was simultaneously image, warfare, news, spectacle, and advertisement for the Pentagon.[19]

Although the immediate effect of the image was to advertise, both at home and abroad, the wonders of hi-tech weaponry, it soon became obvious from public reaction that the spectacle was double-edged. The image and the maneuver it represented were almost "too clean," and as countless phone-in radio and television talk shows registered, had the unappealing simplicity of a video game.[20] But apart from the emasculating and desensitizing associations of war-as-video-game, there was an aspect to the image that was profoundly disturbing. The defining feature of this image and sound was its inherent and intractable disembodiment—because no human body could be in the position of its recording, the images and sounds were available *only* to an electronic eye and ear. Disembodiment was announced within the image flow by the abrupt termination of transmission at the point of the bomb's impact. Operating on a physical, symbolic, and televisual register simultaneously, this termination was an index of absence and loss: the absence of the body, the severance of the television eye, and with it, the loss of the viewer qua viewer. It signaled the impossibility of embodied perception and at the same time presented a death or disconnection of telepresence, indicating the limits of television as the limits of the screen. For when the low-resolution image of the bomb's trajectory was, on impact, suddenly replaced by video "snow"—unorganized transmission—there was nothing to *see* except for the presence of transmission itself.[21] Reversing the logic of the screen as mirror, the viewer glimpsed pure data, data that signaled that the "window to the world" was, after all, an electronic relay, undecipherable, unseeable by the human eye. In that a-televisual moment, the viewer, locked into the narrative of television, was unable to witness the moment of climax, the "death" of the bomb. What the viewer witnessed instead was their own unscrambling as an embodied subject, for not only was it physically impossible for a human eye to be "behind" the camera on the nose cone, but the video snow, the singular sign of the bombs impact, represented a code that only technology could unravel.

Only a few days after its first appearance on the networks, the image of the smart bomb was constantly repeated, evolving into the sign, almost the logo, of not only hi-tech, but of television's dilemma. Its repetition was often accompanied by voice-overs comparing the "almost surreal" if somewhat sterile beauty of Gulf War images with those bloodied and affective pictures from Vietnam— "television's other great war."[22] Thus the "impersonal" image of the smart bomb, showing, after six days of fighting "not one single image of a dead soldier" came to represent that which television was prohibited from showing, and acted as a springboard from which discussions of the nature, indeed the raison d'être of television, could be launched. Never have I seen television so concerned with its nature, so divorced from itself that it would constantly acknowledge its failures or lament its "unseen." Nor have I seen television in such a peculiarly paradoxical position: like the statement "everything I say is a lie," television was forced to preface all reporting with the qualifier that censorship had applied from all sides. Television reacted to this odd position by developing a metacritical relation to itself; it formed itself as an object of analysis and declared that it was, in this instance, severely incapacitated. As if ushering in the post-televisual age, it pronounced the death of its present form, suggesting that a media metamorphosis was underway.

Post-television: Virtual viewers

Allucquere Stone describes cyberspace as a "locus of intense desire for refigured embodiment," and refigured embodiment was precisely what the Gulf War was all about.[23] In the trajectory of Western techno/philosophical development, a circularity forms: the desire for (Cartesian) disembodiment and severance from the "there" of worldliness and mortality enables the activity of war; war, especially the mutilations of a Vietnam, creates a disgust for the body; and hi-tech weaponry eliminates the "Vietnam syndrome" by sanitizing the body through technology. The body of the victor sparkles in its metal jacket, while the body of the victim disappears without a trace. With virtuality, the circuit is completed: floating above the carnage, the pilot initiates actions, the consequences of which are seen only via the snow of signal termination. This "sight," in both senses of the word, belongs to the spirit freed from flesh, the spirit that, in the metaphoric circuitry of virtuality, becomes an analogue to pure signal. According to Lt. Col. Jim Channon, U.S. Army, the advantage the free world has over the world of nonbelievers is that the free world has "God and microelectronics. The beauty is that you can use the microelectronics to project the spirit."[24] The "free" world however, was (and still is) addicted to the projection of visible bodies rather than phantasmic signals. As signal, the virtual body might represent the apotheosis of technological and cultural sophistication, yet viewers were made aware of this sophistication only via the contrast with the unsophisticated military technology that the "unfree" world displayed. It is interesting to note that while the narrative closure of the smart bomb was left to the imagination, the destruction caused by SCUD missiles was frequently shown, barring actual bodily damage. The aftermath of the SCUDS could be seen with the unaided eye and recorded by television because, as Pentagon spokespersons and news reporters intimated, the SCUDS were "stupid" unsophisticated things; they reminded one of outdated warfare with its unwelcome proximity to (outdated?) bodies.

Both sophistication and simulation hide their object as a secret, the revelation of which always exacts a price. The price in this case is the body, whose disappearance from sight via the determinations of virtuality coincides with the disintegration of "reality" as a humanly inhabitable topos in the wake of hi-tech culture. As if initiating the withdrawal inherent in virtuality, flight simulators such as SIMNET were developed by the military as a retreat from the costly real estate of terra firma.[25] And as if registering its own demise as an "effective" tool of the military, television attempted to wean the viewing public away from the desire to see, and therefore vicariously experience, the body in its war-torn state: in other words, to see and experience *itself*.[26] The only claim to the here-and-now of embodiment that television could make was via the sound accompanying and overflowing the impact of the smart bomb. The sound was identifiably "technological" despite its low fidelity, but unlike the video-game image, the sound of its muffled and distorted voices conjured up memories of early ham radio transmissions rather than of hi-tech maneuvers. As opposed to the clean and sophisticated image, the noise of the soundtrack was, like the SCUDS, a reminder of the body's presence. As such, the sound was more easily associated with an era prior to television, an era historically situated within the celebration of technology, radiophony, and the utopian dream of democratic participation via the "freedom" of the ether. Transferred to the tropic landscape of virtuality, the sound of two men communicating both within and about the purely technological sphere, accompanied by eerie and atopic frequency distortions and tones, evoked more of the utopian aspects of virtuality—that is, a reconnection of people through the "space" technology provides.

However, like the image, the sound was also profoundly disturbing. For if one listened to it closely, it was difficult not to wonder about the bodies of whom these voices "spoke." With no discernible speech to distract from the *sound* of the voice (which, after all, constituted the only possible representation of the bodies "behind" the bomb), the listener heard voices mauled by electronic transmission, riddled with the high-pitched scream of a lo-fi, stratospheric, military signal. Thus the "presence" of these voices, returning the listener to a nostalgic sign of technology's past, also revealed the terror of technics: the human voice, so precious to notions of individual authenticity, mutilated by the overriding will of the technology and screaming not from the pain of war but from the evisceration of electronic transfer.[27] Being outside a techno/cultural system characterized by "easy (televisual) listening," these shrieks communicated the fear and aggression of techno-war, piercing the smooth surface that the rhetoric and technology of the war had been tirelessly constructing.

Derrida writes that the ear is

> the distinct, differentiated, articulated organ that produces the effect of proximity . . . an organ whose structure (and the suture that holds it to the throat) produces the pacifying lure of organic indifference.[28]

In the context of Western metaphysics Derrida asks if it is possible to "violently penetrate philosophy's field of listening," to "puncture the tympanum of a philosopher"[29] without rendering philosophical praxis mute. In the same way, one wonders if the mutilated, disembodied voices of hi-tech militarism can be heard without the disquieting recognition that they belong to no-body, since the body has already been denied, first by the rhetoric and then by the sound itself. These voices not only open up the "suture" that holds mind and body together in a metaphysical unity, but they sonorize it, replacing the once silent, invisible point of elision incorporated in the techniques of philosophy and media production alike, with the ear-piercing, surface-rupturing, virtual, and aleatoric scream. This scream is also the call of virtuality, beckoning to a sociality already primed by television, planetary breakdown, and the threat of nuclear annihilation. It calls to and calls forth a New World Order in which the Third World becomes a viable alternative to Mutually Assured Destruction, in which civilian infrastructure is destroyed abroad while social and ideological infrastructure is transformed at home, and in which the viewer is also targeted. One matrix of operations is replaced by another, but the logic remains the same, and the locus of exchange continues to be the body and its metaphors.

Alberto Moreias writes that:

> Cyberspace is a receding space, a withdrawing space, a space as recess. To break into the perpetual recession: such is the addiction that dreams cyberspace as a private clearing for its human interfaces. It produces anxiety, as it is a melancholic exercise in endless loss.[30]

At the conjunction of television, virtuality, and war, the telepresence of the smart bomb represents a loss of narrative closure, of the master narrative itself: death in the bloom of the apocalypse. Shortly after the war, as if to guarantee the success of its surrogates, television delivered its postscript to the war coverage in the form of the Rodney King beating. Repeated with the same degree of fetishism that shrouded the smart bomb's appearance, exploiting the same low-quality, low-resolution images, the King beating transported the body, the technology that appropriated the body, and the truth, justice, and incontrovertible evidence that the body has thus far represented, back into the living room of the people via the now comparatively "sophisticated" medium of television.[31] At the same time, the similarity between the King footage and the image of the smart bomb allowed the authenticity of the former to be retroactively transferred to the latter, reaffirming the "truth" of both the documentary genre of television and the narrative structure of war. Like sound, the King beating was a way to evoke the irrevocable, to recuperate the loss, to reveal what could not be seen by the nose-cone eye, to create a "pacifying lure" through the organic ambience of repetition. Rodney King became the human cormorant of a militarized media operating in the field of the virtual. King's cries, inaudible to the viewer, nonetheless reverberate: crackling in the fires of Persia; echoing through the riots in Los Angeles; and calling, from the terminal purgatory of virtual transmissions, for an in/quest of presence.

Notes

1. Referring to VR, Michael Benedikt uses the common catchall "cyberspace," which he defines as "a globally networked, computer-sustained, computer-accessed, and computer generated, multidimensional, artificial, or 'virtual' reality. In this reality, to which every computer is a window, seen or heard objects are neither physical nor, necessarily, representations of physical objects but are, rather, in form, character and action, made up of data, of pure information. [Cyberspace includes] 'virtual reality' (VR), 'data visualization', 'graphic user interfaces' (GUIs), 'networks', 'multimedia', and 'hypergraphics'." Michael Benedikt, "Cyberspace: Some Proposals," in Cyberspace: First Steps, ed. Michael Benedikt (Cambridge: MIT Press, 1991), 122–23.

2. Michael Heim writes: "With its virtual environments and simulated worlds, cyberspace is a metaphysical laboratory, a tool for examining our very sense of reality." Michael Helm," The Erotic Ontology of Cyberspace," in Benedikt, Cyberspace, 59.

3. Italian Futurism or the North American fascination for things electronic are good examples of proto-virtual engagements. See Futurist Manifestps. ed. Umbro Apollonio (London: Thames and Hudson, 1971); and Carolyn Marvin, When Old Tec   hnologies Were New (Oxford: Oxford University Press, 1988).

4. Cf. Jaron Lanier: "You go home and you're in your living room and you put on the glove and then suddenly you're in the room again, but . . . there's a big rack of fish tanks, and in the fish tanks there are little people running around doing things . . . you put your hand into one of these bowls and you experience yourself flying into the scene." Interview in Afterimage, 1991.

5. Alberto Moreiras, "The Leap and the Lapse: A Private Site in Cyberspace,,," unpublished paper quoted courtesy of the author, 1992.

6. Ibid.

7. As Michael Heim writes: "Only a short philosophical step separates [the] Platonic notion of knowledge from the matrix of cyberspace entities. . . . Both approaches to cognition first extend and then renounce the physical embodiment of knowledge. . . . Now, with the support of the electronic matrix, [the Platonic] dream can incorporate the smallest details of here-and-now existence." Heim, in Cyberspace, op. cit., pp. 63–65.

8. See Eric Partridge, *Origins: A Short Etymological Dictionary of Modern English* (New York: Macmillan, 1966), 711: "theory" and 701 "L. *contemplare.*" For additional etymological readings, see Mark Krupnick, introduction to *Displacement: Derrida and After,* ed. Mark Krupnick (Bloomington: Indiana University Press, 1987), 22.

9. Heim, "Erotic Ontology," 74 –78.

10. As Alan Williams points out, if sound is understood as vibrating air, then reproduced sound is in effect an ontologically different sound. See Alan Williams, "Is Sound Recording Like a Language?" in *Yale French Studies* 60 (1980).

11. Benedikt, *Cyberspace,* 3.

12. See Walter J.Ong, *The Presence of the Word* (Minneapolis: University of Minnesota Press, 1967); and Richard Kostelanetz, ed., *John Cage* (New York: Praeger, 1968), 167. Cf. *cyberphantasia:* "We will all become angels, and for eternity! Highly unstable, hermaphrodite angels, unforgettable in terms of computer memory." Nicole Stenger, "Mind is a Leaking Rainbow," in Benedikt, *Cyberspace,* 52.

13. Benedikt, *Cyberspace,* 10.

14. Allucquere Rosanne Stone, "Will the Real Body Please Stand Up?: Stories about Virtual Cultures," in Benedikt, *Cyberspace,* 98.

15. One such electronic community developed from the "Communi-Tree Group," whose tree-structured conferencing network with its Star Wars rhetoric and spiritualist overtones was nonetheless overloaded and eventually destroyed by the "obscene and scatological messages" of young male hackers. See ibid., 91.

16. According to Susan Douglas "The coming of wireless telegraphy has made it possible for the private citizen to communicate across great distances without the aid of either the government or a corporation, so that the organization of the American Radio Relay League actually marks the beginning of a new epoch in the interchange of information and the transmission of messages." Susan Douglas, "Amateur Operators and American Broadcasting: Shaping the Future of Radio," in *Imagining Tomorrow,* ed. Joseph J. Corn, (Cambridge: MIT Press, 1987), 50.

17. For a rendition of this event and these sounds, see my audio work *Highways to Virtuality,* ABC Radio, May 1991.

18. From Bruce Cumings, *War and Television* (New York: Verso, 1992), 109. Ed Turner, in response to a caller criticizing CNN for trying to interview a wounded woman on a stretcher, said: "I don't believe a CNN reporter was trying to interview that woman; more likely they were trying to get natural sound, that is, picking up the sirens and the bricks being moved. . . ." (Friday, 25 January, CNN). This was the first image of the wounded, and interestingly the image of the bloodsoaked body was immediately connected to or justified by the "need" for sound.

19. Cumings, *War and Television*, 122.

20. For instance, in a conversation between Larry Benski and Lenny Segal on radio station KPFA, a caller responded to the lack of coverage of the devastation by saying, "One of the things I find particularly pernicious about video games is the instant gratification . . . the fact that you press a button, something happens and it's instant . . . and there's no complexity to the development of events and I think that's the mentality that we're facing in the Middle East right now." This theme was repeated by Segal: "The pilots over there grew up on video games—you fire a weapon and it hits a target and it goes poof!—disappears. That's not the way it happens in the real world. . . . I've heard a report from pilots who say that they're so far away from the planes that they're firing at that they don't even know whether they've downed the aircraft. That's the stand-off weapons that we're putting in there where you don't really see the target, you don't really know what you've destroyed. . . . The other side of it of course is that it all seems so clean . . . with the video game approach to war . . . you fire a weapon, the blip on your screen disappears and you chalk up a point. One of my fears in this war is that Bush is hoping he'll get such a high score in this game that he'll get to do it again . . . that's one way in which technology has transformed warfare . . . made it more of a game." Lenny Segal, representing the Military Toxics Campaign, Pacific Studies Center, 222B View St., Mountainview, CA 94041.

21. In reference to cinema, Stone associates the "flatness" of the screen with a lack of corporeal interactivity, and takes the potential for interaction as one of the distinguishing characteristics of computer simulation: "Interaction is the physical concretization of a desire to escape the flatness and merge into the created system. . . . It is the sense in which the "spectator" is more than a participant, but becomes both participant in and creator of the simulation. In brief, it is the sense of unlimited power which the dis/embodied simulation produces, and the different ways in which socialization has led those always-embodied participants confronted with the sign of unlimited power to respond." Stone, in Benedikt, *Cyberspace*, 107.

22. For instance, in a report on radio station KPIX, San Francisco, 30 January, the narrator Bob McKenzie commented that "these surreal broadcasts from the eye of Desert Storm have truly made all of us part of a global village. According to a survey just released by the Times/Mirror center, 81 percent of Americans are keeping their TV's or radios tuned to news. . . . There is still the question of whether that coverage is telling the full story. On TV we've seen many pictures of sophisticated military equipment doing its job, but so far we have not seen much of what war is truly about— human beings . . . and in that respect this war differs from TVs other great war—Vietnam. It was pictures like these that burned into the minds of viewers. By contrast, pictures of the Gulf War have tended to be almost antiseptic: high tech pictures from a high-tech war . . . amazing pictures

kept coming showing the marvels of precision bombing: a smart bomb drops neatly into an air vent on the top of a building . . . there's an eerie impersonal beauty about some of these pictures as there is in the sight of a Patriot missile in the sky over Tel Aviv. . . . Perhaps the first time the war took on a human face for many of us was when Iraq paraded POWs in front of a camera . . . they were a jolting reminder that hi-tech war has human consequences. . . . "

23. Stone, in Benedikt, *Cyberspace*, 108.

24. Cited in Chris H. Gray, "The Cyborg Soldier," in *Cyborg Worlds*, ed. Les Levidow and Kevin Robins (London: Free Association Books, 1989), 60.

25. "In view of the price of land and fuel, and of the escalating costs of staging practice maneuvers, the armed forces felt that if a large-scale consensual simulation could be made practical they could realize an immediate and useful financial advantage." Stone, in Benedikt, *Cyberspace*, 92.

26. As Cumings writes, "In place of sincere inquiry into exactly what the weapons were doing to Iraq, television proffered yet another hero: however deaf, dumb and blind the medium may have been during the Gulf War, the weapons were smart. Since this was one of the few technologies Americans could be proud of in the recent period, it also got wrapped into the patriotic aura. And here, television for once was also 'smart': the weapons were television-guided or television-observed." Cumings, *War and Television*, 124.

27. For an elaboration of the "presence" of the electro-voice, see my "Towards a Genealogy of the Radio Voice," in *Radio Rethink* (Banff: Walter Phillips Gallery, forthcoming).

28. Jacques Derrida, "Tympan," in *Margins of Philosophy* (Chicago: University of Chicago Press, 1981), xvii.

29. Ibid., xii.

30. Moreiras, "The Leap and the Lapse."

31. A factor in the semiotics of the King images was their context: these were decidedly a-televisual images belonging to the sphere of the people. In particular they belong to citizens recording abuses against the people.

3 Consumer Culture and the Technological Imperative: The Artist in Dataspace*

Simon Penny

In many discussions of computer arts, the conversation has focused upon a dialectic between the sciences and the arts—a recapitulation of C. P. Snow's somewhat dated dualism.[1] I want to insert a third term, without which such a discussion can have only limited relevance to contemporary culture: consumer commodity economics.

Unless artists are in direct contact with research labs, their access to "science" is via commodities, and their product, as a product of those tools, can also be regarded as falling within that system. Science, moreover, has achieved its authority in our culture by virtue of the fact that it is the ideology that allowed industrial mass production to occur. Technologies have been brought to market amid complex rhetorics that subscribe to scientific/technical virtues such as speed, precision, and the "saving" of labor, and, at the same time, call upon humanistic utopian notions such as democracy and leisure. Artists, as members of consumer culture, are immersed in and subject to these systems of persuasion. An artist cannot engage technology without engaging consumer commodity economics. I intend here to explore

---

*A previous version of this paper was presented at the Artificial Games Symposium, presented by Medien Labor München, Germany 1993, and has been translated into German for an anthology arising from the symposium, edited by Florian Rötzer (forthcoming). Several paragraphs in this essay also appear in *Virtual Reality as the End Point of the Enlightenment Project*, which was simultaneously published in two anthologies: *Culture on the Brink; Idologies of Technology*, Ed. Bender and Druckrey, Bay Press 1994, and *Virtual Reality Casebook*, Ed. Anderson and Loeffler, Van Nostrand 1994.

in various ways, the position of the artist who uses technological tools, with respect to the larger formations of technologically mediated culture. [2]

Disappearing aesthetics

In 1990, Canadian artist Nancy Paterson completed a piece called *Bicycle TV* in which an interactive laser disc was interfaced with a bicycle and its rider. The monitor displayed video sequences of travel on country roads. Three years later, exercise cycles were available with simulated travel on graphic displays. The release of a consumer commodity conceptually identical to Paterson's artwork places the esthetic worth of the piece in jeopardy. Alternatively: the consumer items are all artworks. Or: the piece, though it made claim to exist in the realm of "art," in fact did not. These three equally unpalatable alternatives throw into high relief the crisis of meaning for electronic media artwork.

In this liminal territory, "art practice" and technological invention overlap. What is conceived as an art project can become a product to be marketed, a potential moneymaker. I attach no value to this slippage between one role and another; it simply indicates the soft edges of art discourse in this territory.

What if Delacroix's *Raft of the Medusa* had become aesthetically redundant due to the proliferation of copies of it on mass-produced vinyl shower curtains only a few years after its completion? A conventional response might be to ascribe value to the "originality" of Delacroix's work, of which the curtains were only "copies." But in the late twentieth century, both theoretically and technically, that notion of intellectual property residing permanently in the "original" is tenuous. The notion of originality is so closely linked to the notion of "inspiration" that it completely denies that artists work in a cultural and historical context in which they, at best, "reprocess" ideas. And if the work consists of a manufactured bicycle and a laserdisc, these are both already mass-produced, and any traces of the precious "hand of the artist" are scarce.

Unrequited consumption

Electronic technologies are consumer commodities. Technological "progress," the relentless arrival of new models and updates, is fueled not necessarily by a cultural or societal need, but by corporate need for profit. Markets are constructed in order to sell the new model.

Artists who engage these technologies also simultaneously engage consumer commodity economics. They are induced to upgrade continually. This creates a financial burden and a pressure to continually retrain, to learn the newest version of the software. The need to upgrade is not necessarily a product of the artists' aesthetic development. Thus they are caught in a cycle of unrequited technological consumption. Artists can barely learn the new technology before it is replaced with another. Art practice requires a holistic consideration of the cultural context of the subject matter, but the pace of technological change prevents just such a consideration.

There are numerous cases over the last twenty-five years of artists who feel compelled to develop a technology to realize their ideas, because they feel their aesthetic ideas are intimately linked to the technology of realization. There is a history of artists' fascination with technology, from the Cybernetic Serendipity and Experiments in Art and Technology to Survival Research Laboratories and the Banff Center (Canada) Virtual Reality initiative. One pitfall of this fascination is due to the inherent complexity of electronic technology: artists (who generally lack at least some of the required technical skills) get bogged down in technical problems and the less tangible esthetic and cultural aspects of the work get lost.

Given the slippery slide of technological change, what is it that artists want with this stuff? There is often a geekiness, a boys-with-toys mentality, a fascination with mechanism. But as members of consumer culture, artists are also not immune to the successive waves of liberatory and democratizing utopian rhetoric. They hear, like everyone else, that video puts TV in the hands of people, or that VR is the best-yet manifestation of the space of dreams, or that one must reach out and touch someone.

As in the case of Nancy Paterson described above, if the artist is lucky, s/he gets the project finished before the corporate R&D labs release a consumer version. But at most s/he'll have a year or two in the sun before there's a Nintendo or Panasonic version. At that point the aesthetic value of that work evaporates.

Is this what art will be in technological times: way-out-there (unpaid) R&D for the military infotainment complex? (And would we prefer it if we were paid?) There is a history in the U.S. of research labs (Atari in the early 80s, Xerox PARC in the 90s) offering artist-in-residencies. There is good evidence that artists' use of emerging technologies is very useful (and cheap) beta-testing for manufacturers. In these ways, artists sometimes inadvertently support the creation of new markets for technological commodities.

The pace of technological change can also render whole classes of work obsolete. A perfect example is artwork on half-inch video, which has effectively disappeared due to the disappearence of playback equipment and breakdown of tape. So here is a dual problematic, with both aspects related to the rapid change in technological commodites. One pertains to art and industrial production, and the other to art and the dynamics of consumer culture:

1. the pressure to retrain (elaborated below: technofatigue)
2. aesthetic obsolescence forced by the irrelevant criterion of advancing technical standards, or arrival of consumer commodities of similar form.

Contrary to the beliefs of the art and technology movement of the 70s, I am arguing that in important ways, this technological system may prohibit art practice, or at least any sort of art practice that takes a critical position. If rapidly increasing standards make the computer artist feel forced to continually upgrade and retrain, then little time is left to do the work of artmaking: the creative analysis and questioning of the relationship between these technologies and culture.

Beneath this lies the vicious possibility that although the tools change, the *underlying value systems* do not. We are confronted with a paradoxical condition in which we are challenged to keep up with a changing technology whose philosophical agenda is stagnant or retrogressive. This technology, moreover, may have the insidious ability to reify a value system that precludes art practice.

Technofatigue

I recall a Gary Larsen cartoon in which a cretinous-looking student stands up in class and says to the teacher, "May I be excused? My brain is full." I feel like that a lot lately. My brain is full of function keys for dozens of obsolete software packages. The prospect of learning a new software application, or even an update, fills me with dread. My professional situation exposes me to this more than most people, as I'm expected to be able to teach a range of these things. I would like to look at the question of changing technologies and time management from this perspective.

As a teacher of computer art, I am forced to put in long hours learning new peripherals and their software. I just took a new job. I have to learn the resident software packages, the peculiarities of the lab and campus network, and so forth. This load translates into hours of rote learning. Imagine if every two years the tools of a painter went out of date and the painter had to retrain: if drawing paper suddenly became multidimensional, paintbrushes were motorized, and color-mixing was achieved by numerical operation!

In the context of this changing landscape, my pedagogical strategy has been to emphasize conceptual skills that the student may "port" from one package or platform to another, rather than to encourage fetishization of a particular product that will likely be obsolete before he or she graduates. But it becomes clear that what I had considered to be general conceptual notions almost universally applicable to computer art are also subject to obsolescence. As machines become more powerful and more procedures become transparent, basic structural understandings are subsumed into deep levels of software and hardware, and become irrelevant to the end-user.

This is a burden that the pace of technological change and the "irrelevant criterion" of technological up-to-dateness forces upon us. One is bound to ask: will this ever slow down? My current guess is that a consumer resistance will force a change in the cavalier way that new packages are introduced to the market. To some extent that is beginning to happen.

Ossification of interfaces

I learned to drive a car twenty years ago, and I can still jump into any car and drive it away. The automobile user-interface has reached a level of maturity at which it has ceased to change, a level that software has not yet approached. What constitutes this moment of maturity? The conventional answer would be that the automobile-user technology reached a maturity, at which time it was fully adopted by the market, the user base. But perhaps this "maturity" was forced by cultural inertia: when fifty percent of the population learned to drive in their late teens, the interface stopped changing. That doesn't mean it had become perfect at that moment but that it had become integrated into the cultural fabric. Around that time any number of songs about cars appeared in popular music. I recently heard a blues song that went:

> I'm going to Dallas to get my carburetor cleaned,
> 'cause those West Texas women use dirty gasoline.

When MTV has songs about file transfer protocols and hard disc optimization, we'll know we've reached a threshold. Recently I heard the radio personality Garrison Keillor relate a story about a vacation. The list of things to do before locking up the house included putting out the cat, turning off the oven, and backing up the hard drive. It's happening: computer culture is ossifying. Nerd culture leads the way, but it is decidedly a subculture. A few weeks ago a friend remarked that someone "went nonlinear" (they became unpredictable, emotionally unstable). I'll know that computer culture is here when my mother offers me a "core dump" on some issue.

Does this mean that computing, particularly domestic computing, will stop developing at that point? Yes and no: the interface will set, but changes will occur behind the scenes, where they ought to occur. It makes no difference to the user interface if I am driving a car that has a carburetor or is fuel-injected.

It becomes clear that a technology-in-development passes through certain stages to which one might apply an anthropomorphic analogy. It goes through an infancy, an adolescence, and an adulthood. Infancy is marked by high expense, low general applicability, development within closed institutions (research labs, universities). Adolescence marks the moment when the technology is generally available, yet open to substantial change. Adulthood is marked by conventionalization, resistance to change, and full residence and integration in the community. These stages parallel the stages of software development: alpha, beta, and full commercial release. In my lifetime I have watched the adolescence of video, CB radio, domestic computing, desktop interactivity and, most recently, VR come and go. Broadcast multimedia has its adolescence now.

It must be emphasised that this "adolescence" is a critical moment for anyone interested in the form a technology will take in culture. It is the moment when the technology acquires its meaning and use as part of culture. Once it is institutionalized it will acquire a conservatism and will resist change. Institutions resist change, as anyone who has been involved in alternative television projects knows too well.

Artistic knowledge bases

I contend that artists often work with cultural questions long before those questions become relevant to the rest of culture. I have observed previously that conceptual art can be thought of as "cultural software."[3] Conceptual art, as an end point of modernist reductivism, finally arrived at the disembodied artwork, pure cultural information. Disembodied information is software, and conceptual artists worked on many of the problems that would later arise within computer technology.

As computing became visual, the skills of image-makers suddenly became valuable in the computing world. As computing becomes multisensorial and spatial, the skills of sculptors and dancers will become equally valued.

A vast untapped knowledge base for the development of interactive media exists in the corpus of Happening-Environment-Installation-Performance-Fluxus artwork of the last thirty years. These radical, experimental genres took the "user interface" and "interaction" as their subject matter before anyone thought in such terms. Wasn't it Allan Kaprow, Jim Dine, and Claes Oldenberg in the 60s, and a little later Joseph Beuys, Vito Acconci, Adrian Piper, Arnulf Rainer, and a host of others who explored the realm of art as interactive play, of dissolving the artist/audience division?[4] Not only is the cognitive science/computer science community generally unaware of this knowledge base, but the general tendency for art research to preempt technological problems remains largely unremarked.

Lev Manovich[5] has made an engaging argument regarding Paul Cézanne's dictum that, in painting, forms should be reduced to basic geometrical elements. Manovich points out that Cézanne took part in the philosophical development of what Manovich calls the "industrialization of vision," a development that would ultimately find realization in 3-D computer graphics almost a century later.

There is an argument bandied about in certain circles that art practice that uses emerging technology is of value because it is future oriented: by virtue of its tools, it is "progressive." This implicitly puts the artwork in a position subservient to the technology, which, by virtue of the fact that it already exists, must be more "advanced."

I am arguing the contrary: that artists are encumbered by current technologies and realize their ideas in the available technologies as best they can. These are ideas for which the appropriate technologies do not yet exist, and the artists are part of the generating system that will give rise to the technology. In terms of technological development, this argument is hard to refute: the intellectual and scientific groundwork for the A-bomb *had to* exist before the bomb was made. The difficulty would seem to be in allowing that artists can take some active part in the evolution of ideas that create (the desire for) technologies.

Construction of the viewing paradigm

As Jonathan Crary has argued in *Techniques of the Observer,*[6] the cultural training that a viewer brings to an artwork is critical in that person's experience of the work. Modes of consumption of conventional art media are culturally inculcated; behavior at a football match is different from that at a ballet. One common criticism of interactive media art is that the technology or the techniques are in a developmental stage, i.e., not mature. This may well be, but it is also true that the techniques of the user are also in a nascent stage. Into this vacuum pour paradigms from other areas, most commonly those from electronic gaming arcades, from the desktop computer, from television, and from the art gallery. Not only in the artworks themselves but in the responses of the users we find a curious condition of "paradigms in collision." This was illustrated graphically by the fate of *Machine in the Garden* (a piece in *Machine Culture* [see footnote 10] by Nancy Paterson), built on the model of a poker machine. Its handle was ripped off by users keen to "win" the game; they were porting their arcade battle game behavior into this new context. Some interfaces have become standardized, become genres. The arcade game is one. I know what to do in a general way before I walk into the arcade. If the arcade game paradigm is applied generally in interactive art, "interpassivity," a Pavlovian interactivity of stimulus and response, will be induced.

There is a burden of responsibility on the visitor to these interactive works, because the codes and conventions required to "read" the work have not been culturally established. The new audience must take care not to impose critical judgments germane to an older media (be it computer games or painting) upon a new and different medium.

Cultural contexts

There is historically a tendency among the technical community to view their research and production as being outside culture. This is, I believe, a dangerous tendency. A computer is as much a product of the culture that produced it as is a silver tea set or a sacrificial knife. Technological products draw their structure and meaning from the cultural education of their makers.

We hear often that one program is better than another because its interface is more "intuitive" or that its processes are "transparent." These terms are closely related in software-speak. In this jargon they have acquired different meanings from those they possess conventional English. We certainly do not look through the monitor at the circuit boards behind! Nor do we look through the graphical user interface (GUI) at the code from which it is built. This would be "transparent" in the sense of an early work by Alan Rath, a "word processor," in which a pair of lips on the screen would speak the letter of the key the user pressed on the keyboard. *Transparent* means that the computer interface fades into the experiential background and the analogy on which the software is based (typewriter, drawing table, paintbox, etc.) is foregrounded. If the paintbox software is "intuitive," it is only intuitive because the paintbox is a culturally familiar object. I had one when I was a kid, so I know the rules of paintboxes. The computer software models its "interface" on the modes of proper interaction with a paintbox. By the same token, it precludes "improper" interactions like sitting in the paint, eating the paint, or smearing it on places other than the "paper." But paintboxes, and the rules for using them, are culturally specific, and specific (to differing degrees) to the user's gender, social class, and ethnicity. The presumption that any interface is universal is a pitfall for developers of technologies that will cross cultural borders. Rejane Spitz has illustrated this in the case of the introduction of automatic teller machines (which presume literacy) into Brazil, where much of the population is only semiliterate.

You may have seen the T-shirt that says : "Apple gives you the power to be your best." The liberationist rhetoric of computer marketing must be weighed against the reality of value-reification inherent in any complex cultural product such as a computer. No selection process is value-free, by definition. Software projects are shaped by the worldviews of their makers, and their value systems are (often unknowingly) incorporated into the work. The value systems of consumerism are "embedded" in hardware or software. Computer menus are a mirror of diner menus (Ranch? Thousand Island? Blue Cheese? Oil and Vinegar?) or the supermarket array. At the computer, as in the supermarket, one *submits* to the interactive scenario and the limited freedoms it offers: total freedom among a set of fixed options. A postmodern capitalist paradise! In postmodern times, we build a personal identity from novel combinations of manufactured commodities. "I shop, therefore I am."

Computer technology, hardware architecture, and software design reify value systems. The consequences of this reification were clearly evident in the Computers and Sculpture session of the 1992 International Sculpture Symposium in Philadelphia. Here I witnessed numerous presentations by sculptors who had harnessed the (awesome) power of the computer to generate variations on their sculptural ideas and control production directly through robotic milling machines, stereolithography, and other computer-controlled tools. Unfortunately, these sculptural ideas were thoroughly outdated, modernist, and formalist, and brought no new understanding of the nature of sculpture or its relationship to the computer technology. The application of the technology created a marvelous monotony of variations on Hans Arp or Isamu Noguchi: a "hyperconformity of difference."[8]

Formalism, canons and algorithms

Formalisms are canonical. Computers are machines for manipulating rule systems, adjusting parameters. An extreme case of the canon is the algorithm. Certain modernist styles are so constrained in their parameters that they can be regarded as rule systems. This has been borne out by the work of Russell and Joan Kirsch, who have built a computer program that produces drawings that continue Miro's *Constellation* series using a technique known as LISP shape grammars. Similar work has been done by Raymond Lauzzana with respect to the drawings of Kandinsky.

Here the potential basic incompatibility of computer systems with art practice is thrown into high relief, for elaboration of a canon is simply elaboration, while it is the quality of invention that we value in art. Invention is not random; it is based on the analysis of canons and codes, and on the inversion of terms. The computer process just generates possibilities, the subtle assessment of value among the choices is beyond the capability of the machine. We may posit a rule system for making choices, but this system will be grounded in another set of assumptions that are held stable. In artistic invention, this set of assumptions would itself come under scrutiny. This situation results in infinite regress when framed in machine hierarchical terms. But in human culture the relation between sets of rule systems is not one of nesting but weighting of terms in a matrix that folds in on itself.

Take, for example, the following statements: 1. It's OK to build an A-bomb, but only when you're currently at war. 2. The scientists are guiltless because science is neutral. 3. If you are a scientist who designs a big gun for a Middle Eastern potentate, then science is not neutral and you are guilty.[9] There is a circularity to these statements and a fluidity in their criteria that discourage their hierarchical arrangement.

Scientific imperative

Throughout the twentieth century, new ideas in the sciences have drifted into the humanities. This process of migration of ideas has much to do with the scientific imperative in twentieth-century culture: science is progress, science is more "true." Early in the century, relativity and indeterminacy left their mark on the humanities, and more recently the technical definition of "communication" in information theory has confused telematic art (discussed below). In computer arts the idea of the "universal machine" (a basic tenet of computer science) is at best complicating, and at worst completely misleading. For although a theoretical Turing machine may be "universal" in a mathematical sense, the computer as a cultural object is anything but. Variously seen as an ominous force aligned with big business or as the receptacle of ill-defined cyberculture, the machine is highly coded. Whatever appears on the screen, it is framed by the monitor and keyboard.

The question of the universal machine is indicative of the collision of two disciplines that have traditionally been quite separate in our culture: art and engineering. Practitioners in computer art tend to come from within one or the other of these disciplines. In general, the works that these two types produce seem to be quite different.

Computer scientists, having been trained in a deterministic discipline, tend to dislike multivalent information, the counterposed, the complex. They seem to shy away from holding an opinion, desiring political neutrality. The artwork is formal and work arises out of an abstract appreciation of the elegance of an algorithm, a clever application of a mathematical notion, or similar ideas. The final product tends to be a "readout" of the functioning of that algorithmic system, and an appreciation of the art quality is derived by reading back into the visual display, intellectually "reverse engineering" the work. The user interface "presents" the obscured (mathematical) beauty functioning in the machine.

When this scientific mind-set is applied by a user of an interactive artwork, it can have dire aesthetic consequences. It can lead to an approach in which the work is consumed by intellectual reverse engineering. Having (to the user's satisfaction) "solved" the system, the visitor might move on, oblivious to the fact that he or she has sidestepped the aesthetic dimension of the work.

Computer scientists are trained to manipulate conceptual objects, which (like the universal machine) are assumed to have general applicability to various practical applications. Visual artists are trained to manipulate tangible objects with unique and specific qualities, but which (alone or in association) can allude to larger concepts.

Interactive media artists who come from an art background tend to focus their attention on the experience of the user as an act of communication, on the social space of the interface, and on the dynamics of interaction. The work tends to be the elaboration of a position; it is concept driven. The execution of the program may be merely expedient—hacked together from whatever code and hardware will do the job. Contrary to the clear and direct presentation of the technical community, these artists exploit innuendo, connotation, allusion, and sometimes self-contradiction. The information given the viewer tends to be polyvalent, without closure.

The Machine Culture exhibition[10] offered a particularly clear example of these two approaches in two works of interactive fiction. *Edge of Intention* (Joseph Bates et al.)[11] uses artificial intelligence techniques to construct an environment in which several cartoon-like agents "play." It is based on a knowledge base of plot structure and character development distilled from English literature and drama. It is an ambitious project which is still in its infancy. The characters (woggles) possess rudimentary personality and can sense the location of the user via sonar. The audience experience at this point is fairly shallow, amounting to meeting a group of moody jelly beans.

By contrast, Luc Courchesne's *Family Portrait* consisted of four low-tech stations: four laser discs, four Macintosh Classics, and a simple hypercard stack. Yet the simulation of human interaction was uncanny. The artist had intentionally removed the computer and AV hardware from view; even the monitor was missing, and the image was reflected in an oblique sheet of glass. This focused attention on the depictions on the glass, the portraits. Within these portraits, Courschesne displays great finesse at simulating human interaction in the social space of the interface, between the user and the laser disc representation. To heighten the effect, the four virtual characters would occasionally break their exchange with the user to interrupt or contradict each other.

The value system of engineering

Computer engineering, software engineering, and knowledge engineering are heirs to the tradition of engineering, the quintessential industrial revolution science, and are concerned with efficient production by means of standardization of parts and processes. A computer is a device for automating production, and automation of production is dependent upon standardization of objects and categories.[12]

It may be that this process of standardization is antithetical to certain creative goals. It is true that many artistic and cultural movements over the last century have attempted to strategize with respect to the phenomenon of industrial mass production: the writings of William Morris provide an early example, and Walter Benjamin's "The Work of Art in the Age of Mechanical Reproduction"[13] remains a crucial early text. Constructivism, the Bauhaus, and the Futurists were all concerned with these issues, as were, later in the century, artists such as Les Levine, who explored the notion of the mass-produced work of art with "multiples."

Though standardization is one of the central ideas of mass production, ours is a historical moment when ideas of standardization are being questioned in the humanities and the sciences, from social policies of multiculturalism to endo-physics to the instantly reprogrammable robotic production line. The engineering worldview is invested in the possibility of the "objective observer." As Florian Rötzer has noted: "The model of the external observer . . . is gradually being superseded, not only in science but also in art."[14]

It might be asserted that the major ideas that have shaped this century are due to Marx, Freud, Einstein, and Heisenberg. What effect have their ideas had on the development of the computer? The answer must be: Close to none. And what of newer philosophical ideas that actively critique Cartesian rationalism: poststructralism, feminism, and other varieties of postmodern thought? We might ask "What could a feminist computer be? How might it differ from the computer we now have?" Nell Tenhaaf states:

> Contemporary women artists who work in technological media are faced with a contradiction. The domain in which they are operating has been historically considered masculine, yet women's current access to electronic production tools seems to belie any gender barrier. Indeed, women have benefited in the last two decades to the extent that they have offered some freedom from the sexist art historical and critical practices attached to more established media.The philosophy of technology, however, has been articulated entirely from a masculinist perspective in terms that metaphorize and marginalize the feminine. In real social discourse, this claiming of technology has been reinforced by, and has probably encouraged, a male monopoly on technical expertise, diminishing or excluding the historical contributions of women to technological developments.[15]

She asserts that this invisibility of the feminine calls for "a radical reconstitution of technology." We must ask ourselves whether the architecture of the machine as it currently exists and the premises of software engineering are not themselves so encumbered with old philosophical ideas that any "reconstitution" would amount only to surface decoration.

A case example of the culturally "male" perspective is the standard paradigm of navigation in virtual space. Simply stated: "what the eye wants, the eye gets" in this world of unhindered voyeuristic desire. It is a machine that articulates scopic desire. Erkki Huhtamo has traced a historical continuity from the phallic "penetration shot" of cinema—a paradigm of the all-powerful gaze, a colonizing, conquering gaze to which the limitless infinities of virtual space can offer no obstacle. If navigation in VR is the articulation of the phallic gaze, we might consider what a feminine alternative might be. Agnes Hegedus has presented us with such a "radical reconstitution of technology" in her work *Handsight*.[16] In this piece the hand guides a helpless eye, as one might help an elderly person. In conventional VR, the eye can fly and grab, unhindered by the body; in *Handsight*, the body leads the helpless eye about the virtual space. Here the virtual space is not a limitless frontier but a closely bounded domain whose physical boundaries prohibit the illusion of limitlessness. This inversion is experiential; one discovers it through interaction and consideration.

These considerations open out onto a vast field of recent critical theory concerning the body and its relationship with gender, technology, and the mind. My own focus has been on the way the Cartesian mind/body duality has been articulated in computer technology and particularly in VR.[17] Much of the rhetoric around VR focuses on the notion of presence (you will BE there!!). There have been many discussions about the "reality" of virtual presence (Is it real? How real is it?). On the one hand, postmodern criticism has taught us to abandon the "authentic" as a useful criteria, referring as it does to the previous version or iteration or to memories of childhood. On the other hand, the illusion of "being there" is the rhetoric that sold cinema and TV, and any number of theme park rides over the last hundred years. (It probably sold the Sistine chapel.) And any chimpanzee can tell the difference between being at the stadium and watching the game on TV.

In late 1990, when VR had just burst out of the labs into popular culture, I began to examine some of the rhetorical claims concerning "the body" in VR. It has been claimed that VR is a liberation from the Cartesian mind-body duality. This would be a marvelous thing if it were true, as neurological and physiological research over the last fifty years seems to indicate that such a distinction cannot be substantiated. The mind-body split is, at best, a philosophical convenience and, at worst, completely wrong. The notion of a body (virtual or real) "driven" by mind like some kinds of teleoperated robot, an obedient servant, is a basic tenet of nineteenth-century industrialism: the bosses and the workers. To me, VR seems to blithely reconstitute a mind/body split that is essentially patriarchal and industrialist.

It would be an oversimplification to claim that the body is not present in VR interaction, for this would imply that the body is not the device through which we interface with the technology. But it would likewise be an oversimplification to claim that the body is *in* VR. The body, we might say, is partially present. It functions as an "effector," but the sensorial feedback is almost exclusively visual (with the occasional addition of sound).

VR technology, far from including the body in a virtual environment, actively excludes the physical body, replacing it with a body image. One does not take one's body into VR. One leaves it at the door while the mind goes wandering, unhindered by a physical body, inhabiting an ethereal virtual body in pristine virtual space, itself a "pure" Platonic space, free of farts, dirt, and untidy bodily fluids. In VR the body is broken into sensor and effector components, a panoptical eye and a slave body that "works" the representation but is invisible within it. As such it is a clear continuation of the rationalist dream of disembodied mind, part of the long Western tradition of denial of the body. This reaffirms the Cartesian duality, reifying it in code and hardware.[18]

These examples suggest that the value systems reified in computer technology are somewhat behind the times. One might fairly ask if it is possible to build a "post-industrial" esthetic within such a steam-powered technology.

Techno-utopian rhetorics

A blitzkrieg of marketing, replete with gushing techno-utopian rhetoric, has ushered interactive multimedia into the consumer commodity marketplace. Business people, educators, and others now "know" that interactive multimedia not only exists, but is a boon to productivity and creativity. Broadcast multimedia is currently a very hot business opportunity in the U.S.A. This new technology is only the most recent in successive waves of new technologies that have been borne into the world amidst utopian fanfares. Technophilic hype seems to have been an aspect of technological PR since the beginning of the industrial revolution, as is evidenced by this piece of doggerel from the 1830s:

> Lay down your rails, ye nations near and far—
> Yoke your full trains to Steam's triumphal car.
> Link town to town; unite with iron bands
> The long estranged and oft embattled lands.
> Peace, mild-eyed seraph—Knowledge, light divine,
> Shall send their messengers by every line . . .
> Blessings on Science, and her handmaid Steam!
> They make Utopia only half a dream.[19]

It is useful to look at the way these previous technologies have embedded themselves into culture, for the technologies themselves are mute until they become invested with narratives and enmeshed in culture. It becomes clear that the realities of new technologies as they are actually implemented is generally in direct opposition to the rhetorics that heralded them into the market. Artists and inventors imbued with a sincere utopianism often become part of the mechanism by which such technologies become products, but the final implementation of those technologies in their social context is often very different from the utopian visions of these artists and inventors.[20]

One of the classic techno-utopian myths of computers is that access to information will be a liberation, and its results will be, by definition, democratizing. The reality of this technology is an effective centralizing of power. This democratizing myth is strongly reminiscent of some that surrounded the introduction of television. Whether TV encouraged greater participation in the democratic process is questionable; it did prove extremely useful for selling goods and inculcating values, and was highly profitable in the bargain. It becomes clear the "democratizing" is one of those utopian catchcries that is always pinned on any emerging communications technology. Armand Mattelart has observed:

> [I]f information were free, everyone would have access to
> it. If information gave power and were within the grasp of
> everyone, then power would be in the hands of everyone.
> If the planetarization of information engendered interde-
> pendence, then there would no longer be any risk that
> power could be used by some to dominate others. Reality
> reveals what the myth veils. It is through the conflicts of
> social actors that the use values of information emerge.[21]

When camcorders became available in the 70s, there was much jubilation among activist groups: the tools of production were finally in the hands of the people, who could now make community TV. This argument followed a familiar and idealistic left politics. But two difficulties arose. Firstly, though the "front end" of production was available, the technologies of processing and, more importantly, distribution, remained firmly locked up; passwords like "broadcast quality" kept the amateurs out. The "mass distribution" dream shriveled on the vine. On a more subtle level, radical video practice was well nigh impossible, for those who attempted it had absorbed the codes of commercial media production on TV and in cinema, since before they could talk. For over a generation, we were able to purchase the technology of consumption but not of production.

So although the technology of production was in new hands, the codes of production and reading were already so instilled that an irregular production or an irregular reading were very difficult to engineer, and required a thoroughgoing deconstruction of the conventional forms. As Bill Stephenson succinctly asked: "What is harder to do than to denaturalize the medium that shaped our consciousness?"

Network art

A paradigmatic example of technological art that has enlisted the democratizing, liberationist rhetoric is telematic or network art. Arising under the influence of the technological utopianisms of both McLuhan and Buckminster Fuller, the basic premise of this practice was that "global connectivity" would result in democratic communication and peaceful coexistence, by virtue of an all-encompassing electronic forum. Later, under the influence of postmodern critique, experiments by Roy Ascott and others emphasized the possibility of authorless group creative practice through simultaneous joint authorship in dataspace. Network Art has troubled me since I first became aware of it ten years ago. I find several theoretical difficulties in the premises of this practice, which divide into two categories. The first involves the question of technologies of communication and the operating definition of "communication" itself. The second problem is implicit colonialist dynamics and the rhetoric of the global village.[22]

Network art founders on the assumption that communication is actually occurring when groups of people at remote locations on the globe, unfamiliar with each other personally or culturally, exchange digital bits on the net. In one awesomely unsuccessful project, students in Sydney exchanged and reworked faxes with students in Vienna. The documents output at the Sydney end were cultural nonsequiturs, a testament to the faulty premises of the project. The exchanges were reminiscent of those films of pitiful split-brain subjects. The Austrians were hampered in their communications by their limited English, but what was more clear was a series of cultural discontinuities. The Australians assumed their electronic pen pals were just like themselves. Or worse, that they conformed to some ill-conceived Australian notion of the Austrian national character. In this kind of exchange there is less *communication* than speaking to someone you don't know in another country on the phone. Communication requires a set of shared concepts. To the degree that the topology of these concepts held by each correspondent map onto each, communication occurs. Henry David Thoreau observed: "Our inventions are wont to be pretty toys which distract our attention from serious things. They are but improved means to an unimproved end." He continued: "We are in great haste to construct a magnetic telegraph from Maine to Texas, but Maine and Texas, it may be, have nothing important to say."[23]

One defense of this shortcoming was that, in line with conceptualist precepts, the "system" of communication was itself the artwork. This argument confuses me. If the system was the artwork, then it was its own content; but that content was invisible. Being invisible, it would remain entirely conceptual (and therefore need not exist) without some message flowing through it. But the message was irrelevant, because the system was the artwork. So it was no surprise that the messages on these systems were so vapid.

A further irony was that these systems were not markedly different from systems used at the time by stockbrokers and bankers to make global connections for quite different purposes. John Broughton has written on the politics of the computer as a mediator of communications: "The systems approach simultaneously dismantles self and culture, assisting precisely that collapse into biology on the one hand and bureaucracy and technology on the other that is so desirable from the point of view of authority. . . . The stress on functional organisation has a doubly homogenising effect: Both psychological and cultural specificity are occluded."[24]

In the visual arts, this focus on "system" arose from the Art and Technology movement, early manifestions being "Experiments in Art and Technology," organized by Billy Kluver in the 60s, and Jasia Reichardts's exhibition *Cybernetic Serendipity* of 1968. In an era of rapidly expanding technologies, an attempt to understand and harness technological thought and product for artistic ends was, and is, laudable. But in the case of network art, in exploring aesthetic communication across electronic data networks, two distinct and incompatible definitions of communication became conflated. The more recent technologically derived definition (Claude Shannon's "communication theory") was concerned with a reliable match between data despatched and data received. The more familiar humanistic definition considers sender and receiver as communicators, while the technological definition considers only the process of transfer. It was thus mistakenly assumed that if a certain bitstream issued from one place and reached the other as an identical bitstream, then communication was occurring.[25]

MUDs

After a decade of artistic prototyping of the "electronic community," the rapid expansion of computer networking has led to the realization of the telesocial condition: the existence of functioning virtual communities that occupy only telematic space. These communities are spontaneously arising in popular youth culture. MUDs (Multi-User Dungeons) are the telematic communities that network artists of the 80s dreamed about. As with Desert Storm references to the "global village," however, the popular culture version is not quite what the aesthetic researchers had in mind.

An offshoot of complex network games—Dungeons and Dragons was an early incarnation and Nettrek is a recent and highly complex version—MUDs are active anarchic invention spaces: networked virtual environments interfaced through ASCII text. Although there is no competitive game structure, these spaces are highly attractive. MUDs are a virtual costume party, allowing users to adopt arbitrary gender and role play. As a space of fictitious simulation, ones' identity is never truly revealed, yet marriages and divorces occur within the MUD environment. One of the U.S. MUDs has a church, run by a real priest. As these communities arise, they evolve their own social problems. Many participants are socially backward people who are generally retiring and introverted and who become addicted to this virtual social space. They log on for twelve-hour stretches, and flunk out of school due to this ecstasy of communication. But when I asked a MUDer what people did in the MUD, he replied that most people "just hang out and eat virtual donuts."

In Japan, a visual MUD called Habitat (originally developed at Lucasfilm) has eighty-five hundred regular inhabitants. Real-time gaming is supported in the Habitat environment and social groupings spontaneously arise. There is a community newspaper and local government, but the preconstructed visual environment does not allow the variety of invention that the text-based MUDs allow. Here emerges a characteristic common to other digital media, that as the bandwidth and resolution increase, the proscription of possibilities also increases, so the space for creative invention seems to decrease.

Volker Grassmuck has suggested that a new branch of sociology will emerge to study telesocial groupings in MUDs. Certainly MUDs are already causing obsessional and neurotic behavior. But will the sociologist observe on-line social behavior from the comfortable distance of a desk chair in front of a computer or will such a sociologist set up a virtual consulting room or research center in the MUD itself?

What happens when more and more human institutions drain out of the physical world and into MUDs? Its quite easy to imagine all manner of social behavior occuring in MUDs. Clearly universities and shopping malls are an easy step in the visual MUDs like Habitat. Some of the activities proposed for interactive TV, gaming in particular, map easily onto MUDs. The possibility of a virtual sound studio or a virtual art gallery is very real.

Cruising the information superhighway

The exponential growth of digital network communications has sent movie studios, computer companies, cable TV companies (particularly the "shopping channels"), TV networks, and telephone companies all scrambling for a piece of the interactive TV action.[26] The "information superhighway" looks poised to become a gargantuan virtual Mall, with consumer commodity capitalism as its guiding philosophy. In true American spirit, the network will be privatized and society will benefit from all the varieties of progress that money can buy (and none of the others). At Siggraph 92, I heard Marc Canter, ex-head of Macromind, relate his vision of interactive broadcast multimedia. He described an interactive MTV in which Johnny, in his bedroom, can download multiple camera angles and MIDI-code for all the instruments, can mix his own Madonna video, and can jam along. This consumption-oriented paradigm contrasts starkly with the democratic interaction paradigm of Network Art.

The impending unification of the telephone, television, and computer will create commercially mediated telesocial information spaces. The following current developments indicate the likely shape of these spaces:

• MUDs, as discussed above
• "Mosaic" is a hypertextual interface to a worldwide multimedia information network with more or less transparent access

on-line to sound, color. image, and video
  • Video conferencing
  • Interactive digital TV, promising real-time ratings surveys, interactive TV games, and the proliferation and pluralization of TV programming

Video gaming has exploded over the last decade from an arcade amusement to domestic TV plug-ins to handheld portables to personal computers with CD-ROM drives. In these transitions, games have followed the major trends of digital technology. Now, with profits from games skyrocketing, most major movie houses are producing game versions of their movies, or interactive features. SEGA released its stereoscopic (VR) game interface for Christmas 1993. Graphical networked multiuser gaming is close at hand.

The cultural ramifications implied by the concatenation of these technologies is mindboggling, as is the pace with which the change will occur. We can reasonably expect these things to be a reality within five years.

The emerging digital media phenomena—interactive media, on-line multimedia and their hybrids—promise new territories for artistic practice. The new contexts, technological, commercial and (tele)social, demand a reconsideration of methodologies of art production and conventions of consumption. The new forms will inevitably generate new cultural institutions. With these potential realities in mind, it would seem appropriate to begin to plan what kind of art we are going to make in these spaces, what kind of audience we will have, and what kind of interaction will occur—ultimately, to consider what art will become in this context.

Conclusion

Though most arguments in this paper have been posed with examples set in the third person, they are my dilemmas as a practitioner in the field. When one is involved in the generation of an artwork that requires the techniques and tools of engineering, the nature of the work *as art* can become tenuous. The work of R&D engineering is the same whether one is building an interactive sculpture or a washing machine. In an interdisciplinary field such as electronic media arts, what I have referred to as the "technological imperative" encourages artists to attempt to be unassailable technically. Even among artists, aesthetic issues can often take a back seat because they are more ephemeral. "Once the system is working and robust, then there will be time to deal with aesthetic issues" is a common rationalization. Yet in some cases, that time never comes. It is easy to know if the technology isn't working. It's harder to know if the aesthetics aren't working.

Attempting to make art with these technologies may require redefinition of precisely what we imagine "art" to be. The era of online digital interactivity and virtual community will evolve an art genre that may be unrecognizable from a traditional art viewpoint. We call some cinema "art," yet one wonders if Leonardo would have possessed the cognitive and aesthetic techniques to perceive or assess cinema. Techniques of the user will evolve along with techniques of the maker, and these media will "grow" cultural contexts. Cinema did not find its place in museums; it evolved a new cultural context and a new code of behavior. Television evolved a new context, simultaneously domestic, real-time and networked, though the real-time networking is limited to a paradoxical reverse panopticality: we all see the newsreader, but s/he does not see us.

This process of building new contexts, new codes, should not be unfamiliar to makers or viewers accustomed to the flow of modernism. Art in the modern period has propagated itself by continually disproving itself, by continually reinventing itself in response to changes in culture and technology.

Whatever art is to become in the realm of consumer electronic culture, it is critical that some sort of autonomy be maintained from the pressures of the technological imperative. Otherwise the politics implicit in the technological manifestation will override the necessary anarchic liberty of art.

Notes

1. C. P. Snow. *The Two Cultures* (Cambridge: Cambridge University Press, 1959).

2. In this discussion, the terms "computer artists," "electronic media artists," and "artists who use technology" are used interchangeably, as I know of no useful and brief blanket term. There will be some specific reference to interactive media artpractice.

3. See Simon Penny, "The Intelligent Machine as Anti-Christ," *SISEA 1990 proceedings* (Groningen, Netherlands, 1990).

4. Interdisciplinarity has recently become a buzzword in universities. It was in art, specifically in the emergence of inter-arts and multimedia

curricula, that the notion of interdisciplinarity was broached a full two decades before university campuses began to explore the idea.

5. This paper was given at the Techne Symposium, organized by Elliot Anderson, at the Seybold Conference, San Francisco, October 1993.

6. Jonathan Crary,*Techniques of the Observer: On Vision and Modernity in the Nineteenth Century* (Cambridge: MIT Press, 1992).

7. Rejane Spitz, "Qualitative, Dialectical and Experiential Domains of Electronic Art," FISEA conference, Minneapolis, October 1993.

8. To apply a term originated by Tony Fry to another context. See "Art Byting the dust . . . " in *Culture, Technology, and Creativity in the Late Twentieth Century*, ed. Philip Hayward (London: John Libbey, 1990).

9. I must confess my lack of training in formal logic. For a more competent elaboration of similar themes, see *What Computers Still Can't Do: A Critique of Artificial Reason*, by Hubert Dreyfus (Cambridge: MIT Press, 1992).

10. *Machine Culture* was an international survey exhibiton of interactive media art, curated and organized by Simon Penny, which was presented at the Siggraph '93 conference, Anaheim, California, 1–6 August.

11. Joseph Bates of the School of Computer Science, Carnegie Mellon University, heads the "O_3" group that is building *Edge of Intention*.

12. See Manuel DeLanda, *War in the Age of Intelligent Machines* (Cambridge: MIT Press, 1991) for a discussion of the history of automated production.

13. "The Work of Art in the Age of Mechanical Reproduction," in Walter Benjamin, *Illuminations*, ed. Hannah Arendt (New York: Schocken, 1968).

14. Florian Rötzer, "Interaction and Play," in *Machine Culture* exhibition catalog, ed. S. Penny. *Siggraph 93 Visual Proceedings*, ACM 1993.

15. "Of Monitors and Men and Other Unsolved Feminist Mysteries," included in this volume. First published in *Parallelogram* 18, no. 3 (1992).

16. See the *Machine Culture* catalog for discussion of this work.

17. See "Virtual Bodybuilding," a paper delivered at the TISEA conference, Sydney 1992. Published in *Media Information Australia* 69 (August, 1993).

18. I have previously argued that there is a familiar Christian theme of denial of the body in this technology. See "2000 Years of Virtual Reality" published in *Through the Looking Glass: Artists' First Encounters with Virtual Reality*, ed. Cirincione and D'Amato (N. p.: Softworlds, 1992). William Gibson's Cyberpunks proclaimed that "the body is meat," but neglected to notice just how similar their position was to that of Saint Augustine.

19. From the *Illustrated London News*, quoted in *The Cult of Information*, by Theodore Roszak (New York: Pantheon, 1986), 45.

20. Thomas Edison imagined that his phonograph would be used to record the voices of aging relatives and act as a family record like a painted

portrait or photo album. He did not forsee a highly profitable sound com-modity industry.

21. Armand Mattelart and Hector Schmucler, *Communication and Infor-mation Technologies: Freedom of Choice for Latin America?* translated from the French by David Buxton (Norwood, N. J.: Ablex, 1985), 152.

22. In 1989 I heard of a transcultural network project that seemed to epitomize many of my misgivings about network art. The Pittsburgh-Sene-gal project of the DAX group at Carnegie Mellon University was for me a case study in the pitfalls of naïve global-villagism. (I learned of this project in 1989, from Bruce Breland, when it was in the planning stages, but received no reports concerning the event itself.) The idealistic intent was that a real-time jam session between Senegalese musicians in Dakar and U.S. musicians in Pittsburgh would represent some sort of transoceanic communion, even perhaps an atonement for the slave trade. I was con-cerned because the initiator of the project had never been to Africa and seemed to have very little understanding of Third World dynamics. In a brief visit to Dakar he was treated royally by members of the Wolof upper class and did not move far from hotels and hired cars. It was decided that the Senegal side of the event would occur on Isle de Goreé, a highly sym-bolic site, as the island was the major staging point for the slave trade from West Africa to the Americas.

The question of the local Senegalese politics was never addressed. Like many African nations, Senegal inherited colonial borders that thrust together antagonistic racial and religious groups, and the country was sim-mering on the edge of armed struggle at the time. The Wolof, Muslim Africans from the north of the country, held power over the southern groups, who are ethnically neither Wolof nor Muslim. On the international front, the Senegalese were expected to obtain and employ U.S.-made technology, and presumably would access U.S.-owned satellite networks in order to take part. The language of exchange was to be English. English, we might guess, was tacitly assumed to be "universal," a global language. This reap-plication of nineteenth-century colonialist values is endemic on the net.

This project was very troubling to me because it combined a well-inten-tioned desire for international communication with a somewhat naïve con-ception of global village that contained within it xenophobic, colonialist, and technologically imperialist values. It brought strongly to mind lines from a song of the 70s by Randy Newman:

> every city, the whole world round
> will just be another american town
> Oh how peaceful it'll be
> We'll set everybody free... .

Randy Newman, "Political Science," on *Sail Away*, Warner Brothers 1972.

"In whose interests . . . ?" is the question that must be asked. Not in the interests of the Senegalese poor, who in some areas still use talking drums for long-distance communication. (Talking drums are a historically early [first?] example of a nodal networked wireless communications technology, and offer thought-provoking possibilites as a model for culturally related network art research.) In the interests of the musician participants on both sides of the Atlantic? Perhaps. In the interests of manufacturers of the communications technologies? Very likely, as an exercise in the creation of demand. Then there is the question of values: might the hardware, designed, constructed and owned by Western interests, inherently purvey Western attitudes? These are pressing questions in postcolonial theory, an aspect of cultural studies that has specific relevance to the realm of intercultural network communication.

The question of infrastructure is often elided in these discussions of communications technologies with liberatory potential. Some years ago I was astonished to see, in a bank in India, clerks at row upon row of desks, keeping books. Blithely ignorant of the necessity to create as many jobs as possible in highly populated countries, I suggested to the teller that one small computer would do all that work. He responded apologetically: "You don't understand, we only have electricity three days a week." And indeed, there was no electric light in the building. A telematic piece by Eduardo Kac exhibited at Siggraph 92 included a fully dressed human skeleton sitting on a chair and holding a telephone. "Eduardo explained to me that the skeleton was meant to be a humorous commentary on the ineffectiveness of telephones in some areas of Brazil. 'You can wait forever to get a line,' he chuckled." Quoted by Mariá Fernández in "The Globalization of Culture" (TISEA , Sydney 1992).

The reality of global connectivity has not resulted in the realization of the utopian ideals. McKenzie Wark has argued that the Tiananmen Square massacre was the result of a telematic feedback loop, with the new (to the Chinese context) technology of fax transmission as the main electronic link to and from the Chinese radicals and with current affairs mass media forming the connections outside China. This instantaneous communication with Westerners, who were perhaps unfamiliar with the military-political realities of modern China, may have induced the cycle of escalation and official repression that resulted in a human and political disaster. Similarly, Frances Dyson records that on 30 January, during Desert Storm, on KPIX San Francisco, commentator Bob McKenzie said: "These surreal broadcasts from the eye of Desert Storm [referring to the smart bomb footage] have truly made all of us part of the global village. . . ." (Frances Dyson: "In/quest of Presence: Virtuality, Aurality and Television's Gulf War," included in this volume). Not quite the global village we might have hoped for.

23. Henry David Thoreau, *Walden*, ed. Owen Thomas (New York: W. W. Norton, 1966), 35.

24. John Broughton, "Machine Dreams: Computers in the Fantasies of Young Adults," in *Individual, Society and Communication*, ed. Robert Reiber

(Cambridge: Cambridge University Press, 1989), 229.

25. See Katherine Hayles, *Chaos Bound* (Ithaca: Cornell University Press, 1990) for a discussion of Shannon's theory.

26. It is ironic that the strategic requirements of ARPAnet (the origin of internet) forced an essentially anarchic solution, in contrast to the centralized heirarchical solutions historically preferred by military thinkers. It was found that in order for the ARPAnet to remain robust against geographically indifferent ICBMs, any sort of centralized control must be dispensed with. A horizontal, parallel, and distributed system of nodes was more robust. It is a further ironic twist that techno-utopian hype the democratizing possibilities of the Internet rests on a technological base designed for military superiority. The internet is anarchy in perfect action, but it derives its economic support from universities. As network use diversifies and consumer demand increases, the attention of snoozing private enterprise is stirred. The telephone companies know that many people are making free international calls over the net, and they're unlikely to watch the net drain their profits away for long. The Internet could only survive as a "democratizing" tool as long as it was encapsulated within a small and elite subsection of society.

The structural identity between the Internet and the idea of the "rhizome" proposed by Gilles Deleuze and Felix Guattari is a curious example of philosophy and technology traveling on parallel tracks. (See Gilles Deleuze and Felix Guattari, *A Thousand Plateaus*, University of Minnesota Press 1987.)

4

Technology is the People's Friend: Computers, Class, and the New Cultural Politics

Richard Wright

I am talking to my father when a thought occurs to me.

"What did you think when I first told you that I wanted to be an artist?"

"A bit puzzled really. No one else in the family had ever gone into that area. We did wonder how you were going to make a living at it. But then you moved away from all that when you were at art college."

"What do you mean?"

"You started out with painting and then you went into computer graphics. And now of course you've changed again and you're doing computer animation."

"Is that different, then?"

"Well, it's got a lot more possibilities than what you were doing before. It's a new field."

As technological media is absorbed into wider and wider areas of society, its demands begin to strain traditional cultural institutions, realigning or exploiting cultural and social groups and threatening to disrupt the established art world and the operation of its aesthetic standards. The working practices of artists are undergoing changes not only in their technical facilitation but also in their relations with other practices and in their function as social constructions. Electronic media and computer processing do not necessarily support the traditional differentials of cultural production and their implicit hierarchies—fine art, independent arts, academic, commercial, activist, community orientated, hobbyist and recreational. Traditional boundaries between media are collapsing as each discipline is computerized and merged with others to create new forms. The tendency to replace the physical basis of media such as photography, cinema, graphics, and painting by reduction to digital information has undermined a large part of their artistic identity. A frame of film can now be digitized, retouched, or recomposed as if it were a painting. A line of text in an illustration program can be placed in an "envelope" and manipulated as though it were a wave form in a sound synthesizer. And a file of dry, abstract numerical data can be interpreted as a kaleidoscope of pulsating colors.

Driven by the notion of computer manufacturers that they are fufilling an artistic desire for unlimited formal innovation, little structural or historical basis is offered for the variety of means of expression made available by the formal freedom enjoyed by computer processing. There is no indigenous studio practice or aesthetic linked to any particular arts practice, form, or genre—they all meet together as interchangeable data entities in the digital environment. A software package such as Adobe *Photoshop* can be used by fine artists, commercial designers, illustrators, and photographers as a complete studio system in itself. The artistic specialists and experts that previously dominated each of their separate disciplines now find themselves working at the same machines as a wide range of "users," and their skills and tools are now encoded down to a list of menu options. The relevance of Walter Benjamin's famous statements about mass reproduction dispelling the aura of the privileged object can now be extended to the aura of the means of production and to the reproduction (or more accurately the simulation) of the means of production.

We can see about us many ways in which institutional bodies and commercial computer vendors have reacted to the situation, playing one social class off against another in order to define and secure a new market or to aestheticize new media to reestablish cultural demarcations and art-world values. This has led to phenomena such as the emergence of alternative exhibition circuits based around academic and industrial collaborations, each one struggling to identify with whatever artistic ideology looks set to rise to dominance. Credit for the democratization of media, global access to culture, and the unification of art and science have been laid at the door of digital media and telecommunications. But the differing backgrounds and interests of the forces at work in these areas— commercial, institutional, academic and artistic—can lead to conflicts of context with bizarre results. In this sense digital media provides a highly charged area in which the pluralist and multivalent approaches that were associated with the rise of poststructuralist theory can find direct (almost trivialized) application. New opportunities for cultural alliances and initiatives come hand in hand with confusion and exploitative colonization as "technoculture"[1] creates a new landscape into which cultural strategies can be mapped.

This essay divides the cultural sociological study of this emergent technoculture into three main motions. Firstly, democratization—the increased access (both economic and social) to production provided by new technologically based means, as against the centralization of production by its dependence on and consumption of the same technology. Secondly, mobility—electronic media operates as a space for interdisciplinary encounters. Here, the emergence of an expanded field of players is caused by the introduction of new extracultural forces such as scientists, business people, and educationalists who discover they have overlapping interests in the application of technology to media and the arts. Finally, aestheticization—mainly a recuperative force concerned with establishing and promoting standards of excellence, either by reinforcing old hegemonies or by constructing new ones around emerging power structures, but it can also function as the search for fresh languages and means of expression, and ultimately return us to notions of cultural identity and empowerment. This essay hopes to provide a series of snapshots of contemporary electronic arts practice that are articulated by these three themes, and to use them to confront and provoke.

The three highly contested areas just mentioned are themselves grounded in a history of interclass conflicts, oppositions, and relations. The same means of production is now not only used by people working in different artistic disciplines, but by people working in and for different social classes and needs. It is not, as many try to suggest, as trivial an argument as trying to describe a pencil as a great leveler because everyone uses one to draw with. Electronic media is not just a random collection of tools for making pictures, but a system of interlocking artistic, technological, and commercial interests that are coming together in new cultural and social formations. It has now become impossible for cultural institutions to ignore the pressure being applied by previously marginalized groups and formations as they exert their newfound economic influence, made possible in part by the commercial traffic in technological media. In turn, the potential appears for a space to be created where a wide range of cultural interests can develop, gain confidence, and begin to operate.

Democratization

We are having a computer graphics open house day at our college and I am demonstrating some software to a potential student. He is working in an office job at the moment and has no formal art and design background but is interested in our short course in computer animation. I prepare myself for the question he will inevitably ask.

"So if I take your course will I be able to get a job in computer animation?"

"This course is an introduction to computer animation and covers the basic techniques, and gives you some hands-on experience of a typical animation system. We also teach you the basic principles of animation as a starting point for any further studies"

"I don't mean to be rude, but that doesn't answer the question."

"O.K., its an introductory course—we can't give you experience with the kind of studio you'd find in a facilities house, but we give you a grounding in the basic techniques. People can spend years studying animation or computers. It's up to you how far you take the skills you learn and to work towards putting together a portfolio. Does that answer your question?"

"No."

Migration

I am at a major computer graphics conference and have been looking at some exhibits in a special section dedicated to new designs and applications of interactive interfaces. There is one particularly entertaining exhibit that catches my attention and appears to have been produced by some scientists working for a well-known computer manufacturer. I decide to see if I can get some background information on this installation.

"Do you have any documentation on this installation?" I ask a young lady. "Oh, no," she replies, "it's not a commercial product. We're artists." I enquire further, pointing out the connection with the computer company that seems to be sponsoring their work. "No. It's not research. We're really just artists that happen to be working at this company." "Is there perhaps an artist's statement available then?" I

persist. "*Er, no, we don't have anything like that either—but perhaps that would be a good idea though. . . .*"

Aestheticization

I have received an invitation to participate in an interactive networking event planned for a number of up-and-coming art shows and cultural festivals. The theme is described as an "international creative exchange through advanced technology" in which artists from different countries will each contribute a panel to a kind of "electronic quilt." Visitors to the event will also be able to electronically paint some sections of a video wall reserved for that purpose. The accompanying leaflet points out the curator's "long-term commitment to making the technology available to artists everywhere." What are the criteria for artists wishing to participate? For the "world-class artists" that are selected, "selection is on the basis of their work in the fine arts. Computer experience is desirable and they should be recognized in their own country." But— "those with limited experience in utilizing the electronic art medium will be trained. . . ." Send a resumé.

Bullshit

A friend who illustrates and produces his own highly contentious style of comic books is telling me how to get a bank loan. "I take in all my computer work and spread it out on the bank manager's desk and start telling him about how it's all done. He doesn't understand a word but just nods and says, 'Mmm . . . computer graphics . . . yes . . .' Then he asks me how much I want."

Mobility: From Big Science to Big Art, and Back

"I use a computer . . . because I hope that the assistance of this tool will permit me to go beyond the bounds of learning, cultural heritage, environment—in short, of the social thing, which we must consider to be our second nature . . . to produce combinations of forms never seen before, either in nature, or in museums, to create unimaginable *images." Vera Molnar, computer artist, 1979.* Quoted in PAGE, the Computer Arts Society Quarterly, 1980.

"*In morphogenetic research, we have striven to apply all of our knowledge both technical and artistic, to create more insightful images, and to develop more advanced algorithms for the creation of sensual objects. Thus, it is hoped, the union of analytic theory and aesthetic sensibility, that is, the fusion of art and science, can be achieved."* Yoichiro Kawaguchi, IEEE Computer Graphics and Applications Journal, *April 1985.*

"Leaving our protected ivory tower for this first exhibition proved a unique learning experience for us. We found ourselves confronted with challenges very different from those which we were accustomed to in our professional lives. This was particularly true for the catalogue in which the scientific background of the pictures was to be explained to the general public." Hans Peitgen and Peter Richter, The Beauty of Fractals, *1986.*

Computer graphics provides an example of a field with a history of pioneers who crossed over between the disciplines of computer science, engineering, mathematics, art, and design. It is also the case that the mobility between workers in the academic, industrial, commercial, and entertainment sectors has long been accepted as a beneficial transference of knowledge and skills. Many of the most successful production houses were founded by artists, who first developed the commercial potential of digital imaging after working in collaboration with computer scientists. Much of the impetus for art and design applications of computing has come from an academic research base at educational institutions—from a mixture of artists, designers, architects, mathematicians, engineers and other scientists. Behind this situation is a unique intermingling of the needs and interests of science, commerce, and art.

Computation and graphical interfaces have become integral to the practice of contemporary science over the last few decades. As the ambitions of science to represent more sophisticated and multi-variate phenomena have increased, so the problem of monitoring these systems in an efficient and accessible way has become more urgent. Computer simulations of complex physical processes have become an important strategy in trying to understand the conditions necessary for certain phenomena to arise.

High-bandwidth data acquisition techniques have also been developed, allowing astrophysicists to record huge amounts of information for later scientific analysis. Both these methods typically produce many millions of raw numbers that threaten to bury the research scientists before they can convert them into an understandable form. The only technique efficient enough to display vast quantities of information in an easily assimilable form is to turn them into pictures. Relationships between elements are quickly picked out by the discriminating eye, color gradients can be apprehended, and signs of movement detected. This pressing into service of the intuitive faculties finds easy acceptance in today's laboratory, where the principles of scientific objectivity, truth, and the pursuit of knowledge have become obscured by the need to *perform*—to provide workable solutions to practical problems, and to provide technological innovation and commercial stimulus rather than abstract explanation of the mysteries of nature.[2]

A feature of this new methodological license has been the appearance of "interdisciplinary teams" of researchers. Groups consisting of physicists and mathematicians are joined by more technically oriented computer scientists and engineers, and then by experts in perceptual psychology and cognitive studies, and artists. Although scientists had worked with artists before on rare occasions, such as during the Art and Technology projects of the 1960s, more recently the impetus has come from the scientists themselves. As well as invitations to artists to assist in visualization projects, scientists have become more and more seduced by the results of their own experiments, and artists have been looking with interest at the imagery trickling out of computer labs. The mid-eighties saw the increased availability of high-resolution color graphics in scientific research centers, and with it came the phenomenon of "scientific" forms of "art" almost completely autonomous of mainstream culture. The most well-known examples are Chaos Art and Fractal Art, forms that by the late eighties had received widespread attention from artists and critics.

One of the first and most publicized of these manifestations was "Map Art," originating from a traveling exhibition of the work of a group of mathematicians and physicists at the University of Bremen. They had been generating images of fractal Mandelbrot sets for their work on dynamical systems until sometime after 1981 when "the idea for an exhibition came up."[3] They were invited by a bank in Bremen to exhibit their work to the public and to produce an illustrated catalog. The success of this show led quickly to two more by the end of 1984 and culminated with their work being added to the cultural program of the Goethe Institute. What was most interesting was the pressure put on the scientists to account for their work in the catalog in cultural and ideological terms, an account that they had not expected would be required from such an audience and at variance with the conception of art that they, as typical scientists, possessed. "What had been quite simply fun in the context of our scientific work suddenly became the topic of very serious discussions. The viewers demanded an explanation of that context and wanted to know its importance."[4] Peitgen and Richter go on to explain the effort it took to ease themselves out of the relatively narrow frame of reference in which they worked and to try to bridge the gap in mind-sets between mathematicians and the wider public. In fact, on reading their description, one might be forgiven for getting the impression that these scientists had been leading some kind of alienated monastic existence before their reintroduction into the real world through their participation in art.

As media interest in these swirling masses of color and crystalline structures increased, a still unresolved ideological tension emerged over the function of these images and the status of their producers. If the images that scientists were now using in their research were attractive enough, could they be called art? Were their properties as hypothetical models of natural phenomena (still hotly debated within the scientific community itself) relevant to their "meaning" as artworks? And really, could someone who had never been to art college and had never heard of contemporary French philosophers command the authority to hold a major international touring exhibition of their pictures?

By 1989 fractals and chaos theory formed part of the subject matter of an art show at the New Museum of Contemporary Art in New York. The theme of the show *Strange Attractors : Signs of Chaos* was the relation between order and randomness, logic and the irrational, in the context of the new scientific ideas that were becoming popularized through their attractive graphical imagery. The work exhibited was a mixture of photographs, installations, and sculptures by artists that addressed chaos and served to contextualize the scientific discourse that was represented by just a few images of strange attractors and fractal landscapes produced by scientists. A passage in the catalog by the curator, Laura Trippi, is instructive in its indication of a contemporary attitude of the art world towards this new extracultural force. "In 1986–7, James Welling [exhibiting artist] produced a series of 'circle paintings' that bear a striking resemblance to the 'sphere fractals' of Mandelbrot, among the least obviously 'fractional' of fractal images, printed in black and white in the book (*The Fractal Geometry of Nature*). In Welling's paintings, the massing shapes come across at once as vaguely ominous and profoundly pop, suggestive in this context of a deadpan commentary on the "promiscuity" of fractal graphics (even, more generally, on that of simulation), the near-contagion of their allure."[5] Although Trippi had based the show on new scientific concepts in nonlinear systems, it still seemed necessary to criticize the scientific graphics for their vague aesthetic threat.

One of the most bizarre features of this "mathematical art form" is its ability to almost completely negate the practice of aesthetic creativity and craftsmanship. To produce a hypnotic fractal vision of the Mandelbrot set for example, one merely types in the computer program from a book or magazine—about a dozen lines—and enters about four numbers (almost at random within a specified range), to define which part of the image to "zoom in" to. To animate the result is even more simple—just load the image into a basic paint program and "color cycle" it (a simple electronic paint function) for a surprisingly authentic-looking psychedelic effect. Although the diversity of imagery that can be found in the Mandelbrot set begins to pale after a few days exploration, there is now a vast array of mathematical objects to chose from: fractals, graftals, cellular automata, bifurcation diagrams, chaotic systems, and iterative mappings. Catalogs of mathematical and scientific software are full of programs with names like "Fractal Explorer" used to generate, explore and save all kinds of fractal exotica. It takes no more than a training in high school mathematics to begin writing one's own functions based on the standard forms of equations. Most importantly, mathematical art like this introduces a way of making imagery in a formal way without any visual understanding of images themselves. Highly decorative and intricately structured forms are designed numerically using the language of the scientist, and performed at the keyboard, not at the easel. This presents us with the prospect of an aesthetic developing from a nonaesthetic practice and divorced from the usual cultural sensibilities.

The modernist promotion of individualism as creativity, subjectivity, and originality became part and parcel of a popular ideology of art that has been used to support everything from psychoanalysis to capitalist entrepreneurship. It is this construction of the integrity of "the subjective" that informs most popular discourse about art, especially outside artistic circles. As the pursuit of pure science has come under political attack from the New Right, there is a real sense in which the arts have become a notional haven for scientists wishing to pursue idealistic goals in their work. For many scientists, notions of artistic integrity or autonomy have provided a space in which they can escape from the commercial pressures of modern scientific research and pursue their more personal interests in an atmosphere of refined and enlightened tolerance. Research institutions have sometimes recognized the value of supporting activities if they are immediately suited to media coverage and can be directly exploited for very considerable publicity—quite apart from the projects that are specifically for application in the entertainment industry. It is not so much the case that research of the purest and most speculative kind is in the process of migrating to the artistic arena. Rather, those seeking a kind of open-ended research and having a comparatively escapist or dilettante attitude seem most attracted to this position. Art seems to provide a way for the "blue sky" research centers to give a certain direction to their work and attract publicity; perhaps it provides a way to introduce an element of play into their methods not normally considered proper. At the same time, art has become a way for scientists wishing to follow an exploratory line of enquiry not directly related to marketable outcomes to avoid committing themselves to any rigorous program, and from defining the exact function that their most speculative work fulfills in a wider social, commercial, or even contemporary cultural context. Questions even in the most general terms related to the purpose behind a project can be deflected by stating "It's just art . . . " followed by a respectful silence.

If "pure" science is retreating into "purer" art (or a rarefied modernist conception of it), it can also be observed that over the last decade artists under attack from similar reactionary forces are seeking legitimation by identifying with science and technology. In the past, government funding bodies in Britain such as the Science and Engineering Research Council (SERC), which validates Ph.D. research programs, has twisted itself into knots when considering proposals that contain a strong art and design component. During the eighties the massive investment of technology in the media industry spawned a demand for research that stimulated a new response in the academic research sector. Art and Design faculties found their postgraduate students applying for doctorates to do work in computer imagery and animation, often prompted by the hope of lucrative placements in commercial production houses. After receiving an increasing number of research projects that would result in nothing more conclusive than a computer program to produce a realistic-looking forest of trees or a cloud, SERC accepted in principle the concept of scientific research in art and design media, deciding that at the very least a Ph.D. project must result in some kind of formal written documentation to support an otherwise practical component.

In 1990 the Roith Report Committee published their policy document, entitled *Research in the PCFC (Polytechnic Central Funding Committee) Sector*. The new categories of research in academic institutions were laid out and described, covering all areas from basic or pure research, to strategic research and applied research, to scholarship and creative work. Though not concerned with any specific level of research, the Roith Report tried to allow for such areas as art and design with its category of "creative work," which it described as "the invention and generating of ideas, images and artifacts including design. Usually applied to the pursuit of knowledge in the arts." The ground is thus prepared for the formal inclusion of a far wider range of academically funded activities than before. Because most British art colleges had been merged with polytechnics since the 1960s and were upgraded to university status, a large proportion of artists may find material attractions in considering their next project as a piece of "research." Likewise, with the continuing universal disdain for pure research that has demoralized so much of the scientific community, those that have stayed to fight have sometimes found allies in unexpected quarters when moving into the expanding field of media technology. We can perhaps look forward to interesting discussions at research committee meetings between heads of Physics, Architecture, and Art and Design as they try to agree on research priorities and common resources. They may need to find a common ground in order to secure these new sources of funding. Quite frequently that common ground is computer imaging and media technology.

By rallying around the flag of technology, then, artists and scientists have found new ways to legitimate their aspirations, and at the same time provide implicit channels of access into each other's disciplines. It is this effect of bringing the world of cultural production to wider groups that we will now probe further.

Democratization

"The Only Limit is Your Imagination"
—*W Industries promotion, 1991*
(simulator and VR games manufacturer)

The phrases "democratization of media," "empowerment of the individual," and "access to the means of production" have functioned as everything from popular aesthetics, to artistic manifestos and cultural hypotheses, to advertising slogans. For the Mac it was the "user friendly" graphical interface, for the IBM PC it was a stream of references to the great Renaissance "universal man" of art and science, for the Commodore Amiga it was the cheap and cheerful video studio in a box. For computer manufacturers the short-term aim of popular computing was apparently to provide access to processors not previously available to the mass user. But there are two distinct senses in which the idea of democratization as access can be used: that of physical and economic access to production, and that of cultural and social access to production. Technological media introduce important new features into both of these, as well as revealing new relations between the two.

The strategy behind the commercial development of mass-user electronic media has been to focus on the individual as the ideal producer/consumer. This has produced low-cost general purpose computers that can be bought by people with very diverse needs— towards art and design or otherwise—and a software base of specialized application packages and a range of peripherals: printers, styluses, tablets, storage media. By making a selection of software and hardware products, a user can build a computer workstation to suit his or her production needs. This has become known as the "desktop production" revolution, comprising desktop publishing, desktop CAD, and now multimedia and desktop video. Applications software exists to supply the technical functions for most design disciplines and processes: drawing, illustration, 3-D design, typography, layout, presentation graphics, and so on. Each of these areas of expertise is *encoded* into the user's workstation as a piece of software and a set of tutorial manuals. Whereas before if you needed some airbrushing done on your artwork you would have had to hire a specialist airbrush artist to do the work, it is now just another option in the menu lists of a digital paint system. The whole history of technical skills in design is sitting in front of you at your terminal. You sit at the desktop, click the mouse, and you *access*.

In this new studio environment the interactions between people and materials become narrowed down and focused onto the VDU screen on the table. This *desktop fetish* results in a centralization of the studio practice in the single lone user. Whereas before a design job would have needed a team of art directors, visualizers, illustrators, graphic designers, typographers, and pasteup people, now it can be tackled by one person without getting up out of their chair. Buy a Mac and become a design company.

What emerges is an increased number of freelancers, all offering a wide range of design services. (The question of whether the skills provided are of a consistent quality across so many different areas is debatable.) There is less need for production to be based around groups of specialists rather than individuals, and this may tend to diminish the social interaction that stimulates people in such a community of workers. In some ways this is analogous to the development of multitrack recording, which allowed one musician to perform all the instruments in a piece. This does not necessarily mean an inevitable decline in cultural production as a social process, but computer marketing is always in terms of the primacy of the individual consumer; computer media strategies stress *individual* rather than *social* access.

In larger design studios, problems have been caused by the introduction of design technologies for the same reason. For the first time in history, designers are using one tool to develop every phase of a project, blurring the distinction between tasks and making job demarcations difficult to define. Normally, the process of designing is a hierarchical one. After the client's initial brief to the art director or creative director, the basic design is passed to a team of designers and their assistants. This team may include illustrators, copywriters, typographers, and photographers. After the presentation has been approved by the client, the production artists and assistants prepare the final artwork for the printer. With the introduction of computers, the boundaries between these different areas have become unclear. Designers have found that they could have too much control over a project; taking on too many ancillary technical tasks that should have been done by specialists. In a field of semiautomated production, technical knowledge can be critical, and one mistake can easily lead to wasted time and unusable work. This has resulted in some managers imposing severe restrictions on exactly who is allowed access to what machines and software. (In some educational institutions, as well, design students are not allowed to use a computer until they can show they have a finished design to work from.) But for other design companies this is seen as throwing away the creative potential of exposing designers and artists to new techniques. Insisting that designers work "away from the terminal" must discourage the playing around with technology that is often seen as essential to the development of new ideas. An alternative strategy is developing that combines the specialist knowledge of a designer's main area of work with a general knowledge of other areas, all supported by increased communication between different members of the team. As larger studios increase their amount of computer equipment, firms will be able to divide the responsibilities for projects as they used to, but people's roles will still overlap more than they did and creative teams and production teams will need to know more about each other's duties and technologies.

Previously, the design process was thought of as a linear chain from designer down to printer. It was hoped that the computer would simply speed things up a bit, remove a few links from the chain, and improve communications. Now, with a new common ground between specialists, design organization is seen as more of a *heterarchy* than a *hierarchy*, with shared responsibilities for the work between different colleagues. The specialist areas of activity still exist, but no longer as isolated or privileged. What we really see here is how new technology that is applied to previous methods of organization highlights the limitations of those systems and prompts a new way of tackling the problem. For both the independent designer and the company employee, electronic design can both broaden the creative opportunities of each individual artist and reveal the necessity of his or her interdependence with other workers.

The emergence of people from scientific and technical backgrounds as a necessary part of the cultural workforce has been a prominent feature of the electronic media industries. "Animators," "technical directors," and "paintbox operators" in studios and facilities houses are often graduates of computer science and engineering courses who have been hired for their familiarity with computing principles. Production houses also typically employ a group of technical experts expanded to include programmers, system managers, network technicians, and hardware and software engineers. The gap between the work of a technician and a graphic designer or model builder has become less distinct. The problems involved, for example, in inputting 3-D data into a computer are frequently of a rather technical nature, or may simply demand more of a superhuman level of patience than a surfeit of creative insight. The difficulties that occur when trying to digitize an object such as a hand can more often be appreciated by someone with an understanding of sampling theory, mathematical surface modeling, and 3-D computer interfaces than someone who knows how to animate a bouncing ball. (It could also be argued that the tedious repetitive tasks that accompany much production work can be more easily passed on to someone from a nonartistic background who is grateful for the chance to enter the glamorous world of media at however low a level.) There is, therefore, a large and integral area in media production that is of a highly technical character, requiring specialist skills (or temperaments) usually beyond the scope of art and design graduates and resulting in an unusually rich diversification of peoples and backgrounds. Indeed, for an intensely pressured production company the prime requirement of a new colleague is that they can communicate well with others and work with them as a team.

The realignments that result when a technology is introduced into a cultural practice are often discussed with a historical reference to the development of photography. There are many fundamental differences between photography and computer media, the most important being that the computer is a nonspecific technology. Unlike a camera and a collection of darkroom equipment, the computer is a generic technology that has been implemented across a wide range of art and design disciplines, and across an even wider range of applications throughout the whole of society. The crucial similarity is the *industrialization* and *commercialization* that occur when a sphere of cultural production is "technologized." When production becomes dependent upon a technology, let's say a camera and film, it becomes dependent upon an industrial and economic structure in order to support itself. Photography needs an industry to make its cameras and process its films. To make this feasible in a modern capitalist economy, the operation needs to have a commercial rationale behind it. There is a marketing strategy that identifies the potential users and of the product and their desires, and a program of research and development that meets these needs and provides the technical innovations to stimulate new ones. On top of this are the forces that determine business plans, the need to diversify and expand markets, to compete in terms of technology, and to identify its applications to optimize returns. These commercial interests have targeted many different classes and social groups in an effort to generate a mass market of users of art and design software.

The technical nature of computer media as applied to the art and design process also provides new channels of access and exposure for classes of people who cannot take the traditional routes. There are wider social groups of people who are trained in neither arts nor science but who find the technical aspect of electronic media appealing and an incentive to get involved. For many people it is more important that an image has been generated digitally than that it is fine art, research, or advertising. In this way social access to production is stimulated and interest in culture that has a technological component is encouraged. For some social groups technology can be a neutral ground in which new activities can be sampled, isolated from their historical baggage.

The image-making technology of photography proved to be very amenable to commercialization, and the business strategy employed was that of the mass cultural—the social construction of photography as "the world's most popular hobby." Photography as a cultural form bypasses the traditional routes of access through institutions and class; it has a vast supporting structure of popular magazines, amateur groups, conventions and exhibitions, often functioning at a local level; and it compensates for the level of skill and dexterity needed for drawing by a partly technical knowledge of lighting conditions, filters, and shutter speeds. But what are the forms of cultural practice it has motivated? Photography has a central role in commercial art—in advertising, design, and graphics; it has a function in documentation, in photojournalism, as judicial evidence. It figures in the media, often providing the pivot for magazines and pictorial publications. It has certainly been used to reinforce the identity of commercial and academic culture, but what of the realm of the "popular"—what is commonly referred to as the realm of the amateur photographer? There is no doubt that photography has become a means of mass cultural expression, but the forms it has taken seem to promote cultural hegemony as much as to sidestep it. The common genres of amateur photography are well-known—the holiday snapshot, the births, marriages, and deaths that have become photographic rituals enshrined in the family album, the new home, the kids in the paddling pool, the graduation ceremony. The popular becomes conflated with the personal, a petrified subjectivity beyond the reach of anyone outside the family circle. Attempts to expand the genre of the popular (through the contradictory strategy of state arts support) have resulted in the endless projects of social documentary photography—old people sitting in a park, shopkeepers laughing, and mothers pushing prams—all finally ending in a poorly attended exhibition of "community art" in a municipal gallery space. Problems of developing the cultural identity of the community, from the confines of the familial into the social realm and the shared experience, are coupled with problems of consumption and distribution. It is at this point that democratization as the promotion of a popular culture demands a different aesthetic and social program as well as an economic one.

Although the manufacturers are eager to sell digital media to as wide a selection of social groups as possible, they do not normally consider it necessary to address the issue of widening the range of what these new users can actually do with their packages beyond applications that are part of the intentional design of the package. Software packages are increasingly targeted at specific user and professional groups as primary consumers, new forms of cultural production are difficult to imagine and risky to explore (note the continual confusion over what the nature of the "multimedia industry" is, or even more problematic, the "virtual reality industry"). But occasionally efforts are made to place an electronic medium somewhere in the cultural hierarchy. For example, the most obvious strategy for Quantel—the manufacturers of the electronic paintbox and digital video effects suites used in all the top facilities houses—was to give its products the kind of high-art prestige fitting to their place in expensive high-end professional video production. In the BBC TV series *Painting with Light*, transmitted in 1987, it invited a selection of famous painters to produce a work on the company's paintbox system (with which the painters had no previous experience) while being filmed. Apart from the blatant pitch for "serious" cultural superiority, the result was to denigrate the status of an independent "computer artist" practice in favor of a more traditional fine art discipline. And as critic Philip Hayward later wrote, "The irony of involving traditional fine artists such as painters with the medium of television is of course that in changing the context of their work (from the easel to the screen), the very specific qualities of their traditional practice coveted by the media (their precise composition and the *aura* of the original) are of course dispensed with."[6]

On other occasions commercial forces have taken quite different approaches, such as JVC's sponsorship of the Tokyo Video Festival. Since 1978, the festival's aim has been explicitly to promote the use of video making among as wide a group of the general public ("our customers") as possible, inviting both amateurs and professionals to participate, and frequently awarding the top prizes to the former. The range of work covers everything from video diaries, documentaries, and campaign work to back-garden features and lyrical abstraction. From the start, the intentions of the organizers seemed to be to present video as a new medium distinct from either film or

TV and driven by a logic of general technological proliferation. Despite the rush to promote "video culture," the festival catalog presents anything but the united front expected in the usual corporate showcase. In the judges' comments, quaint terms like "citizen's video" are tempered with the desire to avoid categorization based on the abilities of participants and to avoid efforts to define the nature of the video medium. The whole catalog is peppered with disagreements over the merits of the prizewinners and various calls for more original or more "expressive" work—inconceivable in the manufactured consensus of the corporate art events that we are commonly subjected to. Sometimes the differences in cultural politics from aestheticization to democratization can be reflected in business strategies, revealing how the interests of commercial and cultural forces can either coincide or contrast.

A quest to locate a popular electronic media practice might lead us to speculate on the possibility of an "amateur computer artist," operating in a similar fashion to the amateur "Sunday painter." Such a creature would be defined by the reflected glory of another practice of higher cultural status, that of the professional fine art painter. But if we look around at some well-known applications of media technology to popular arts genres, we see anything but a desire to emulate the practice of high culture in a computer-based form. For one thing, there is no properly identified "high-culture" for "computer art," or or at least not one that has become entrenched in the mainstream. What we do see is a continuation of forms of popular culture extended in various ways—like digital sampling and recording in music or forms of independent publishing stimulated by desktop technologies. Otherwise, completely novel forms, (in terms of their social functioning) seem to have arisen—like networking as a means of distribution or game playing as a form of interactive fantasy or fiction.

A relation between high and low art is still articulated at the digital level, though in rather bizarre terms. It is now possible to buy a modest software package that applies filters to digital images to give them the appearance of having been created by an artist's hand. One called *Gallery Effects* by Aldus includes sixteen "master effects" to turn scanned photographs into "Charcoal, Watercolor, Fresco, Film Grain," and many others. The software is advertised as *"Everything you need to transform images into art."* High art has been brought into the domain of computer media, but now it is merely a style—a *"sophisticated professional-looking artistic effect."* Although this software only changes the surface finish or texture of an already completed picture, other software products exist that assist in higher-level problems such as composition. These packages are mainly aimed at business users, who use them in the production of information graphics, but there is no reason why this strategy could not be gradually extended, using artificial intelligence techniques to automate all sorts of aspects of the art and design process.

This kind of phenomena reveals a very ambiguous attitude to high culture. On the one hand, software companies accept it as a desirable standard to be achieved in as painless a way as possible. On the other hand, it is seen as just a mechanized process, drained of its "aura" and reduced to a commodity. As a way of promoting cultural activity it can also be seen as taking the path of least resistance, resulting in a negation of original expression by its simulation of traditional aesthetics and genres. But perhaps it is only the beginning of the end of the popular status of fine-art aspirations: just a Baudrillardian endgame for high art before it is absorbed and dissipated as a digital encryption, and the field is cleared for new players to emerge.

Aestheticization

The final goal of the avant-garde—the destruction of art as an institution and its introduction into daily life—couldn't be achieved. It became clear that the effects of art were in fact determined by its status as an institution and by the social framework in which it exists. . . . The intended proximity between art and life has been realized, but at the cost of a total aesthetization of daily life."
—Isabelle Graw, "Interview with Peter Burger,"
Flash Art 144 (Jan/Feb 1989).

The problem of access to the technology of production is soon replaced by the problem of access to a language. Never before have the means of production become so ahistorical, so dislocated from the framework of cultural praxis. For the amateur, the "low-end" user, the situation has always been to walk a tightrope of class identity between the introversion of the personal and the irrelevance of the concerns of high culture and "artiness." But there are certain forces that are now eager to develop new languages for electronic media and to define a practice that will fit comfortably into the aims and objectives of the mainstream art world.

Although "the arts" are commonly characterized as a socially monopolized activity—usually confined to the middle-class intelligentsia—through arts education and the exposure it intermittently receives through the media it can still function as a cultural standard of excellence. Despite the social program of the modern avant-garde to destabilize perception and cultural codes, art is still a strong normalizing force, defining what is aesthetically in good taste, what is creative, what is most worthy of serious attention. This ability to valorize what might originally be quite unencumbered by intellectual baggage has the effect of elevating non-art or the mundane into the respectable, but always in terms of values that are specific to certain classes and interests (recall the elevation of graffiti art during the eighties). Art is not democratic; it is individualistic. It does not provide a space for the social articulation of desires, but provides a platform for the subjectification of the experience of selected individual artists. Attempts to challenge the privileged mode of address afforded to the artists by participatory, collaborative, or retrograde approaches and yet retain a position on the moral high ground of contemporary art perspectives are faced with impossible contradictions.

By the mid-eighties we could see a resurgence of interest in electronic media of all kinds by artists, curators, and funding bodies. Once technological culture had become unavoidable through its prevalence in popular forms like videographics, computer games, and music, it was as though the time had come for digital media to now be saved from its vulgar origins and a process of aesthetic upliftment to begin. What better people were there to show off the enlightened things you could do with a computer than artists themselves? By the beginning of the nineties there were numerous calls for artists to become more and more involved in new media, computer technology, and electronic imaging, to use their "unique powers of creativity and imagination" to show what computers could do when put to "nondestructive ends." As one writer put it, "It is as if somehow (by sheer weight of numbers?) artists are able to rescue [technology] from bad uses."[7]

"Computer art," "electronic media," and "interactivity" have become the art-world clichés of the decade, an identification with innovation and progress that is part of the ritualized radicalism of mandarin taste. Promoted by the emergence of regular shows and competitions during the mid-eighties and appearing as an outgrowth of older festivals for experimental film, video, and music, shows of interactive installations and screenings of electronic imagery are now de rigeur for the arts venue of the nineties. The "art and technology" show has resurfaced as an exhibition genre in its own right, with the occasional proviso that the work take a "critical" stand towards machinery and rationality. Curators and organizers scramble about desperately for any examples of computer animation, interactive multimedia, and global networking that they can massage into their selection criteria. Computer animation is now being produced at a manic pace—partly because it is now a component in one form or another of so many different kinds of activity. But curators find that many artists are only able to produce a minute or two of computer animation on their home computers, and often not to sufficiently accomplished standards. To ensure that their screening programs are long enough, curators must approach educational institutions, research centers, and commercial production houses to find enough pieces with that elusive level of razzle-dazzle that will satisfy their audiences' expectations.

The democratization of art was proposed as one of the goals of technological and computer art by commentators like Jasia Reichardt since the 1960s.[8] The intention was for those outside of the artistic community to plug in their computers, learn a programming language, and start producing mathematical art. The cerebral skills of logic were considered to be more within the abilities of an average person than the manual dexterity necessary for fine craftsmanship. Though it is questionable whether mental skills are more universal than manual ones, computer programming at least had the social advantages of avoiding the contentious medium of canvas and paint, with their long association with the elitism of art colleges and academies. In many ways this goal of widespread computer literacy has been achieved, not through cultural movements but through the aggressive marketing of commercial computer vendors seeking to expand their consumer base. As far as programming as a democratic form is concerned, by the 1990s the result is the opposite of what was hoped for. Now that graphical interfaces have become the normal means of using the computer, programming is no longer a necessary discipline to engage with. In the effort to differentiate a specific computer arts practice from other formations, a fine arts emphasis is now placed on art "which could only have been produced by the computer."[9] In effect this means work not produced using interactive packages but using specially written software—the implication being that now only serious artists learn to program.

This has been the direction taken by the annual Prix Ars Electronica competition, associated with the Ars Electronica festival held in Austria every year. In 1992 it deliberately set out to restrict prizewinners to those working in computer-specific artistic genres (effectively defining computer art as algorithmic art), with the result that nearly all that year's prizewinners were people who wrote their own software. A peculiar result of this policy was that most winners were from computer science and engineering backgrounds, since they were the main group possessing the right technical abilities. As Peter Wiebel states in the catalog "[W]e are dealing with scientific artists (or artistic scientists) who develop those custom programs necessary for the creation of their images."[10] The likely prospect is that future "computer artists" will exclude not only those from marginal social groups, but also most artists as well. The irony, however, is that the group benefiting most from this kind of definition will still be from outside the art-world establishment, namely, the scientific community.

Many "computer art" events have developed out of non-art organizations such as academic conferences and commercially sponsored trade shows. The friction this caused in the early days with the established art-world means that this is still a highly contentious area. Computer art shows tend to swing between actively courting art critics and curators with invitations to take part in seminars and committees, and developing their own alternative festival circuit with its own "stars," publications, and ideological gurus. At first, those active in academic and commercially based art shows would bemoan the fact that the work of their colleagues was ignored by the mainstream art world.[11] Their neglect was frequently rationalized by arguments that the immaterial nature of digital media meant there were no unique art objects that commercial galleries could exploit, quite ignoring the fact that most public and noncommercial galleries had exhibited conceptual art, photography, and installations for years. More recently the public interest in high-tech media and the shortage of electronic art work has resulted in curators being more tolerant of including this more academic kind of work in their programs. Also, the attraction of artists to institutions boasting state-of-the-art equipment has meant more of a dispersal of talents and resources between these two "cultures."

The technological art form that has come closest to carving itself a space of sorts in the established art world is that of the "video art" and electronic media groups, who managed to come to terms with their derogatory associations with television and military technology and set up their own festival circuits and support organizations at the end of the 1970s. The video art world has since then negotiated an uneasy marriage with the TV industry to the extent that broadcasters have become an indispensable sponsor of cultural institutions, a situation made more imperative by changing political tastes in state funding. It is this collection of cultural organizations and its links to distributors, galleries, critics, and curators that often seems to be caught between opposing the encroaching computer technology with its artistically naïve pretensions and "politically incorrect" associations with state power and the military-industrial complex, and wanting to embrace a new field of activity that may bring an increased public interest in the arts and the promise of new forms of corporate and institutional sponsorship. More recently events have brought these two factions closer together as their power bases have felt the need to expand and break their isolation. The computer industry has the financing to support the conferences and exhibitions that it has built up, and arts organizations have the infrastructure and political connections to extend the range of these activities into the cultural sphere.

Scientists and members of the media industry are now frequently invited to art conferences and seminars to lend an aura of scientific legitimacy to the discussion. The academic institutions that fuel research in the computer industry provide a source of information and background for the writers and critics who feel acutely embarrassed by their ignorance of technological media and whose art-theoretical tools have not progressed since they read Virilio's *War and Cinema*. Panel sessions at arts seminars typically display an extraordinary degree of theoretical cross-referencing, mixing of terms, and plain word juggling. An "art and technology" conference will frequently veer wildly between discussions of interactivity, "virtual reality," computer animation, and surveillance systems, each criticism being haphazardly reapplied to each new phenomenon in turn. Spurred on by a continual barrage of eloquent descriptions of new technological innovations, current theories become unable to keep up the pace and often collapse into attempts to redefine the basic terms of debate: What is Art? What is Technology? The sight of our leading cultural commentators making hopelessly inaccurate or overgeneralized statements about digital media causes a feeling of bewildered inadequacy in the audience. Scientific "experts" invited to provide objective accounts of information technology look on, seemingly at a loss to understand why a simple thing like making pictures with a computer should be causing so much concern for the arty types.

The range and diversity of digital media, graphics software, and electronic effects continue to grow unabated. Computer systems and packages are superseded by enhanced and expanded versions at a rate that defies the user to keep up. It is a struggle to absorb the special abilities and applications as technology lurches inexorably onwards, a struggle matched only by the efforts of writers and critics to elucidate their cultural and aesthetic implications and possibilities. Every attempt to clarify and categorize one of these manifestations is soon made obsolete by its next incarnation. The efforts of critics to determine the poetics and grammar of the new aesthetic are relentlessly overtaken and rendered trivial or hopelessly shortsighted by another barrage of inventions and products. Computers consume theory. For every "theory of the new media," supporting examples can be found, and contradicting ones. The pure symbolism that underlies the functioning of the computer frees it from the physical constraints and structural properties that anchor thought to fact and ground theory. This unbounded formalism ruptures and fragments theoretical work until it becomes a game of rhetorical space invaders. Discourse becomes introverted, contingent, without currency.

But it is this relentless tide of innovation that technological commerce demands that can provide the space to resist the reactionary ideologies of aestheticization and keep the channels of cultural access from clogging. Technological art-forms become a way to continually defer the recuperative powers of cultural hegemony, a way to keep it off balance by always taking on a new guise, ready to introduce some new sector of the non-art community onto the scene. From this vantage point we take the opportunity to work in a new space between the gregarious snobbism of state-sponsored arts and the tasteful foyer-art of corporate monoculture. The development of electronic media as new means of expression is therefore not only an aesthetic challenge but takes on a social and political dimension outside the usual parameters.

iF

The year 1991 saw the release of *Mental*, "Britain's first computer-generated comic."[12] It emerged as the third issue of *iF Comix*, an independent title started a few years ago by Graham Harwood. The previous issues had contained a similar polemical thrust, with post-situationist references, plagiarized imagery, and varying degrees of digital post-processing. Most noticeable about this issue, however, is its distinctive "look." Every graphic appears to be cut out of sheets of anodized steel, with hard and crisp tones. The graphics are simplified in some places but greatly detailed in others, and frequently broken up by sharp horizontal bands. The metallic appearance is not like the usual look of pristine computer-generated geometries; it is more as though the drawings have been etched or burnt into steel plates, leaving tarnishes and rivulets of molten metal.

These effects are achieved by image-processing software that Harwood has developed himself, which is applied to the images once they have been scanned into his computer. Nearly all the artwork is culled from nonoriginal sources, ranging from s.f. comics to the *I Spy Handy Craft Book.* The scanned pictures are processed into a single style—sharp and glistening, but also gritty and even dirty looking. "It's about the Gulf War and technology and the metallic look suited that," Harwood explains. "Also, cyberpunk never really had an aesthetic of its own, and I wanted to produce a style for it that fit the present. I wanted it to look like the images were pressed out of steel, stark and hard." Included in the comic is an A2 poster and a 45 rpm record, composed by sampling and collaging sounds and dialogue from war films, s.f. films, and CNN news broadcasts— "but it's still danceable," says Graham. The text tells the story of a working-class fighter pilot in a Gulf War type scenario, but the script is mainly pieced together from documents and leaflets like Marks and Spencer sales promotions, British Petroleum handouts, and more news broadcasts.

Harwood is normally described under the rubric of "cultural activist" and the strong anti-art component of his work has normally revolved around opposition to art-centered notions of genius, originality, and authenticity. An important strategy in this counterculture ethic is to use means of production that are outside high-art practice, especially if such means are familiar to the non-art community. Strongly emphasized is the anti-aesthetic way of working—the ad hoc improvised style that rejects the finely tuned skills of the artisan based on the artisan's submission to a socially constructed system of training and apprenticeship. The use of photocopiers has been particularly highly regarded as a nontraditional medium, lending itself well to the recycling of mass cultural debris into rambling collages commonly found in counterculture publications.

Fig. 4.1. Digital image from cover of iF Comix, "Mental," by Graham Harwood (London: Working Press, 1991). Reproduced with permission.

This rejection of artistic professionalism was an attitude well known to Harwood himself before his exposure to digital imaging methods. Originally attracted to computer graphics as a tool to speed up the process of cutting, pasting and manipulating imagery, Harwood found the quality of work that the computer could effortlessly synthesize suggested a new approach. The collaging techniques now available were of a photographic finish and veracity that far surpassed the confrontational power of what was possible before. Somehow the technical superiority of the production methods available and the seamless recombinations of imagery forced the viewer to take the result more seriously. The finely crafted montages looked almost as though a virus had invaded official mass culture and turned it into a pathological beast, turning around and snapping unpredictably at its keeper. Though sacrificing the counterculture aesthetic of old, electronic media and its subdisciplines like desktop publishing do provide access to some of the means of mass production and a way to colonize the mainstream aesthetic that allows its users to "speak in the voice of the dominant culture." Such techniques point towards a possibility for marginalized groups to be have their position taken seriously *by any other class*, not just as an art curiosity, but as an active cultural agent.

For most cultural activists working on the political margins of art, magazines and pamphlets have been an important channel of expression and opposition. Now the comic book form is proving itself a particularly flexible way for independent producers to make themselves seen and heard. Since the mid-1980s, commercial comics have made important steps in leaving their "kids-only" reputation behind and finding new "serious" readerships. With these new extended markets and the graphic possibilities of combining image and text, comics offer a form of media able to operate as an individual means of "artlike" expression, but also able to take advantage of its function as a reproduced commercial commodity. Comics like *iF* sell in comic shops and bookshops as well as art gallery shops.

Graham had previous project work censored and confiscated from public art galleries, and independently produced comics provide him with unparalleled freedom. The same commercial pressures that compel art curators to compromise prove unexpectedly liberating in the commercial media sector, whose only requirement is to sell. "I can do whatever I like in comics," says Graham. "It's an escape from art to a wider audience and I'm independent of publishers and distributors." (Some years ago Graham helped set up the Working Press to support publications dealing with working class culture.) "You know I see art as a class practice in the U.K., but comics work in a wider cultural context." Graham bases his production around an IBM PC running PageMaker and some image-processing software that he learnt to write while in a part-time course at London Guildhall University. "It's all done on cheap and accessible technology. The PC costs about 1700 pounds, and it costs me about 2500 pounds to print 1500 copies of the comic."

A lot of Graham's source imagery originates from the comic strips of his youth—the Eagle comics, *Voyage to the Bottom of the Sea, Dr. Who*. "It's partly an attempt to reclaim my boyhood culture. The aim is to re-work my culture anew, for myself and for others." He goes on to explain, "[A]fter the loss of Marxism, there's no alternative to capitalism. People say 'but now there's only capitalism, capitalism has won.' So there's no resistance to the dominant culture."

The battle for visibility in mass culture, for submerged forms to develop and reassert themselves, is an area in which new opportunities are emerging. The old forms of working-class culture and other local narratives will not survive unchanged, but new avenues into cultural production, many coming from non-art directions like new technologies or practices like scratch and plagiarism, can bypass the more class-conscious side of the necessary cultural and intellectual baggage. The challenge for these new "cultural workers" now is not just to throw up new aesthetics and reappropriate cultural forms, but to evolve genres that are neither art-based nor propagandist, but relevant, accessible though polemical, and even entertaining.

We can see, then, how the themes of mobility, democratization and aestheticization can come together. The role of computer programming and mathematical design in such areas as image processing brings new resources of knowledge to disciplines previously distanced from them. Combinations of text and graphics merge into a product that takes advantage of commercial channels to operate on more than one level. Democratization appears in the guise of extensions to popular culture and the encroaching into mainstream production values by independents. And aestheticization, instead of enforcing structures of dominance, develops distinctive new styles to reinvigorate a marginalized culture.

Unfortunately there is only room here to describe one example of a future for electronic media practice. Another study could talk about computer networking as an alternative method of distribution, and one not far away from being able to access and play back digital video and animation as well as text and graphics. Still another could extend the independent comic book scenario into moving image culture and the growth of independent electronic cinema. Or the potential for electronic games as fiction and play to combine through interactivity to suggest a new narrative structure. Although past advancements in technological media like radio and TV proved easily centralized and were absorbed into prevailing power structures, it must be stressed that the pace of technological innovation is now so accelerated and diverse that contradictions in its functioning and unpredictability in its control are almost inevitable and ready to be exploited.

Technology acts as a cultural compressor, squeezing practices and languages down onto a single sheet of features and pathways. Media has leveled down our experience to be inscribed into a cartography of forms. Hierarchies of access and discourse have been mapped out on a common terrain and forced to become paper thin. Technological pressure reduces artifacts and craftsmanship to information and digital processes—they are standardized as digital data and yet at the same time able to perform signifying functions and resist entrenchment. When the top and bottom of cultural stratifications are pressed into closer proximity, it is easier to overcome barriers between parts and for the potential for new cultural strategies to emerge. The impact of technology will not be to just provide economic access to the means of production, but also to restructure in new terms the practices and modes of expression that have confined any activity to a social class.

In our college we run courses in computer graphics that typically attract students from a wide range of backgrounds—artistic and social. Every year we take students who have not been through the usual art-school system—perhaps from scientific or technical backgrounds, or perhaps people who are artistically self-taught or come from sectors of society where their position precludes any involvement with what they perceive as the cultural establishment.

One student I have been tutoring recently is of the latter type. He comes from one of the most deprived areas of northern England—he shows me photos of young kids playing in a muddy wasteland of broken timbers and sewer pipes against a backdrop of concrete tower blocks and washing lines. Working as an artist for some years now, though completely outside the art-world or design industry, he sells his work to local people where he lives. After building up his skills he was able to leave the town he was brought up in to take a job on the sup-

port staff of a computer vendor and now finds the confidence to take a course in art and design.

He can only afford to put in the minimum number of hours on the course, but he works hard and uses his own computer at home. Recently he has been having difficulties on the course. He sometimes feels isolated from the rest of the class, unsure as to what direction his work should take, not knowing how to gain approval, unable to identify with the attitude of the typical art student. He hates the egotism of the world he finds himself in, can't understand its introspection, resents its hypocrisy, is alienated by its values—but with a little support from us he will see the course through.

Notes

1. Constance Penley and Andrew Ross, eds., *Technoculture* (Minneapolis: University of Minnesota Press, 1991).

2. Richard Wright, "Computer Graphics as Allegorical Knowledge : Electronic Imagery in the Sciences," in *Siggraph '90 Art Show Catalogue: "Digital Image-Digital Cinema,"* (N. p.: Pergamon Press 1990).

3. H. O. Peitgen and P. H. Richter. *The Beauty of Fractals* (London: Springer, 1986).

4. Ibid.

5. Laura Trippi, *Strange Attractors: Signs of Chaos.* Exhibition catalog, New Musuem of Contemporary Art, New York, September 1989.

6. Philip Hayward, "Beyond Reproduction," *Block* 14 (Autumn 1988).

7. Andy Darley, "Big Screen, Little Screen. The Archaeology of Technology," in *Digital Dialogues* , special issue of *Ten8* 2, no. 2 (1991).

8. Jasia Reichardt, *Cybernetic Serendipity* (N. p.: Studio International, 1968).

9. Peter Weibel, "Jury Statement," in Prix Ars Electronica catalog, (Linz: Veritas Verlag, 1992).

10. Ibid.

11. Delle Maxwell, "The Emperor's New Art?" in Isaac Kerlow, ed., *Computers in Art and Design*, ACM Siggraph '91 Art Show Catalog (New York: ACM, 1991).

12. Graham Harwood, "Mental,"*iF Comix*, no. 3 (London: Working Press, 1991).

5

Utopian Plagiarism, Hypertextuality, and Electronic Cultural Production

Critical Art Ensemble

Plagiarism has long been considered an evil in the cultural world. Typically it has been viewed as the theft of language, ideas, and images by the less than talented, often for the enhancement of personal fortune or prestige. Yet, like most mythologies, the myth of plagiarism is easily inverted. Perhaps it is those who support the legislation of representation and the privatization of language that are suspect; perhaps the plagiarist's actions, given a specific set of social conditions, are the ones contributing most to cultural enrichment. Prior to the Enlightenment, plagiarism was useful in aiding the distribution of ideas. An English poet could appropriate and translate a sonnet from Petrarch and call it his own. In accordance with the classical aesthetic of art as imitation, this was a perfectly acceptable practice. The real value of this activity rested less in the reinforcement of classical aesthetics than in the distribution of work to areas where otherwise it probably would not have appeared. The works of English plagiarists, such as Chaucer, Shakespeare, Spenser, Sterne, Coleridge, and De Quincey, are still a vital part of the English heritage, and remain in the literary canon to this day.

At present, new conditions have emerged that once again make plagiarism an acceptable, even crucial strategy for textual production. This is the age of the recombinant: recombinant bodies, recombinant gender, recombinant texts, recombinant culture. Looking back through the privileged frame of hindsight, one can argue that the recombinant has always been key in the development of meaning and invention; recent extraordinary advances in electronic technology have called attention to the recombinant both in theory and in practice (for example, the use of morphing in video and film). The primary value of all electronic technology, especially computers and imaging systems, is the startling speed at which they can transmit information in both raw and refined forms. As information flows at a high velocity through the electronic networks, disparate and sometimes incommensurable systems of meaning intersect, with both enlightening and inventive consequences. In a society dominated by a "knowledge" explosion, exploring the possibilities of meaning in that which already exists is more pressing than adding redundant information (even if it is produced using the methodology and metaphysic of the "original"). In the past, arguments in favor of plagiarism were limited to showing its use in resisting the privatization of culture that serves the needs and desires of the power elite. Today one can argue that plagiarism is acceptable, even inevitable, given the nature of postmodern existence with its techno-infrastructure. In a recombinant culture, plagiarism is productive, although we need not abandon the romantic model of cultural production that privileges a model of *ex nihilo* creation. Certainly in a general sense the latter model is somewhat anachronistic. There are still specific situations where such thinking is useful, and one can never be sure when it could become appropriate again. What is called for is an end to its tyranny and to its institutionalized cultural bigotry. This is a call to open the cultural database, to let everyone use the technology of textual production to its maximum potential.

> Ideas improve. The meaning of words participates in the improvement. Plagiarism is necessary. Progress implies it. It embraces an author's phrase, makes use of his expressions, erases a false idea, and replaces it with the right idea.[1]

Plagiarism often carries a weight of negative connotations (particularly in the bureaucratic class); while the need for its use has increased over the century, plagiarism itself has been camouflaged in a new lexicon by those desiring to explore the practice as method and as a legitimized form of cultural discourse. Ready-mades, collage, found art or found text, intertexts, combines, detournment, and appropriation—all these terms represent explorations in plagiarism. Indeed, these terms are not perfectly synonymous, but they all intersect a set of meanings primary to the philosophy and activity of plagiarism. Philosophically, they all stand in opposition to essentialist doctrines of the text: They all assume that no structure within a given text provides a universal and necessary meaning. No work of art or philosophy exhausts itself in itself alone, in its being-in-itself. Such works have always stood in relation to the actual life-process of society from which they have distinguished themselves. Enlightenment essentialism failed to provide a unit of analysis that could act as a basis of meaning. Just as the connection between a signifier and its referent is arbitrary, the unit of meaning used for any given textual analysis is also arbitrary. Roland Barthes's notion of the *lexia* primarily indicates surrender in the search for a basic unit of meaning. Since language was the only tool available for the development of metalanguage, such a project was doomed from its inception. It was much like trying to eat soup with soup. The text itself is fluid— although the language game of ideology can provide the illusion of stability, creating blockage by manipulating the unacknowledged assumptions of everyday life. Consequently, one of the main goals of the plagiarist is to restore the dynamic and unstable drift of meaning by appropriating and recombining fragments of culture. In this way, meanings can be produced that were not previously associated with an object or a given set of objects.

Marcel Duchamp, one of the first to understand the power of recombination, presented an early incarnation of this new aesthetic with his ready-made series. Duchamp took objects to which he was "visually indifferent" and recontextualized them in a manner that shifted their meaning. For example, by taking a urinal out of the rest room, signing it, and placing it on a pedestal in an art gallery, meaning slid away from the apparently exhaustive functional interpretation of the object. Although this meaning did not completely disappear, it was placed in harsh juxtaposition to another possibility—meaning as an art object. This problem of instability increased when problems of origin were raised: The object was not made by an artist, but by a machine. Whether or not the viewer chose to accept other possibilities for interpreting the function of the artist and the authenticity of the art object, the urinal in a gallery instigated a moment of uncertainty and reassessment. This conceptual game has been replayed numerous times over the twentieth century, at times for very narrow purposes, as with Rauschenberg's combines—done for the sake of attacking the critical hegemony of Clement Greenberg—while at other times it has been done to promote large-scale political and cultural restructuring, as in the case of the Situationists. In each case, the plagiarist works to open meaning through the injection of skepticism into the culture-text.

Here one also sees the failure of Romantic essentialism. Even the alleged transcendental object cannot escape the skeptics' critique. Duchamp's notion of the inverted ready-made (turning a Rembrandt painting into an ironing board) suggested that the distinguished art object draws its power from a historical legitimation process firmly rooted in the institutions of Western culture and not from being an unalterable conduit to transcendental realms. This is not to deny the possibility of transcendental experience, but only to say that if it does exist, it is prelinguistic, and thereby relegated to the privacy of an individual's subjectivity. A society with a complex division of labor requires a rationalization of institutional processes, a situation that in turn robs the individual of a way to share nonrational experience. Unlike societies with a simple division of labor, in which the experience of one member closely resembles the experience of another (minimal alienation), under a complex division of labor, the life experience of the individual turned specialist holds little in common with other specialists. Consequently, communication exists primarily as an instrumental function.

Plagiarism has historically stood against the privileging of any text through spiritual, scientific, or other legitimizing myths. The plagiarist sees all objects as equal, and thereby horizontalizes the plane of phenomena. All texts become potentially usable and reusable. Herein lies an epistemology of anarchy, according to which the plagiarist argues that if science, religion, or any other social institution precludes certainty beyond the realm of the private, then it is best to endow consciousness with as many categories of interpretation as possible. The tyranny of paradigms may have some useful consequences (such as greater efficiency within the paradigm), but the repressive costs to the individual (excluding other modes of thinking and reducing the possibility of invention) are too high. Rather than being led by sequences of signs, one should instead drift through them, choosing the interpretation best suited to the social conditions of a given situation.

It is difficult to believe that a method of production as simple as plagiarism could have revolutionary effects within the institutions of culture. Yet if one reflects on this issue for a moment, it becomes readily apparent that plagiarism challenges the stagnant paradigm of privatized and exclusive culture around which these institutions are structured. If plagiarism were to be recognized as a legitimate and inventive act, bureaucracies in general and the university in particular would have to completely rework their criteria for hierarchical mobility and their notions of cultural production and cultural management.

Cultural production, literary or otherwise, has traditionally been a slow, labor-intensive process. In painting, sculpture, or written work, the technology has always been primitive by contemporary standards. Paintbrushes, hammers and chisels, quills, paper, and even the printing press do not lend themselves well to rapid production and broad-range distribution. The time lapse between production and distribution can seem unbearably long. Book arts and traditional visual arts still suffer tremendously from this problem, when compared to the electronic arts. Before electronic technology became dominant, cultural perspectives developed in a manner that more clearly defined texts as individual works. Cultural fragments appeared in their own right as discrete units, since their influence moved slowly enough to allow the orderly evolution of an argument or an aesthetic. Boundaries could be maintained between disciplines and schools of thought. Knowledge was considered finite, and was therefore easier to control. In the nineteenth century this traditional order began to collapse as new technology began to increase the velocity of cultural development. The first strong indicators began to appear that speed was becoming a crucial issue. Knowledge was shifting away from certitude, and transforming itself into information. During the American Civil War, Lincoln sat impatiently by his telegraph line, awaiting reports from his generals at the front. He had no patience with the long-winded rhetoric of the past, and demanded from his generals an economy of language. There was no time for the traditional trappings of the elegant essayist. Cultural velocity and information have continued to increase at a geometric rate since then, resulting in an information panic. Production and distribution of information (or any other product) must be immediate; there can be no lag time between the two. Techno-culture has met this demand with databases and electronic networks that rapidly move any type of information.

Under such conditions, plagiarism fulfills the requirements of the economy of representation, without stifling invention. If invention occurs when a new perception or idea is brought out—by intersecting two or more formally disparate systems—then recombinant methodologies are desirable. This is where plagiarism progresses beyond nihilism. It does not simply inject skepticism to help destroy totalitarian systems that stop invention; it *participates* in invention, and is thereby also productive. The genius of an inventor like Leonardo da

Vinci lay in his ability to recombine the then-separate systems of biology, mathematics, engineering, and art. He was not so much an originator as a synthesizer. There have been few people like him over the centuries, because the ability to hold that much data in one's own biological memory is rare. Now, however, the technology of recombination is available in the computer. The problem now for would-be cultural producers is to gain access to this technology and information. After all, access is the most precious of all privileges and is therefore strictly guarded, and this in turn makes one wonder whether to be a successful plagiarist one must also be a successful hacker.

Many artists and writers exhibit a fear of new technology. For some, the fear is that the technology will functionally replace them, while for others it is the fear that they will be merged with the machine in an undesirable manner. These worries are difficult to understand. Humanity has been merging with technology for millennia, ever since the tool became an extension of the body. Inventive technology has always required an active agent, and still does. The real fear is that the *sole* variety of technology produced in the future will be a kind that reduces the agent to the role of passive spectator. To prevent this possible scenario, cultural workers must create a sensibility for active technological participation. This cannot be accomplished by treating the use of technology as a sacrilege.

To some degree, a small portion of technology has fallen through the cracks into the hands of the lucky few. Personal computers and video cameras are the best examples. To accompany these consumer items and make their use more versatile, hypertextual and image-sampling programs have also been developed—programs designed to facilitate recombination. It is the plagiarist's dream to be able to call up, move, and recombine text with simple user-friendly commands. Perhaps plagiarism belongs rightfully to post-book culture, since only in that society can it be made explicit what book culture, with its geniuses and auteurs, tends to hide— that information is most useful when it interacts with other information, rather than when it is deified and presented in a vacuum.

Thinking about a new means for recombining information has always been on twentieth-century minds, although this search has been left to a few until recently. In 1945 Vannevar Bush, a former science advisor to Franklin D. Roosevelt, proposed in an *Atlantic Monthly* article a new way of organizing information. At that time, computer technology was in its earliest stages of development and its full potential was not really understood. Bush, however, had the foresight to imagine a device he called the Memex. In his view it would be based around storage of information on microfilm, integrated with some means to allow the user to select and display any section at will, thus enabling one to move freely among previously unrelated increments of information.

At the time, Bush's Memex could not be built, but as computer technology evolved, his idea eventually gained practicality. Around 1960 Theodor Nelson discovered something when he began studying computer programming in college:

> Over a period of months, I came to realize that, although programmers structured their data hierarchically, they didn't have to. I began to see the computer as the ideal place for making interconnections among things accessible to people.
>
> I realized that writing did not have to be sequential and that not only would tomorrow's books and magazines be on [cathode ray terminal] screens, they could all tie to one another in every direction. At once I began working on a program (written in 7090 assembler language) to carry out these ideas.[2]

Nelson's idea, which he called *hypertext*, failed to attract any supporters at first, although by 1968 its usefulness became obvious to some in the government and in defense industries. A prototype of hypertext was developed by another computer innovator, Douglas Englebart, who is often credited with many breakthroughs in the use of computers (such as the development of the Macintosh interface). Englebart's system, called Augment, was applied to organizing the government's research network, ARPAnet, and was also used by McDonnell Douglas, the defense contractor, to aid technical work groups in coordinating projects such as aircraft design:

> All communications are automatically added to the Augment information base and linked, when appropriate, to other documents. An engineer could, for example, use Augment to write and deliver electronically a work plan to others in the work group. The other members could then review the document and have their comments linked to the original, eventually creating a "group memory" of the decisions made. Augment's powerful linking features allow users to find even old information quickly, without getting lost or being overwhelmed by detail.[3]

Computer technology continued to be refined, and eventually—as with so many other technological breakthroughs in this country—once it had been thoroughly exploited by military and intelligence agencies, the technology was released for commercial exploitation. Of course, the development of microcomputers and consumer-grade technology for personal computers led immediately to the need for software that would help one cope with the exponential increase in information, especially textual information. Probably the first humanistic application of hypertext was in the field of education. Currently, hypertext and hypermedia (which adds graphic images to the network of features that can be interconnected) continue to be fixtures in instructional design and educational technology.

An interesting experiment in this regard was instigated in 1975 by Robert Scholes and Andries Van Dam at Brown University. Scholes, a professor of English, was contacted by Van Dam, a professor of computer science, who wanted to know if there were any courses in the humanities that might benefit from using what at the time was called a text-editing system (now known as a word processor) with hypertext capabilities built in. Scholes and two teaching assistants, who formed a research group, were particularly impressed by one aspect of hypertext. Using this program, they believed it possible "to peruse in a nonlinear fashion all the interrelated materials in a text. A hypertext is thus best seen as a web of interconnected materials."[4] This description suggested that there is a definite parallel between the conception of culture-text and that of hypertext:

> One of the most important facets of literature (and one which also leads to difficulties in interpretation) is its reflexive nature. Individual poems constantly develop their meanings—often through such means as direct allusion or the reworking of traditional motifs and conventions, at other times through subtler means, such as genre development and expansion or biographical reference—by referring to that total body of poetic material of which the particular poems comprise a small segment.[5]

Although it was not difficult to accumulate a hypertextually linked database consisting of poetic materials, Scholes and his group were more concerned with making it interactive—that is, they wanted to construct a "communal text" consisting not only of the poetry, but also one that could incorporate the comments and interpretations offered by individual students. In this way, each student in turn could read a work and attach "notes" to it about his or her observations. The resulting "expanded text" would be read and augmented at a terminal on which the screen was divided into four areas. The student could call up the poem in one of the areas (referred to as windows) and call up related materials in the other three windows, in any sequence s/he desired. This would powerfully reinforce the tendency to read in a nonlinear sequence. By this means, each student would learn how to read a work as it truly exists, not in "a vacuum" but rather as "the central point of a progressively-revealed body of documents and ideas."[6]

Hypertext is analogous to other forms of literary discourse besides poetry. From the very beginning of its manifestation as a computer program, hypertext was popularly described as a multidimensional text roughly analogous to the "standard scholarly article in the humanities or social sciences," because it uses the same conceptual devices, such as footnotes, annotations, allusions to other works, quotations from other works, etc.[7] Unfortunately, the convention of linear reading and writing, as well as the physical fact of two-dimensional pages and the necessity of binding them in only one possible sequence, have always limited the true potential of the traditional type of text. One problem is that the reader is often forced to search through the text (or forced to leave the book and search elsewhere) for related information. This is a time-consuming and distracting process; instead of being able to move easily and instantly among physically remote or inaccessible areas of information storage, the reader must cope with cumbrous physical impediments to his or her research or creative work. With the advent of hypertext, it has become possible to move among related areas of information with a speed and flexibility that approach finally accommodating the workings of human intellect.

> The recombinant text in hypertextual form signifies the emergence of the perception of textual constellations that have always/already gone nova. In this uncanny luminosity the authorial biomorph has been consumed.[8]

Barthes and Foucault may be lauded for theorizing the death of the author; the absent author is more a matter of everyday life, however, for the technocrat recombining and augmenting information at the computer or at a video editing console. S/he is living the dream of capitalism that is still being refined in the area of manufacture. The Japanese notion of "just in time delivery," in which the units of assembly are delivered to the assembly line just as they are called for, was a first step in streamlining the tasks of assembly. In such a system, there is no sedentary capital, but a constant flow of raw commodities. The assembled commodity is delivered to the distributor precisely at the moment of consumer need. This nomadic system eliminates stockpiles of goods. (There still is some dead time; however, the Japanese have cut it to a matter of hours, and are working on reducing it to a matter of minutes.) In this way, production, distribution, and consumption are imploded into a single act, with no beginning or end, just unbroken circulation. In the same manner, the on-line text flows in an unbroken stream through the electronic network. There can be no place for gaps that mark discrete units in the society of speed. Consequently, notions of origin have no place in electronic reality. The production of the text presupposes its immediate distribution, consumption, and revision. All who participate in the network also participate in the interpretation and mutation of the textual stream. The concept of the author did not so much die as it simply ceased to function. The author has become an abstract aggregate that cannot be reduced to biology or to the psychology of personality. Indeed, such a development has apocalyptic connotations—the fear that humanity will be lost in the textual stream. Perhaps humans are not capable of participating in hypervelocity. One must answer that never has there been a time when humans were able, one and all, to participate in cultural production. Now, at least the potential for cultural democracy is greater. The single bio-genius need not act as a stand-in for all humanity. The real concern is just the same as it has always been: the need for access to cultural resources.

> How much longer must we contend with the insufferable condition of an oedipal culture? There is no reason to measure success by the ability of the junior cultural model to eliminate its senior. In fact, such standards should be the measurement of catastrophe.[9]

The book has by no means disappeared. The publishing industry continues to resist the emergence of the recombinant text, and opposes increases in cultural speed. It has set itself in the gap between production and consumption of texts, which for purposes of survival it is bound to maintain. If speed is allowed to increase, the book is doomed to perish, along with its Renaissance companions, painting and sculpture. This is why the industry is so afraid of the recombinant text. Such a work closes the gap between production and consumption, and opens the industry to those other than the literary celebrity. If the industry is unable to differentiate its product through the spectacle of originality and uniqueness, its profitability collapses. Consequently, the industry plods along, taking years to publish information needed immediately. Yet there is a peculiar irony to this situation. In order to reduce speed, it must also participate in velocity in its most intense form, that of spectacle. It must claim to defend "quality and standards," and it must invent celebrities. Such endeavors require the immediacy of advertising—that is, full participation in the simulacra that will be the industry's own destruction.

Hence for the bureaucrat, from an everyday life perspective, the author is alive and well. S/he can be seen and touched, and traces of h/is existence are on the covers of books and magazines everywhere in the form of the signature. To such evidence, theory can only respond with the maxim that the meaning of a given text derives exclusively from its relation to other texts. Such texts are contingent upon what came before them, the context in which they are placed, and the interpretive ability of the reader. This argument is of course unconvincing to the social segments caught in cultural lag. So long as this is the case, no recognized historical legitimation will support the producers of recombinant texts, who will always be suspect to the keepers of "high" culture.

> Who can excuse the nauseating self-importance of the person claiming to have written a document in h/er own words! Artist and poets do not steal the vitality of words; instead they recognize and maintain the autonomy of words. Compelling writing is liberating; it frees us from convention. Now, whose words were they again?

The invention of the video portapak in the late 1960s and early 70s led to considerable speculation among radical media artists that in the near future, everyone would have access to such equipment, causing a revolution in the television industry. Many hoped that video would become the ultimate tool for distributable democratic art. Each home would become its own production center, and the reliance on network television for electronic information would be only one of many options. Unfortunately this prophecy never came to pass. In the democratic sense, video did little more than super 8 film to redistribute the capacity for image production, and it has had little or no effect on image distribution. Any video besides home movies has remained in the hands of an elite technocratic class, although (as with any class) there are marginalized segments that resist the media industry and maintain a program of decentralization.

The video revolution failed for two reasons—a lack of access and an absence of desire. Gaining access to the hardware, particularly post-production equipment, has remained as difficult as ever, nor are there any regular distribution points beyond the local public access offered by some cable TV franchises. It has also been hard to convince those outside of the technocratic class why they should want to do something with video, even if they had access to equipment. This is quite understandable when one considers that media images are provided in such an overwhelming quantity that the thought of producing more is empty. The contemporary plagiarist faces precisely the same discouragement. The potential for generating recombinant texts at present is just that—potential. It does at least have a wider base, since the computer technology for making recombinant texts has escaped the technocratic class and spread to the bureaucratic class; however, electronic cultural production has by no means become the democratic form that utopian plagiarists still hope it will be.

The immediate problems are obvious. The cost of technology for productive plagiarism is still too high. Even if one chooses to use the less efficient form of a handwritten plagiarist manuscript, desktop publishing technology is required to distribute it, since no publishing house will accept it. Further, the population in the U.S. is generally skilled only at receiving information, not at producing it. With this exclusive structure solidified, technology and the desire and ability to use it remain centered in utilitarian economy, and hence not much time is given to the technology's aesthetic or resistant possibilities.

In addition to these obvious barriers, there is a more insidious problem that emerges from the social schizophrenia of the U.S. While its political system is theoretically based on democratic principles of inclusion, its economic system is based on the principle of exclusion. Consequently, as a luxury itself, the cultural superstructure tends towards exclusion as well. This economic principle determined the invention of copyright, which originally developed not in order to protect writers, but to reduce competition among publishers. In seventeenth-century England, where copyright first appeared, the goal was to reserve for publishers themselves, in perpetuity, the exclusive right to print certain books. The justification, of course, was that when formed into a literary work, language has the author's personality imposed upon it, thereby marking it as private property. Under this mythology, copyright has flourished in late capitalism, setting the legal precedent to privatize any cultural item, whether it is an image, a word, or a sound. Thus the plagiarist (even of the technocratic class) is kept in a deeply marginal position, regardless of the inventive and efficient uses his or her methodology may have for the current state of technology and knowledge.

> What is the point of saving language when there is no longer anything to say?

The present requires us to rethink and re-present the notion of plagiarism. Its function has for too long been devalued by an ideology with little place in technoculture. Let the romantic notions of originality, genius, and authorship remain, but as elements for cultural production without special privilege above other equally useful elements. It is time to openly and boldly use the methodology of recombination so as to better parallel the technology of our time.

Notes

1. In its more heroic form the footnote has a low-speed hypertextual function—that is, connecting the reader with other sources of information that can further articulate the producer's words. It points to additional information too lengthy to include in the text itself. This is not an objectionable function. The footnote is also a means of surveillance by which one can "check up" on a writer, to be sure that s/he is not improperly using an idea or phrase from the work of another. This function makes the footnote problematic, although it may be appropriate as a means of verifying conclusions in a quantitative study, for example. The surveillance function of the footnote imposes fixed interpretations on a linguistic sequence, and implies ownership of language and ideas by the individual cited. The note becomes an homage to the genius who supposedly originated the idea. This would be acceptable if all who deserved credit got their due; however, such crediting is impossible, since it would begin an infinite regress. Consequently, that which is most feared occurs: the labor of many is stolen, smuggled in under

the authority of the signature that is cited. In the case of those cited who are still living, this designation of authorial ownership allows them to collect rewards for the work of others. It must be realized that writing itself is theft: it is a changing of the features of the old culture-text in much the same way one disguises stolen goods. This is not to say that signatures should never be cited; but remember that the signature is merely a sign, a shorthand under which a collection of interrelated ideas may be stored and rapidly deployed.

2. Ted Nelson, "On the Road to Xanadu," *Personal Computing* 11, no. 12 (December 1987): 169.

3. Paul Saffo, "What You Need to Know About Hypertext," *Personal Computing* 11, no. 12 (December 1987): 169.

4. James V. Catano, "Poetry and Computers: Experimenting with the Communal Text," *Computers and the Humanities* 13 (1979): 269.

5. Ibid., 269.

6. Ibid., 270.

7. George P. Landow, "Changing Texts, Changing Readers: Hypertext in Literary Education, Criticism, and Scholarship," in *Reorientations: Critical Theories & Pedagogies,* by Bruce Henrickson and Thais E. Morgan (Urbana and Chicago: University of Illinois Press, 1990): 134.

8. If the signature is a form of cultural shorthand, then it is not necessarily horrific on occasion to sabotage the structures so they do not fall into rigid complacency. Attributing words to an image, i.e., an intellectual celebrity, is inappropriate. The image is a tool for playful use, like any culture-text or part thereof. It is just as necessary to imagine the history of the spectacular image, and write it as imagined, as it is to show fidelity to its current "factual" structure. One should choose the method that best suits the context of production, one that will render the greater possibility for interpretation. The producer of recombinant texts augments the language and often preserves the generalized code, as when Karen Eliot quoted Sherrie Levine as saying, "Plagiarism? I just don't like the way it tastes."

9. It goes without saying that one is not limited to correcting a work or to integrating diverse fragments of out-of-date works into a new one; one can also alter the meaning of these fragments in any appropriate way, leaving the constipated to their slavish preservations of "citations."

6

Virtual Worlds: Fascinations and Reactions

Florian Rötzer

Televirtuality is the application of telecommunicative means, allowing rapid communication over long and short distances, on the potential of the virtual world of being able to be at any "place" at will. . . . Once the appropriate networks have been installed, allowing televirtuality, the nature of human communication will change—just as radically as the experience of space and time, due to the knowledge of the millions of symbols involved. Perhaps we will in the long run return to the era of television, which enabled us to flee into stultifying passivity without having to fear the totally interactive involvement required by the new televirtual media. However, we might also overcome the traditional obstacles of communication, whether of a social or a technical nature, and create new communities granting man new possibilities on a local as well as global scale.

—Robert Jacobson

Being able to be at any place at any time, being able to do anything we imagine, even if it is only virtual and not "real": this is the dream of all-round availability that has urged on the development of technology since time immemorial. One world no longer suffices; we want many worlds, between which we can zap to and fro as with the remote control of the television set, by means of which we could basically even produce our own film as a heterogeneous mixture of sequences, released from all referential fetters, including those of time, space or scene. This corresponds with a mobility that is no longer "on the way," but which raves and becomes vectorless in that it converts any recorded phenomenon into digital code, and can

119

therefore mix such phenomena arbitrarily with all others, whether recorded or self-produced. The digital code is a universal code, and the representation of the recorded or created phenomena also becomes arbitrary, because the acoustic can be converted into the visual, and vice versa. Programs can be controlled by our eyes, without the need to use our hands to make the usual entries on the keyboard or to move the mouse. With our breath we can generate visual changes on the screen, which no longer bear witness to any analogy. With our movements, recorded by a video-camera, we can paint pictures in virtual space or play nonexistent instruments. With our brain waves we already can control a cursor on the screen. The real and the virtual enter into hybrid mergers.

More than anything, however, we, the consumers, want virtual worlds that we can step into, and such worlds will have to be just as complex as, but more compact and intense than, the ones we want to catapult ourselves out of. For this reason, these worlds must not only be a "montage of attractions" (Sergei Eisenstein), compressing and accelerating time, but must also be able to react to us. However, to realize this, we, the observers, must become the observed.[1] Even if we have the impression that in the use of interactive and intelligent technologies, we are testing them by trying to find out how they react to us, it is still we who are being tested: the machines observe the answers we give. The price we pay for the freedom of traveling weightlessly in virtual spaces, which are no longer subject to the laws of physics, is the totalitarian control over the environment, over each of our movements and perhaps over every thought as well, should we be successful in connecting the neural CRT to the computer.

The communicating tubes of the electric, electronic, and information technologies shroud us in a cave, in a closed space, which is, at the same time, completely open. As with the fractional worlds of images generated by means of simple recursive algorithms, we can move around endlessly within this space, even if we do not experience anything radically new, but only perceive permutations. The monitor is a window looking out on a world that is, in principle, endless, one that still has to be discovered and invented. Its only restriction is the calculating time required, which allows the real to creep back again into the virtual world.

Moreover, in order to be interesting, to fascinate us, the digital worlds and their inhabitants must also be intelligent, autopoetic, and mysterious—not boring like conventional, trivial machines, which can only reel off their fixed and therefore easily predictable programs, even if, due to acceleration, they produce precisely the kind of intensity (by loss of reality) once enthused about by futurists, when they spoke of the incredible pleasure of acceleration, reaching even beyond the infinity of dreams. It is the exceeding of the inner virtual worlds of dream and fantasy that fascinates techno-aestheticians: the overcoming of the distance to the real and the perceptible that these allow. The virtual worlds of the wishing machines must fulfill the imagination and, at the same time, leave it behind. This is the reason why the accelerated trips made possible by film, video games and video clips, and in a way also by simulation cabins, fascinate us; they leave us no time to reflect, but captivate our glance and our reactions. The situations they create are as tense as situations involving real danger, which explains the frequent representation of danger and horror. In this light, Jonathan Waldern of W-Industries (producers of VR-systems) struck the right note when he pointed out that their potential will, at most, be restricted by the simpleness of the imagination.[2]

The aim embodied by all wishing machines—of reaching beyond the virtual worlds of inner dreams or fantasies by means of technical devices—is objectified by the possibility of leaving the real to immerse oneself in a new and different world. This constructed world must be transparent, woven out of a process of calculation. But this mathematical world should not be a mechanistic universe, as the thinkers of the modern age imagined, a universe moving towards perfection according to ironclad rules in an uneventful cycle or in permanent progress. Despite all the transparency, it should let the unexpected occur and, as in chaotic processes, continually be open to metamorphoses and catastrophes. We want to enter a world that is safe and, at the same time, offers an element of surprise, an inexhaustible horizon of possibilities, from which events can emerge that are not enforceable, yet evocable.

> Free availability of space and time will therefore lead to a new form of urbanization. The old term "town planning" is aligned with the organization of fixed housing and settlements. It does not meet the requirements of a fluctuating way of living. Someone who is not tied down by temporal deadlines or places of residence will scarcely see the point of a permanent dwelling place. He will prefer an unrestrained, nomadic life. He will therefore create

for himself an environment which, with its artificially generated ambience constructions, allows him precisely this
way of life.[3]

Constant's New Babylon was one of many attempts of the sixties to
imagine a totally mobile, and therefore solitary, life, in a virtual or
rhizomatous event architecture; it has now come one step closer
through cyberspace. The media environment, in which we move
with ever better connections, is a first realization, if only a partial
one, because so far it only exists on the screen. With the ramified,
network-connected information technologies, the architecture of
built space, that is, space laid still, will have to change drastically.
With the advance of televirtuality, public matters will happen more
and more in intimate places. Perhaps the outside will be drastically
relieved of passengers, or be abandoned entirely to indifference.
Since the striking disappearance of the great city utopias, there has
been a continual architectural search for temporary arrangements
with only a fleeting existence and instant changeability. Along these
lines, the media and information technologies are bringing about a
process-related communication network that, due to its virtual and
nonmaterial nature, is widely indifferent to spatial form. Basically
independent of location and the form of the enclosed area, the image
and information channels replace the physical traversing of space
and allow an urban way of life without real urbanity. The space of
locations is replaced by a space of flow-line processes.[4]

A really modern person who wishes to build himself, for
example, a house, will feel as if he were trying to bury
himself alive in a mausoleum.[5]

Domotik allows images on the wall to be replaced by screen walls,
with continually changing images and the capacity to project the
inside to the outside or the outside to the inside. Even architecture
becomes mobile; it becomes the design of the interface, a vehicle of
images with which one no longer needs to travel and yet can be
everywhere at the same time. This mobile life could entrench itself
again in permanent dwellings, yet constantly be in virtual movement. But will anything still happen in the course of this?

In the virtual world of simulation, there is no irreversibility and
everything is concentrated into a symbolic economy, which insu-
lates itself from the real, even if interactivity is possible by means of

a structural coupling. It is never more than timeless and utopian images, sounds, signs, or numbers circulating among themselves. Whereas, during the era of the real and representation, people tried to reach the realm of signs, of illusion, and the imaginary in order to escape the experience of reality, the reverse is pursued in digital spaces: what we are now searching for is the gap in the web of the communicative tubes, through which the real can enter as an event, no matter how terrible or trite this may be. This reversal could be observed even as early as the days of romanticism, when not only the trite and the commonplace, but also the evil and the irrational, were provided with an aura as a protest against the Hegelian system. Its origin can also be traced back to the epistemological systems of the modern age, which not only produced technologies but also created prisons everywhere. Access to the real, to the "thing as such," was barred. Recognition is granted only to phenomena, images surrounded by the unknown, and this shirks any direct involvement. In this way, man is locking himself, no matter how effectively, in inner rooms, in projections without any windows, with simulacra—still images themselves—appearing or disappearing on the walls. Modern epistemologies suggest that we are all pilots on a blind flight or in the simulator cabin, merely orientating ourselves by means of data on the mental CRT. But blind flights give rise to the wish to break through the giddiness and deception of simulation and experience failure, the only possibility in which the real still shimmers. No wonder that pain, a sign of resistance and human materiality, and shock, a sign of the victory over the data-processing "consciousness" by the sublime, and war, the spectacle of intensity and destruction, also became the aesthetic attractions of a confirmation of existence, which had to destroy semblance. Wherever reality, or rather the experience of reality as an event, as a coincidence, and as the essentially nonmade, is in short supply, it must be supplied with an aura to enhance its quality, now marked by uniqueness, nonreproducibility, and fatefulness.

The occurrence of events in time corresponds with the materiality of things in space. It is no longer the image bearer or the bearer of the symbolic, but it has become, in its nonreproducible quality, the aesthetic object of a phenomenological sign and presentation, which has, indeed, governed the arts as a gesture ever since the beginning of photography. This trend is emphasized by, for example, Lyotard, as the "aesthetics of the unpredictable, material presence,"[6] by way of countermove to the immaterialization and simulation of the digital technologies. With the audiovisual media, the sense of touch is becoming privileged, although there have been efforts to incorporate it into VR technology. It is not the eyes and ears, not the forms, sounds and words, but the collision of the bodies, and finally the accident, that will become the primary indication of reality experience in the age of simulation.

Nothing is more typical of the media than the paradoxical attempt to attest the real as an event by constructing it in full detail, by generating it. This fascination with the event seems to be the imaginary aspect of the media: that is, constant production of images, so as to break through the image prison and allow the real to flare up. The media not only fulfill the wish to flee from "being" into "seeing" (Schopenhauer), they also turn the perceivable world into a web of fluctuating data, into a musical glide that is no longer material, into a "Dionysian frenzy in which no limb is not drunk" (Hegel). In all simulation, the craving for reality prevails. Reality, then, is just another word for event and intensity resisting the principle of representation. The induction of the electronic dream, and therefore of virtual worlds, owes its attraction to the fact that we are jolted into the real, seeing it with completely different eyes, like entering into the daylight from the dark of the cinema. Would it not mean the realization of a secretly harbored dream and trauma, to destroy the hardware simply by manipulation of the software? Something similar can be observed in the craving for realistic representation, which often seems to mark our dealings with computer technology. This is not so much a matter of once more simulating the real; we only do that in order to recognize the way in which reality is perceived and to learn how to build a complex world that has reality content. After all, we want to be drawn into another world, one that, albeit intensified by acceleration and change, abandons to oblivion all that has happened before. Good practice for this are the so-called "mind machines," which, in the same way as rock music or video clips, evoke a state of trance by means of overstimulation, or by exposing perception to a formless noise.

> The observer does not see any images or hear any tones, as is usual in films and video productions. True to nature, the data flow of these media is directed from outside to inside. The activity of consciousness is reduced to the processing of these data. "The inner cinema," on the other hand, provides only minimal optoacoustic basic information. The psycho-active pulse conveys neither

content nor aesthetics, it should exclusively arouse the observer's own, subjective imagination.[7]

The media have changed not only the understanding of the real, but also, and above all, the expectation of it. We no longer want to flee from the real by means of fiction; on the contrary, we now want fiction to evoke reality: simulation as a trap for the event. Though some deconstructivist theoreticians try to prove that the expected event never takes place, or the original event never happened, and that we always move within sign sequences, these aesthetics of futility, of emptiness, and resentment should be regarded not only as a reaction to the pressure of expectation of the telematic society, but also as an affirmation of all self-organizing systems that shut themselves off from the outside and only process the self-produced. The environment of such systems is beyond their knowledge; it is merely the supplier of disturbances that stimulate the "autopoiesis," and hence may have to be evoked as disturbances to keep the machine running.

The biologists Humberto Maturana and Francisco Varela use the term "autopoiesis" to characterize complex and closed living systems that, by means of reversible processes, produce themselves and preserve themselves.[8] In short, systems whose elements mutually interact. Living beings are linked to their environment in a structural way only; they do not adjust to their environment. Influences from the environment only serve to disturb the autopoiesis, thus provoking more complex internal dynamics, through which the urge of these living systems to survive within their environment is increased. In other fields of science, the concept of autopoiesis is applied to other complex systems, such as societies and knowledge transfer systems. The philosopher Vilem Flusser, for example, sees the approaching "telematic society" determined as a whole by the search for the creation or experience of improbable events, marked by fateful unpredictability as in an accidental disaster. In an adroit redefinition of the cybernetic concept of information, Flusser forces the principle of simulation, and so, presumably, the calculation of the future, into a paradox:

> He who predicts, does not see what he is heading for. . . .
> All future prediction is future destroying. The computer
> screen is our witness. Developments, tendencies, curves,
> can be projected out from the present, and we can play
> with these projections. And the factor of error can be

> defined precisely as we wish. Yet, such projections show us the results of the calculation, and not what really matters. There is no future. The predicting computer has devoured the future. . . . Genuine disasters are new information. They are, by definition, surprising adventures. . . . The telematic society is a structure to evoke disasters.[9]

The announcement of radical changes caused by technologies, or even simply by the prospect of such, has pervaded the futuristic awareness of man since the initial utopias of the dawning modern age, whether they were apocalyptically or optimistically tinted. The disappearance of distance and duration, due to the new communication technologies that enable us to send words and images across the globe in real time and so allow for telepresence, is accompanied by a certain neutralization of the forces of gravity: not only can matter and bodies stay where they are, but space traffic also cancels out all boundaries between cultures. Physical borders can only be preserved because the organization of space transport of people, information, objects, and matter is time-consuming and can therefore be stalled temporarily. The demise of the Berlin Wall, that tangible relic of a border and at the same time symbol of a conservatism only secured by bunker mentality, is the sign of a general fluctuation as prescribed by the ramified media networks. We are now approaching a global society, prepared long ago by the capitalist system at the level of goods and capital flow. With astonishment we notice how badly communication is functioning; how we hang on to passivity, in spite of the general encouragement of creativity; how resistance is stirring everywhere, against larger units and even more against the global village; how the need to develop ever smaller identity systems is growing. The latter could eventually lead to the breaking up of single people—after all, the realization of the "individual" (Stirner)—into competing systems that can no longer communicate with each other: a psychoticization that goes hand in hand with the pluralization and relativization of reality, with the insight that worlds are constructed, and that, for this reason, there are many worlds that can exist alongside, or merge with, one another. However, the function of the media is perhaps not so much that of creating new worlds, detached from space, time, and physical locality, but rather that of producing an unstable, chaotic world of worlds that constantly penetrate one another, merge into one another, dissolve, appear, and disappear without any possibility of orientation. Perhaps the joint media are bent on triggering a frenzy in which man no longer knows whether he is coming or going: from the deception of illusion to the illusion of giddiness.

It is possible that in cyberspace, technically still mostly virtual itself, there is now a state-of-the-art in computer technology that also creates a problem horizon for consciousness in general. If it is fundamentally possible to enter a completely artificial world, wander through it, interact with other people, or even with artificial intelligent beings within this world, then this virtual reality, in which everything is basically manipulatable, triggers the wish to experience this at some time. This is a wish not only inherent in technology, but also in our expectations of art, which has always constructed "wishing machines."

In fact, cyberspace demonstrates best of all that computer technology tends to make the dividing line with the media disappear. This implies effort to put the digitally created worlds in the place of the ordinary world as we experience it, or at least to incorporate the digital world into it. This is perfectly analogous with the aesthetisizing of the real as it is practiced, for instance, in installations or "environments" in art. Such works turn the real into art, while art is freed of its limitations. Since the beginnings of kinetic art, but above all due to the impulse from the idea of the "happening" that arose in the sixties, the involvement of what once was the spectator in the work of art—now characterized by openness—has moved into the center, of electronic art in particular. The dominant factor in this was the intention that was also the basis of the concept of the *Gesamtkunstwerk* and that determined psychedelic art in the sixties: the idea of creating an "environment" that triggers interaction between work and spectator, so that together these will constitute a whole. The "best" *Gesamtkunstwerk* in this sense corresponds to Plato's Cave, a technically constructed total illusion. As critics observed at the time, entry into an artificial world is only possible by temporary or permanent suspension of reality, so that we lose our standards of comparison and can immerse ourselves entirely in the artificial world.[10]

Cyberspace is an intersection between media: the expression of a media association orientated towards a virtual total reality and a *Gesamtkunstwerk*, a *Gesamtdatenwerk*, and in which there are no longer any spectators but only participants or parties involved. The usual aesthetic distance to the image (screen) world is thereby canceled out, and this has many different consequences.

The novelty of cyberspace is, on the one hand, that by necessity it still shields the environment, which allows us in fact to enter the digitally produced three-dimensional space with the entire body. Whereas we used to be led as spectators through the spaces and scenes by the moving camera, we can now move within them on our own, just as in the real world. At the same time, we are integrated into the scene as observable actors, insofar as others, who are also wearing the data suit, are telepresent in the same virtual reality in a body mask basically chosen at will, whether they are "real" or participating as actors in a more or less fixed event from the ego-perspective. The anchoring of man in his body, in a bodily world without arbitrary time-space situations, is therefore removed, although cyberspace connects the senses and the human body to the computer in an almost psychotic manner, and so crossbreeds the real with the simulated. As in a cockpit protected from the outside world, one in which only data from the outside are admitted, we fly through the world without having to move from the spot, and without knowing whether we are actually flying or not. In this "final vehicle," says Paul Virilio, "the vehicle of the image merges with the image of the flying vehicle."[11]

On the other hand, by now we have learned how difficult, if not impossible, it is to bring about total simulation of the world of natural perception—the famous paradox of computer sciences. The furthest advanced, so far, is the audiovisual dimension. Experiments with tactile experience indicate that the weight or resistance of the virtual objects can be experienced via the data glove or the data suit, which would naturally strengthen the impression of reality. This requires mechanical application of some kind of pressure on the hand or other parts of the body. However, it is easy to imagine that the infinite variety of materials that can be touched by far exceeds the mechanical reproduction possibilities of simulation. There is not even the recording equipment for the universe of smells and taste, and the thought of a "data tongue" or a "data nose" is not only farfetched, but, most likely, also technically impossible.

Even if we take the simple example of a simulated drive by car, comparable to a flight in a simulator cabin, dramaturgic problems arise: we would have to be capable of "virtually" steering a car along a road, which logically also implies the possibility of branching off or driving somewhere else. This could be accomplished, although with great difficulty, as long as we remain inside the car. But what happens if we want to get out of the car? To maintain the perfect illusion, would there not have to be a bodywork to get out of, in real space? It is precisely the connection in cyberspace technology between virtual space and physical gestures that hampers perfect simulation. No wonder that, after the first experiences gained with it, technologists are already dreaming of canceling out the interface between machine and body, so as to solve the connected problems of representation. It is probably not only the considerable limitations in the simulation of a complex reality, but also the unpleasant conditions of cyberspace technology, that will be a motive for future development of close interesections between computer and man. There is thought of possibly connecting the computer directly with the central nervous system. Impulses would be conducted directly from the human brain into the computer, or the brain would be stimulated directly, without the interface between the peripheral input and output systems of the computer and those of the human body. Of course, this still belongs to the distant future, if it will ever be possible at all. But even as a transitional technology, cyberspace has raised the concept of virtual realities into general awareness, and the consequences of that will keep us busy for a long time to come.

> Just as it can be assumed that glasses or contact lenses will one day become integrated prostheses in a species whose eyesight has disappeared, it is to be feared that artificial intelligence and its techniques could also become the prostheses of a species whose thinking will have disappeared.[12]

Perhaps we should spell backwards, so to speak, the question of the influence of the electronic media on society and art, and start from the reactions they evoke, which lead to an apparent return of threatened dimensions of experience. This reversal would seem useful, as each diagnosis of change is based on processes of disappearance, often relying on facts whose meaning is only perceived when an obvious novelty appears.

Therefore, disappearance should not be placed in a context of destruction, but in one of discovery or even invention of, say, naturalness or humanity. Great shifts of consciousness come to mind, such as the high regard for body and senses as anchors in reality and as a newly reclaimed primary orientation of life—a perception that did not arise until the nineteenth century. Only when the body becomes more than a matter-of-fact existence, only when it is consciously ours to use in its presence and real structures, does it become a phenomenon at issue and one of libidinous inhabitation, which has to be maintained, protected, and cultivated because of its potential. Something similar can be recognized on a trip into virtual realities, which to some extent generate the uniqueness of the unavailable real as an echo, to reveal it, for the first time, in its full complexity. Of course, such contemplations are not meant to define actual causalities, but rather to suggest sources of enigmatic influence, which did not start with the electronic media but with the first locomotion and image-production techniques—even if, at a certain time, they were, or still are, only imaginary. The question is whether we will grow accustomed to the immaterial, virtual worlds, to our cooperation with machines, to the mutual penetration of the real and the virtual (with which we live, saved by science, even without media), or, as justified as ever, cannot live without yearning for a world of facts and resistant materials that we eventually wish to control, so as not to succumb to the feeling that we are always bumping into our own software walls?

Notes

1. See Florian Rötzer, "Observers and pictures of the first, second and n-th order," in Karl Gerbel and Peter Weibel, eds., *Die Welt von Innen: Endo und Nano, (Linz: Ars Electronica '92 / PVS Verlager, 1992).*

2. Jonathan Waldern, "Virtuality—The First Workstation to Create Virtual Reality," in *Cyberspace,* ed. Florian Rötzer and Peter Weibel (München: Boer Verlag, 1993).

3. Constant, *New Babylon,* in *Amsterdam: Catalogue of the Städtische Kunstgalerie* (Amsterdam: Bochum, 1961).

4. See Florian Rötzer, "Telecommunications and the world without frontiers," in *Telesculpture,* ed. Richard Kriesche and Peter Hoffmann (Graz: Kulturdata, 1993).

5. Friedrich Nietzsche: *Menschliches, Allzumenschliches* 1, 23, in *Friedrich Nietzsche: Werke I,* ed. Karl Schlechta (München: Carl Hanser Verlag, 1969).

6. Jean-François Lyotard: *Nach dem Erhabenen, Zustand der Ästhetik,* in J.-F. Lyotard, *Das Inhumane* (Wien: Edition Passagen, 1989).

7. Zelko Wiener and Konrad Becker, "Mind Cinema," in *Ars Electronica 90: Virtual Worlds,* ed. Gottfried Hattinger and Peter Weibel (Linz: Veritas Verlag, 1990).

8. Humberto Maturana, *Der Baum der Erkenntnis* (Bern-München: Scherz Verlag, 1987).

9. Vilem Flusser, *Angenommen: Eine Szenenfolge,* (Göttingen: Immatrix Publications, 1989).

10. See Florian Rötzer, "Virtuelle und reale Welten," in *Cyberspace,* ed. Florian Rötzer and Peter Weibel (München: Klaus Boer Verlag, 1993).

11. Paul Virilio, *Der rasende Stillstand* (München: Carl Hanser Verlag, 1992).

12. Jean Baudrillard, "Der Xerox und das Unendliche," in *Cyberspace,* ed. Florian Rötzer and Peter Weibel (München: Klaus Boer Verlag, 1993).

7 Transforming Mirrors: Subjectivity and Control in Interactive Media

David Rokeby

A technology is interactive to the degree that it reflects the consequences of our actions or decisions back to us. It follows that an
interactive technology is a medium through which we communicate with ourselves—a mirror. The medium not only reflects back,
but also *refracts* what it is given; what is returned is ourselves, transformed and processed. To the degree that the technology reflects
ourselves back recognizably, it provides us with a self-image, a
sense of self. To the degree that the technology transforms our
image in the act of reflection, it provides us with a sense of the relation between this self and the experienced world. This is analogous
to our relationship with the universe. Newton's First Law, stating
that "For every action there is an equal and opposite reaction,"
implies that everything is a mirror. We discover our "selves" in the
mirror of the universe.

The purpose of this text is to explore the implications of interactive media through the lens provided by interactive artists and
their work. Interactive artworks are revealing because the artists
creating them have taken literally McLuhan's oft-repeated dictum,
"The medium is the message." The mirror is used as a technique of
expression. While engineers strive to maintain the illusion of transparency in the design and refinement of media technologies, artists
explore the meaning of the interface itself, using the various transformations of the media as their palette.

The expressive power of the interface, in conjunction with the
increasing "apparent" transparency of interface technologies,
raises complicated ethical issues regarding subjectivity and control.
Interactive artists are in a position to take the lead in generating a

discussion of these concerns, but are also in danger of becoming apologists for industrial, corporate, and institutional uses of these technologies. An awareness of the contradictions inherent in mediated interactivity is essential if we, as a society, are to move into the future with our eyes open.

Interaction in the context of art

Although the focus in interactive artwork is usually on work that incorporates technology, the implied transformation of the relationship between art and audience can be traced back to roots that predate the existence of interactive technologies.

Itsuo Sakane, the Japanese journalist and curator, suggests that interactive art is simply art that involves the participation of the viewer. He goes on to remark, "All arts can be called interactive in a deep sense if we consider viewing and interpreting a work of art as a kind of participation,"[1] an echo of Marcel Duchamp's famous declaration, "The spectator makes the picture."[2]

While all artworks are to some degree open to multiple interpretations, some artists work to discourage subjective readings and others work to encourage them. An early example of work that encourages subjective readings is Laurence Sterne's novel, *The Life and Opinions of Tristram Shandy,* finished in 1766. Throughout the book, the reader's expectations and assumptions are variously addressed in a surprisingly postmodern manner. Here are some passages from chapters 37 and 38 of volume 6.

> Let love therefore be what it will,—my uncle Toby fell into it.
> —And possible, gentle reader, with such a temptation—so wouldst thou: For never did thy eyes behold, or thy concupiscence covet any thing in this world, more concupiscible than widow Wadman.

> To conceive this right,—call for pen and ink—here's paper ready to your hand.—Sit down, Sir, paint her to your own mind—as like your mistress as you can—as unlike your wife as your conscience will let you—'tis all one to me—please but your own fancy in it.[3]

After leaving a blank page, he continues:

—Was ever any thing in Nature so sweet!—so exquisite!
—Then, dear Sir, how could my uncle Toby resist it?
Thrice happy book! thou wilt have one page, at least,
within thy covers, which Malice will not blacken and which
Ignorance cannot misrepresent.[4]

Sterne may be accused of excessive cleverness, but he actively addresses issues that are central to interactive work. His novel is intended to be physically modified by the reader, making literal and visible the implicit inscription of the reader's subjectivity into the body of the book. In fact, there has always been a strong interactive character to the process of reading; the reader takes the role of universal renderer, using his or her imagination to construct a subjective world upon the skeleton of the text. For a brief moment, Sterne clarifies the mirror provided by the text, showing us ourselves staring into the page.

Marcel Duchamp expresses the idea of the artwork as a mirror in his work *The Bride Stripped Bare by Her Bachelors, Even*. In his discussion of this work, Octavio Paz notes:

> Duchamp's painting is a transparent glass; as a genuine monument it is inseparable from the place it occupies and the space that surrounds it; it is an incomplete painting that is perpetually completing itself. Because it is an image that reflects the image of whoever contemplates it, we are never able to look at it without seeing ourselves.[5]

The work is mirror, image, and window combined. The spectator's reflection mingles with the images inscribed on the glass, and with the gallery space, the viewing context, seen through the glass.

A book or a painting appears capable only of passive response under the subjective gaze of the spectator. The artist may, however, have acted in anticipation of the spectator's interpretations by combining elements into the work so that their significance is transformed by the shifting perceptions of the viewer. Again commenting on Duchamp, Paz suggests: "A work is a machine for *producing meanings*. In this sense Duchamp's idea is not entirely false: the picture depends on the spectator because only he can set in motion the apparatus of signs that comprises the whole work."[6]

An examination of how "interactive" artists incorporate interaction into their work reveals a correspondence with Paz's view.

The reactive behavior of most interactive works is defined by a computer program that is written in advance by the artist, or by a programmer realizing the artist's wishes. This program is, in most cases, a static text that is *read* and *interpreted* by the computer. Each reading of the program by the computer depends on the activity of the spectator. Like the artist constructing an "apparatus of signs" that anticipates and supports subjective readings, the interactive artist, according to pioneer interactive artist Myron Krueger, "anticipates the participant's possible reactions and composes different relationships for each alternative."[7] Although, in both Duchamp's and Krueger's cases, the artist has made room for the spectator's subjective readings of the work, what this involves is a partial displacement of the machinery of interpretation from the mind of the spectator into the mechanism of the artwork, a *fracturing* of the spectator's subjectivity. The external machinery is partly, as McLuhan contends, an extension of the spectator, but the relationship between the spectator and this extension is externally defined.

As the role of the spectator is questioned and transformed, so is the role of the artist. Most artworks start as a set of possibilities: the blank canvas, the empty page, the block of marble, and so forth. The act of realizing a work is a process of progressively narrowing the range of possibilities by a series of creative choices until one of the possibilities has been manifested in the finished work. One might say that the interactive artist decides at some point in this process not to choose from among the remaining possibilities but to create some sort of audience-actuated choosing mechanism. The immediate precedent for this is found in John Cage's chance compositions. In each of these works, Cage defined a set of rules and then used the tossing of coins to choose a specific composition from the range of possibilities allowed by these rules. Cage's intent in reducing the control he had over the final result can be inferred from his suggestion that "the highest purpose is to have no purpose at all. This puts one in accord with nature in her manner of operations."[8] However, as the composer Henry Cowell commented in a discussion of these compositions:

> It is evident that much more remains to be done in this direction, for in spite of his best efforts to the contrary, Cage has not succeeded in eliminating his highly refined and individual taste from the music derived from the

I Ching. Unfortunately, from the point of view of this group of composers, no order of tossings can give anything more than a variety of arrangements of the elements subjectively chosen to operate upon.[9]

In later works, Cage further removed himself from the compositional process through what he called "indeterminacy." In these works, the rules themselves were left intentionally ambiguous, leaving them open to subjective interpretation by the performers as well.

The structure of interactive artworks can be very similar to those used by Cage in his chance compositions. The primary difference is that the chance element is replaced by a complex, indeterminate, yet sentient, element: the spectator. Whereas Cage's intent is to mirror nature's manner of operation, the interactive artist holds up the mirror to the spectator. There is an additional and important difference that this creates. Unlike Cage's work, interactive work involves a dialogue between the interactor[10] and the system making up the artwork. The interactive system responds to the interactor, who in turn responds to that response. A feedback system is created in which the implications of an action are multiplied, much as we are reflected into infinity by the two facing mirrors in a barber shop.

Whatever the differences, interactive artists like Cage are looking for ways to give away some of the control over the final actualizations of their works. The extreme of this position, in some sense corresponding to Cage's notion of "indeterminacy," is found in the creation of learning and evolving systems. One might take the extreme position that a significant interaction between an artwork and a spectator cannot be said to have taken place unless both the spectator *and* the artwork are in some way permanently changed or enriched by the exchange. A work that satisfied this requirement would have to include some sort of adaptive mechanism, an apparatus for accumulating and interpreting its experience. While few interactive works currently contain such mechanisms, many have exhibited a form of evolution, not through internal mechanisms but through the refinements and adjustments made by their creators—responses to observations made of interactions between the work and the audience. The inclusion of learning mechanisms in interactive works will no doubt become increasingly common.

Models of interaction

There are a number of distinct models that can be used to represent the interaction between an artwork and an interactor. I will examine four models that I find particularly useful. The artwork can be conceived of as a navigable structure or world, a creative medium in its own right, a transforming mirror, or an automaton. While each interactive work can be profitably examined in the light of several of these models, each model offers a unique perspective on the issues involved in interaction.

Navigable structures

The navigable structure can be thought of as an articulation of a space, either real, virtual, or conceptual. The artist structures this space with a sort of architecture and provides a method of navigation. Each position within the conceptual space provides a point of view, defined and limited by the surrounding architectural structure. Exploring this structure presents the spectator with a series of views of the space and its contents. The sequence in which the spectator experiences these vistas forms a unique reading of that space. In virtual reality systems, the architectural metaphor can be taken literally. In other works, the architecture is more like a conceptual paradigm, a method of organization of intellectual perspectives, opinions, or emotions.

The architecture can be regular and highly formalized. On the other hand, it can be highly idiosyncratic. The possible structures range from the latticework of a regular and highly interconnected network to the single serial path of a narrative. Navigable structures present the audience with a series of options and the consequences for each possible decision, but there are several distinct models defining how these paths diverge and recombine.

Some works utilize an open plan resembling a city map, a structure that tends to invite wandering. In Jeffrey Shaw's work *The Legible City*, this metaphor is presented literally. The spectator uses a stationary bicycle to navigate through the computer-generated, three-dimensionally rendered representation of a city projected on a large video screen. Instead of buildings, the streets are lined with letters of the alphabet, transforming the street facades into texts:

> Bicycling through this city of words is consequently a journey of reading. Choosing direction, choosing where to turn, is a choice of texts and their juxtaposition, and the identity of this city emerges in the conjunction of meanings these words generate as they emerge along the bicyclist's path.[11]

Hypermedia-based works use a treelike branching structure in which one moves from a fairly general starting point into greater and greater specificity, encouraging a more focused and structured exploration in which each choice carries with it a responsibility. In Paul Sermon's work *Think About the People Now*, the interactor makes a series of decisions that increasingly define their place in time and space, relative to a single event, that of a protester burning himself to death during the two minutes silence on Remembrance Day in Whitehall, London. Navigating through the structure, one may miss the event altogether, hear an ambulance go past, or overhear someone's horrified words. On the other hand, one's decisions may lead to the time and place of the protest and the choice to watch or look away. One may even find oneself in the role of the protester, covered in gasoline, faced with the decision of whether or not to light the match. Through a series of decisions, the interactor moves into a highly specific position for which he or she is, in a sense, accountable. Alternatively, the interactor can adopt different roles in what Sermon calls the "social construction,"[12] and can experience a variety of conflicting perspectives on the event, the metaexperience that the work as a whole represents.

Navigable structures have some of the characteristics of a maze or labyrinth, except that the interactive work does not usually have a goal or exit, a reward in the conventional sense. Discussing another of Jeffrey Shaw's works, *Point of View*, in which the structure of a labyrinth is intentionally invoked, Erik Colpaert comments that "The correct route is unimportant—It doesn't even exist."[13] The reward, if one insists on using such a term, is the unfolding experience of exploration and discovery, the collection of points of view resulting in a personal reading of the work.

The metaphor of the labyrinth has some disturbing implications. Is the interactive artist sending the audience, like rats, through a laboratory maze? Indeed, people sometimes feel irritation when faced with an interactive artwork, because they feel that their "behavior" is being judged. There is some justification for this feeling, as the interactor does reveal something in the process of interacting. One solution to this problem is to make the method of interaction as familiar or banal as the action of pedaling the bicycle used in *The Legible City*. In addition, in Shaw's work, the letters that line the streets are permeable, so that one can bicycle right through them. The street layout exists as a suggestion that the spectator can choose to ignore, rather than an imposition.

In these examples, the artists are clearly addressing the issue of subjective interpretation. Indeed, to some degree, the subjectivity of interpretation is the topic of these works. The artists allow the interactor to establish a personal identity in the context of the work; this identity is a reflection of the decisions that the interactor makes on his or her path through the possibilities presented. It is possible, and generally intended, that the interactor try out other possible identities, to explore alternate readings of the same structure.

It is a mistake to conclude that by presenting a variety of perspectives, the artist is being objective and disinterested. Through selection of the specific points of views offered, how they are linked together, and the design of the method of navigation, the artist holds significant expressive power, which is enhanced by this apparent objectivity. This is analogous to the situation encountered in hypertext databases that presume to completely cross-reference the information that they contain. The system of cross-referencing used remains a powerful expression of the ideas of the creator, emphasizing certain kinds of relationships while effectively discouraging others. Creating such structures is similar to designing the infrastructure of a community or society; it charges the space politically. At the same time, such a structure is comforting, because in limiting the options available at any one time, it assists the interactor in deciding how to proceed. It gives one a coherent structure within which and against which one may establish an identity.

It is ironic that wide-open interaction within a system that does not impose significant constraints is usually unsatisfying to the interactor. It is difficult to sense interaction in situations in which one is simultaneously affecting all of the parameters. It has been my experience that the interactor's sense of personal impact on an interactive system grows, up to a point, as his or her freedom to affect the system is increasingly limited. The constraints provide a frame of reference, a context, within which interaction can be perceived.

While the constraining structure subtly expresses itself, the interactors' ability to navigate the system gives them a sense of freedom. This freedom exists only in relation to the established structure; it is a representation of freedom, a symbolic freedom. By relinquishing a relatively small amount of control, an interactive artist can give interactors the impression that they have much more freedom than they actually do. The clearest example of this can be found in disk-based video games where the system gives the user the impression that he or she is moving at great speed through, or just above, a certain terrain. The video disk is made up of short clips that link together in a branching and merging structure. In the most effective cases, the image presented on the screen is only the central section of a larger image. If the user tries to turn to the left while the system is in the middle of a linear segment, the section of the frame that the user sees is immediately shifted in that direction, giving an immediate sense of responsiveness, but the interactor is, in fact, still traveling along the same restricted path. The illusion that the user has the freedom to roam the entire terrain is maintained for a surprisingly long time, especially if the user is moving at a high "virtual" speed (i.e., without time to reflect on the degree to which his or her actions are being reflected). The navigable structure and its system of navigation together make up a guidance system through which the trajectory of the user through the work may be subtly controlled.

The static artwork can be looked at in two opposing ways. It can be seen as authoritarian in its refusal to reflect the presence and actions of the spectator, or it can be seen as giving the spectator complete freedom of reflection and interpretation by not intervening in this process. An interactive artwork can likewise be seen as loosening the authority of the traditional work, or as interfering in the interactor's subjective process of interpretation.

This irony gets increasingly pronounced as the technology of interaction becomes more and more sophisticated. In the introduction to his book, *Artificial Reality II*, Myron Krueger says, "Imagine that the computer could completely control your perception and monitor your response to that perception. Then it could make any possible experience available to you."[14] Florian Rötzer responds to this scenario by saying, "The freedom in virtual space is sacrificed in the final control over the environment, over every thought, when and if it becomes possible to successfully couple our neurons directly with the computer."[15] When a system monitors interactors to this extent, it has effectively taken control of the interactors' subjectivity, depriving them of their idiosyncratic identity and replacing it with a highly focused perspective that is entirely mediated by the system. Subjectivity has been replaced by a representation of subjectivity. The fact that the system responds to the interactor does not guarantee in any way that the system is responsible to the user; the interactor can fairly easily be pushed beyond reflection to the edge of instinct, capable only of visceral response to the system's stimuli, mirroring the system rather than the reverse.

A variation of the navigable structure is found in the work of communications artists who design interactive communications systems and networks. Instead of creating subjective points of view and offering a method of navigation through or between them, communications artists create systems that interconnect individuals, that offer methods of communication. These artists are inventing alternate communities. An example is *Habitat*, an artificial on-line community developed for Lucasfilm by Randy Farmer and Chip Morningstar. Using simple Commodore 64 computers connected by phone lines, they have created a complex world in which thousands of participants adopt identities, participate in a simulated economy, and exercise democratic control over the course and structure of their community.

In France, a few years ago, I encountered an intriguing device called *Le Flashing*. It was a tiny radio transceiver in the shape of a wearable pin that had a light-emitting diode on the front. The device could be set to transmit and receive on a variety of wavelengths. The wearer selected personal wavelengths from a range representing a variety of sexual preferences. When two people with corresponding frequencies came within a few feet of each other, the diodes on each device would begin to flash. Whereas *Habitat* creates an environment distinctly separate from our conventional reality, *Le Flashing* creates alternative systems of communications that rest invisibly on top of existing social structures.

In *Habitat*, no attempt is made to accurately represent the individuals participating. They are allowed to design identities for themselves. The carrier of communications between participants is therefore not transparent; this is part of the pleasure of participating. The transformations of the communicating medium are quite obvious, especially due to the low-resolution, cartoonlike representations of the participants. Where the transformations of the medium are not made visible, however, the possibility for powerful manipulation occurs. As we become less and less connected in local communities and increasingly involved in virtual communities, we stretch the intimacy of personal communications over longer and ever more complex pathways, making ourselves increasingly vulnerable. Communications systems are inherently vulnerable to surveillance. For example, a device like *Le Flashing*, in another set of hands, could be used to track down "sexual deviants."

Traditionally, so-called common carriers like the phone system have been restricted from introducing information into their own networks; they are allowed only to transmit information from source to destination. We trust that the telephone represents us accurately, transmitting our voice, and therefore, our intentions and meanings, without distortion. But the native intelligence of communications networks is rapidly increasing. Already our voices are echo-canceled, digitized, and multiplexed as they speed from phone to phone. Videophones and teleconferencing rely on significant amounts of data compression to achieve usable transmission speeds. Images are reconstituted at the receiving end with varying degrees of faithfulness to the original. It is a small step from this type of processing to interpretation. Already someone has decided what information is worth preserving in an image, and what is not. The neutrality of communications networks will become an increasingly significant, and at the same time slippery, issue.

The invention of media

It is often said that interactive artworks blur the line between the artist and the audience. The audience becomes creator in a medium invented by the artist. The artist enables the interactors to express themselves creatively.

Myron Krueger has developed a complex set of video-centered interactions that he calls *Videoplace*.[16] The *Videoplace* installation is made up of a video camera, a video projector, and a rack of specialized processors. The interactor's image, as seen by the camera, is interpreted as a silhouette. This silhouette is analyzed in various ways and a response is generated and updated thirty times a second. Writing of a subset of these interactions called *Individual Medley*, he has said:

> Each is a restricted aesthetic medium that can be composed through body movements. In fact, your body becomes a means of creating art. The goal of these

interactions is to communicate the pleasure of aesthetic creation. Since these media are unfamiliar, dwelling as they do on dynamic images controlled by movements of the viewers' bodies, artists trained in traditional static media have no automatic advantage in creating pleasing results.[17]

There is no question that people are given a tangible and "empowering" experience of creativity from an interaction of this sort. This is precisely because the medium is "restricted." Presenting a limited range of possibilities reduces the likelihood that the interactor will run up against a creative block, and allows the medium to guide the inexperienced hand of the interactor, reducing the fear of incompetence. Such a creative experience is more powerful than traditional examples of "guiding" media, such as paint-by-numbers, because the interactor makes decisions throughout the creative process. The interactor is therefore, to some degree, genuinely reflected in the resulting creation.

In the hands of technologists, a medium evolves towards apparent transparency (i.e., the development of a complete range of pigments for oil paints, or the evolution from early low-resolution black-and-white television to natural color high-definition TV). The message (as per McLuhan) that such a medium conveys may be powerful, but it is generally unintentional. Of course, interactive artists intentionally express themselves through the opacities and idiosyncrasies of the media that they create. These media reflect, but also guide and transform, the gestures of the interactor.

The interactor becomes a creator. But, as the conceivers of the media, interactive artists reserve a privileged position for themselves. The product of the spectator's creative interaction is often "pleasing," but would rarely qualify as "serious" art. To quote Krueger: "It is the composition of the relationships between action and response that is important. The beauty of the visual and aural response is secondary."[18]

When the Apple Macintosh first came onto the market, the MacPaint program, which simulates, to a degree, the visual artist's basic tools, sent a shock wave through the creative community. For the first year, MacPaint-produced posters were everywhere, an apparent explosion of the freedom of, and possibility for, self-expression. But while the MacPaint medium reflected the user's expressive gestures, it also refracted them through its own idiosyncratic prism. After a while, the posters began to blend together into an urban wallpaper of MacPaint textures and MacPaint patterns. The similarities overpowered the differences. Since then, graphics programs for computers have become much more transparent, but that initial creative fervor that MacPaint ignited has abated. The restrictions that made MacPaint easy to use were also the characteristics that ultimately limited its usefulness as a medium for personal expression. One can look at the distribution of a creative medium in the form of a software package as a subtle form of broadcasting.

Transforming mirrors

While all interactive works reflect interactors back to themselves, in many works the idea of the mirror is explicitly invoked. The clearest examples are interactive video installations in which the spectator's image or silhouette becomes an active force in a computer-generated context. Examples include aspects of Myron Krueger's *Videoplace* work, Ed Tannenbaum's *Recollections* and Very Vivid's *Mandala*. The spectator sees some representation of himself or herself on a video projection screen. This representation follows the movements of the interactor like a mirror image or shadow, transformed by the potentials with which the artist has endowed the space. These transformations are realized by software running on a computer. In such work, the content is contained in this difference between the gesture and its transformed or recontextualized reflection.

The myth of Echo and Narcissus, told by Ovid in the *Metamorphoses*, provides an interesting context in which to examine the question of reflections and distorted mirrorings. Echo was a nymph who used to tell stories to Juno in order to distract her while Jupiter consorted with the other nymphs. When Juno discovered Echo's deceptions, she punished Echo by removing her ability to source words. She retained only the ability to repeat back the last words said to her. And so, when she saw Narcissus in the forest and fell in love with him, she had only his words of rejection to transform into an expression of her love. The interactive artist transforms what is given into an expression of something other, making Echo a patron deity of interactive art.

Later, in the most familiar part of the story, Narcissus glimpses his image in a pool of water, and falls in love himself. He does not initially realize that it is his own image, and falls into despair that the youth in the pool does not return his love.[19] Noting that the name "Narcissus" is derived from the Greek word *narcosis* (numbness), McLuhan writes

> This extension of himself by mirror numbed his perceptions until he became the servomechanism of his own extended or repeated image. The nymph Echo tried to win his love with fragments of his own speech, but in vain. He was numb. He had adapted to his extension of himself and had become a closed system.[20]

The myth presents two kinds of reflection: the perfect, mirrorlike, synchronous reflection of Narcissus in the pool and the delayed and distorted reflections of Echo's speech. In the "Sounds" chapter of *Walden*, Thoreau, describing the sound of distance church bells, writes:

> The echo is, to some extent, an original sound, and therein is the magic and charm of it. It is not merely a repetition of what was worth repeating in the bell, but partly the voice of the wood; the same trivial words and notes sung by a wood-nymph.[21]

While the unmediated feedback of exact mirroring produces the closed system of self-absorption (the reflection of the self is reabsorbed), transformed reflections are a dialogue between the self and the world beyond. The echo operates like a wayward loop of consciousness through which one's image of one's self and one's relationship to the world can be examined, questioned, and transformed.

In many of Krueger's *Videoplace* interactions the interactor's image is the device through which the "artificial reality" is explored. The transformations of this silhouette are the keys to the understanding of the world depicted on the video screen. The self-image is the known reference against which the phenomena of transformation are registered. In my own work, *Very Nervous System*, a computer looks out through a video-camera and gathers a sense of the physical gestures of the interactor. These impressions are immediately translated into sounds or music, reflecting and accompanying the gestures, thereby transforming the interactor's awareness of his or her body. In both cases, the character of the experienced phenomenon is discovered as a change in a representation of the self.

The relationship between the interactor and the transformed reflection is stereoscopic. When we look into a three-dimensional space, each of our two eyes sees a slightly different image. What transforms the image that the right eye sees into the image that the left eye sees is a change in point of view. The tension that exists between these two points of view is resolved by the brain into the revelation of depth. An interactive artwork presents, in the form of the transformed reflection, an image of the self from another point of view that likewise produces a sort of stereoscopic tension.

Transformed mirroring is also found in *Tumbling Man* by Chico MacMurtrie and Rick W. Sayre. In this work, participants wear jumpsuits wired with sensors that detect the opening and closing of elbow and knee joints and the lowering of the chin. This information is used to control similar joints in a life-size pneumatic robot through a radio link. The robot mimics the general posture of participants, but the robot is carefully designed so that it doesn't follow the participant's gestures exactly. The robot's appendages are constructed of metal pipes containing free-rolling metal balls, and the joints are intentionally loose. This adds a rich complexity and indeterminacy to the movement of the robot, enabling it to rock, heave, and tumble with momenta derived from, but not copied from, the movements of participants. Generally, two participants work together, each with control over a changing fraction of the robot's joints, resulting in movements that are a partial and shifting reflection of both participants.[22] An additional level of interaction exists between the two participants as they work together to gain some mastery over the robot. The robot arouses strong empathy, on one hand as an eloquent reflection of the participants' struggles, and on the other as a subject of domination by the participants.

The question of domination raises an important issue. For many people, interaction has come to mean "control." People look to interactive technology for "empowerment," and such technologies can certainly give the interactor a strong sense of power. This is clearly the attraction of video games. In these games, the mirror transforms the interactor's gestures largely by amplification, but what is actually offered is the amplification of a gesture within a void, a domination of nothingness, the *illusion* of power. In particular, this is a fantasy of power bereft of responsibility. In the recent Gulf War, the video-game fantasy of power was reconnected to the power of actual armaments. In the process, the sense of responsibility was lost; the personal accountability of the pilots was cleverly amputated, dissolved by the interface.

Interaction is about encounter rather than control. The interactive artist must counter the video-game-induced expectations that the interactor often brings to interaction. Obliqueness and irony within the transformations and the coexistence of many different variables of control within the interactive media provide for a richer, though perhaps less ego-gratifying experience. However, there is a threshold of distortion and complexity beyond which an interactor loses sight of himself or herself in the mirror. The less distortion there is, the easier it is for the interactor to identify with the responses the interactive system is making. The interactive artist must strike a balance between the interactor's sense of control, which enforces identification, and the richness of the responsive system's behavior, which keep the system from becoming closed.

Because explicit interactivity is still a relatively new feature in artworks, the audience often approaches the works with skepticism. The audience requires proof that the work is interactive. This seems like a reasonable expectation. In navigable work, establishing the responsive character of the work is not difficult, but in works where the character of the interaction is more complex, providing proof is not always so easy. The proof that will most easily satisfy the audience is "predictability" (i.e., if one makes the same action twice, the work will respond identically each time). Unfortunately, this test only works for simple interactive devices with no memory and no ability to adapt. More complicated systems might perceive a repetition of an action as the establishment of a pattern, and respond to this new quality in the behavior of the participant with a new kind of response.

I noticed an interesting pattern emerging in the interactions between the audience and an early manifestation of *Very Nervous System*. This version would, in fact, respond identically to identical movements. People entered the installation and set about verifying the predictability of the system. They made a gesture, as a question to the space, and mentally noted the sound that that gesture had made. They repeated the gesture once or twice, again as a question, and got the same result. The third repetition seemed to satisfy the participants that the system was in fact interactive. The way they held their body and the look on their face changed. They made the gesture again, this time as a command to the system, not a question. The physical dynamics of the command gesture was significantly different from the previous, more tentative questioning gestures, and the system responded with a different sound.

The complexity of this relationship is, in this case, not so much a function of the complexity of the system but of the complexity of the participants themselves. The system was not programmed to interpret motivation; it merely reflected what it saw. The critical point is that aspects of movement that might reflect motivation were not filtered out. By increasing the amount of filtering that is applied in the perceptual process that the interactive system employs, the designer increases the reliability of the resulting information and therefore the unambiguity of control, but at the same time the richness of that information is reduced.

Interactive technologies are hybrids of communications media and control media. We don't expect to control someone by talking to them on the telephone, except to the degree that a relationship of control has been elsewhere established. We do expect to be able to control the telephone itself, as well as our computers, our automobiles, and our smart bombs. But as our technologies evolve and become more complex, they begin to exhibit human behavior. For example, much current research in the field of human-computer interface is focused on the the creation of computer-simulated anthropomorphic "agents" to whom the user can pose questions and assign duties. Our interactions with such agents begin to take the form of communication, but the relationship is still intended to be one of control. This relationship of control is desirable to the degree that our technologies are extensions of ourselves. But these extensions are not just enlargements of the boundaries of our autonomous individualities; they are interfaces through which our contact with the outside world is mediated. The interface becomes a containing environment; if control over this environment is insisted upon, it becomes a system of insulation and isolation from both otherness and ambiguity.

"Virtual reality" presents an interesting context in which to examine this question. To the extent that virtual reality is intended as a technology for presentation or visualization, its conventional control interface of DataGlove and Polhemus trackers is quite adequate, and the lack of ambiguity appropriate. But the creators of these systems dream of creating comprehensive, shared "realities," in which case we must question the philosophy behind the interface. In virtual reality systems, the participant acts on and moves through the environment with a few linear controllers. As the technology evolves, the visual renderings grow increasingly "real," but the relationship between the participant and the reality remains simplistic. Our interface with the real world and with other people is complex and highly nonlinear, and, from a "control" point of view, very ambiguous. Interface designs appropriate for the cockpit are not necessarily appropriate in our relationships with the world around us.

Many interactive artists create their own interfaces. Without the pressures and restrictions involved in getting a saleable and reliable product "to market," they are free to incorporate a richer complexity and ambiguity into these interfaces. Myron Krueger has been developing the interface technology for *Videoplace* for almost two decades. Unlike virtual reality control technologies, which are primarily "sensing" technologies, his interface is a "perceiving" technology. The Polhemus and the DataGlove involve the sensing of a small number of essentially unambiguous parameters. In *Videoplace* the many thousands of individual pieces of information making up a video camera's image are digested by various processors that attempt to make some kind of sense out of what the camera is seeing. Krueger has gone to great lengths to develop methods that derive relatively unambiguous information from the image, but perception is inherently prone to errors and ambiguity. It interprets what it senses, and therefore exhibits something very much like subjective judgment. Because such perceptual mechanisms are generally very complex, they often display unexpected behaviors as well as those intended by their creator. In *Artificial Reality II*, Krueger writes: "Indeed, one of the strong motivations guiding this work is the desire to compose works that surprise their creator."[23] This apparent contradiction between the desire for control and the desire for surprises is common among interactive artists. James Seawright, one of the earliest creators of interactive sculptures, explained, "My aim is not to 'program' them but to produce a kind of patterned personality. Just as a person you know very well can surprise you, so can these machines."[24] An engineer might suspect that this expressed taste for surprises is a cover for bad design. But an engineer's aims are different. Interactive artists balance control and surprise to suit their "interactive aesthetic."

This desire for surprise rises partly out of the nature of the medium. Computers are the greatest expression of man's desire to control. They are a pure representation of authority. They are constructed of the utterly unambiguous "elementary particles" of presence and absence, on and off, one and zero. Computers are a metatechnology, almost infinitely flexible and bristling with potential. In the face of this medium of absolute determination, artists often feel a kind of loneliness or claustrophobia. Pushing the technology until it surprises is one way of escaping from the numbing effects of staring deeply into your own constructions.

Automata

Although he hopes that his works will surprise him, Myron Krueger feels that "nothing should happen in an interactive medium unless it is a response to some action by the participant"[25] since this would be confusing to the interactor. Other artists create artworks that are not intended to be an extension of the interactor; their creations are essentially self-motivated and autonomous. These automata survey and maneuver through their environment, of which the spectators are only one aspect.

The Holy Grail for these artists is the self-replicating, self-sustaining machine—artificial life. The immediate aims are less lofty. Norman White aims to endow his robots with what he has termed "artificial sanity," which he defines simply as the machine's ability to make sense of its environment.

Whereas most interactive works present acoustic, visual, or conceptual environments, these works present individual entities. As a result, their interactions with the public take on the nature of social behavior and relationships. Although these works use many of the approaches and technologies used by other kinds of interactive works, it is not the individual interactor who is reflected in these works so much as human behavior itself. In a sense, the responsive environment and the automaton complement each other, representing both sides of the relationship between man and the social and natural environment.

A particularly provocative example is White's *Helpless Robot*. This is an unusual robot because although capable of perceiving, it is incapable of moving.

> I see the work behaving as the classic "hustler." For instance, it might initially enlist human cooperation with a polite "Excuse me . . . have you got a moment?" or any

one of such unimposing phrases. It might then ask to be
rotated: "Could you please turn me just a bit to the right?
. . . No! not that way . . . the other way!" In such a way, as
it senses cooperation, it tends to become ever more
demanding, becoming in the end, if its human collabora-
tors let it, dictatorial.[26]

Another of White's robots, *Facing Out, Laying Low*, interacts
with its audience and environment, but can become bored or over-
stimulated, in which cases it becomes deliberately antisocial and
stops interacting.

This kind of behavior may seem counterproductive, and frus-
trating for the audience. But for White, the creation of these robots
is a quest for self-understanding. He balances self-analysis with
creation, attempting to produce autonomous creatures that mirror
the kinds of behaviors that he sees in himself. These behaviors are
not necessarily willfully programmed; they often emerge as the syn-
ergistic result of experiments with the interactions between simple
algorithmic behaviors. Just as billions of simple water molecules
work together to produce the complex behaviors of water (from
snowflakes to fluid dynamics), combinations of simple programmed operations can produce complex characteristics, which
are called emergent properties, or self-organizing phenomena.

These emergent properties, like the surprises that Krueger and
Seawright seek, represent to interactive artists transcendence of the
closed determinism implied by the technology and the artists' own
limitations. While such unexpected characteristics delight artists,
they represent the ultimate nightmare for most engineers. The complex systems within which we already live and operate are perfect
breeding grounds for emergent behaviors, and this must be taken
into account as we move into greater and greater integration and
mediation.

Designing the future

Interactive artists are engaged in changing the relationship between
artists and their media, and between artworks and their audience.
These changes tend to increase the extent of the audience's role in
the artwork, loosening the authority of the author or creator. Rather
than creating finished works, the interactive artist creates relationships. The ability to represent relationships in a functional way

adds significantly to the expressive palette available to artists. The power of this expression is multiplied by the fact that the interactors themselves become referents of the work. The works are somewhat akin to portraits, reflecting back aspects of the interactors, transformed so as to express the artist's point.

Mirrors give us back an image with which to identify. We look at the marks we have made on our world to give us a sense of our significance. We distinguish ourselves from others by the uniqueness of our point of view. We compare ourselves to others like us in order to understand our similarities and differences. By providing us with mirrors, artificial media, points of view, and automata, interactive artworks offer us the tools for constructing identities—our sense of ourselves in relation to the artwork and, by implication, in relation to the world.

It is clear that these relationships, and the images of self that they reflect, are merely representations, simplified symbols that are used to refer to the more complex operations of what we call "real" life. Navigable structures are a way of *representing* subjectivity. Limited media are ways of *representing* creativity. Mirrors, and in a more abstract way automata, are ways of *representing* ourselves. All of these representations are also personal expressions of the artists who made them possible. The artist's act of expression is moved to a higher level of abstraction although the artwork's final manifestation retains a compelling apparent actuality. Rather than lessening the authority of the creator, these works represent a shift in the nature of that authority.

As interactive technologies become increasingly common in our everyday relationships, and as they approach transparency, these simplified representations replace the relationships to which they initially referred. This substitution turns the interesting ambiguities of control and subjectivity in interactive art into serious issues of control, manipulation, and deception.

The trouble begins as the user's awareness of the interface ends. A transparent interface is desirable from a functional point of view because it allows the user to work without considering the interface at all, but no interface can be truly transparent. When an interface is accepted as transparent, the user and his or her world are changed; the transforming characteristics of the interface, no longer contained by a visible apparatus, are incorporated into the user and the user's worldview. In mirroring works like *Videoplace*, we watch our silhouette encounter a world. We may be drawn at times to identify strongly with this "shadow," but it remains clearly separate from us. In immersive environments, rather than observing, we inhabit this shadow, this limited representation. Currently, the technology is cumbersome, but as it evolves toward apparent transparency, the danger arises that we will become, literally, "a shadow of our former selves."

McLuhan often referred to technologies as "extensions of man." But in fully interactive technologies, the flow of information goes both ways; the apparatuses become more like permeable membranes. If there is a balance of flow back and forth across this membrane, then the interactive technology is an intermingling of self and environment. If there is an imbalance, then the technology extends either outwards from the organic boundary of the interactor or inwards into the interactor. If the flow across the interface is predominantly inward,then the technology has become a foreign agent, an infiltrating extension of the outside. If the input is dazzling enough, we are left in a daze, responding only on instinct: unconscious reflex rather than conscious reflection; we become extensions of the technology.

The infiltration can be very subtle. Television expands the reach of our vision, while at the same time filtering the content. We trade the subjectivity of our personal point of view for centrally collected and broadcasted images and information. Interactive media have the power to likewise expand the reach of our actions and decisions. We trade subjectivity for participation and the illusion of control; our control may appear absolute, but the domain of that control is externally defined. We are engaged, but exercise no power over the filtering language of interaction embedded in the interface. Rather than broadcasting content, interactive media have the power to broadcast modes of perception and action.

This broadcasting corresponds to a deeply felt need in our society; our technologies have caused an information explosion, and now we look for technological solutions to the problems that the explosion has produced. We no longer have the ability to take in and interpret the mass of information presented to us. Conscious reflection is painful if not impossible; we are desperate for filters. We welcome anything that will simplify our media-amplified reality. By filtering out apparent irrelevancies, giving us simplified representations of our relationships, interactive media make it easier for us to make decisions. These filters operate like a belief system. In fact, perception itself is a kind of *personal* belief system, without which we would be unable to function. When we forfeit the right or power to decide for ourselves the nature of these systems of generalization, we commit ourselves to an "objectivized" point of view that is entirely in the control of others; we head back into the Middle Ages, when the Roman Catholic Church defined the world. The greater danger is that we may forfeit that control without realizing that anything has been lost. If we are given a sufficiently virtual *representation* of freedom and personal autonomy within a limiting structure, we lose awareness of the artifice; we are unaware that we have adopted a belief system and its attendant simplifications.

Surrendering our subjectivity for "objectivized" viewpoints, we are given, in return, a representation of responsibility, a virtual enfranchisement. Each participant in an interaction receives the *sensation* of responsibility; each has the *ability to respond*. The simplified relations of interactive media provide us with a space in which we can feel and accept responsibility. We cede some of the operations of our conscience to the interface in exchange for a measure of ethical tension that we feel we can endure.

At the other extreme, interactive technologies can also simplify the task of decision-making by bombarding the interactor with decisions at a rate that removes the possibility of thought. Video games provide a familiar example. Speed is intoxicating because it makes us, in some sense, unconscious, incapable of reflection; speed relieves us of the burden of responsibility, because there is no time to measure the consequences of an action. The skills required are programmed into our brains through repetition, so that our responses become instinctive, requiring no conscious thought. We return to the paradise before consciousness and moral dilemma.

Technology mirrors our desires; interactive technologies, in particular, reflect our desire to feel engaged. We feel increasingly insignificant, and so we desire the affirmation of being reflected; we are tired of the increasing burden of consciousness, and so we are willing to exchange it for this sense of affirmation. In this trade, the interface becomes the organ of conscience, the mechanism of interpretation, the site of responsibility. The design of these technologies becomes the encoding of a kind of moral and political structure with its attendant implicit social contract.

Our involvement in the process of this reinvention of society is crucial. If a new sort of social contract is being drawn up, it is important that the terms, conditions, and implications be thoroughly explored before we are committed by default through the momentum of technological development, which is also the momentum of our own frustrated desires. If we allow ourselves to lose consciousness of the influence of the interface, we lose our ability to question the terms of the contract; the contract will be effectively invisible. If we accept the transformed images reflected back through the mediating technologies as images of ourselves, we surrender the ability to control who we are.

Perhaps this transformation of society and humanity is inevitable. Perhaps the "individual" is becoming obsolete. It is already being proposed, by artists like Stelarc and roboticists like Hans Moravec, that the human body is obsolete. In virtual environments, the dematerialization of the body has, indeed, already begun. The idea of the individual changes when the body loses its role or meaning, because our bodies are the experiential apparatuses that define each of our subjective points of view.

The situation is full of contradictions; issues of subjectivity and control flip-flop. The technology that might allow a woman in virtual space to redefine her body, to escape the trap of her socialized identity, is the same technology that would allow that identity to be manipulated from the outside. The technology that provides alternative communications links and invents new kinds of community is the same technology that offers undreamt-of degrees of surveillance. The technology that can connect you to the world in unprecedented ways is the same technology that can isolate you in a fantasy of your own, or another's, construction.

What is clear is that there are many important issues to be explored. There is no question that there are exciting potentials for the use of interactive media, but the utopian rhetoric that, for example, has characterized discussions of virtual reality in the popular press must be countered with responsible examinations of the cultural and political implications of these technologies. Interactive artists, at a privileged position at the junction of culture and technology, have the potential to contribute significantly to this discourse. In the process they must carefully avoid becoming merely public relations devices for government and industry. The artists' role is to explore, but at the same time, question, challenge, and transform, the technologies that they utilize.

Notes

1. Itsuo Sakane, "Introduction to Interactive Art," in *Catalogue: Wonderland of Science-Art* (Kanagawa, Japan: Committee for Kanagawa International Art & Science Exhibition, 1989), 3.

2. Quoted by Octavio Paz, "The Castle of Purity," in *Marcel Duchamp* (New York: Viking Press, 1978), 85.

3. Laurence Sterne, *The Life and Opinions of Tristram Shandy* (Harmondsworth: Penguin Books, 1986), 450

4. Ibid., 452.

5. Octavio Paz, "The Castle," 80.

6. Ibid., 86.

7. Quoted by Cynthia Goodman, *Digital Visions* (New York: Harry N. Abrams, 1987), 134.

8. John Cage, "45' for a Speaker" (1954), in *Silence* (Middletown, Conn: Wesleyan University Press, 1973), 155.

9. Henry Cowell, "Current Chronicle," *Musical Quarterly*, January 1952.

10. No satisfactory term has yet been proposed to describe the person who engages in interaction with an artwork. Roy Ascott has suggested the term "user," but that carries implications that the artwork is at the service of that person, implying an imbalance in the relationship between person and artwork that is potentially misleading. "Interactor" is used here for the sake of simplicity.

11. Jeffrey Shaw, ed., *The Legible City* (Amsterdam: Colophon, 1990), G.

12. Paul Sermon, in *Der Prix Ars Electronica* (Linz: Veritas, 1991), 124.

13. Erik Colpaert, "Here, There and Everywhere," in Shaw, *The Legible City* (Amsterdam: Colophon, 1990), G.

14. Myron W. Krueger, *Artificial Reality II* (Reading, Mass: Addison-Wesley, 1991), xvi.

15. Florian Rötzer in "On Fascination, Reaction, Virtual Worlds and Others," included in this volume.

16. For a full description, see Krueger, *Artificial Reality II*.

17. Ibid., 48

18. Ibid., 86.

19. See Ovid, *Metamorphoses*, trans. Rolfe Humphries (Bloomington: Indiana University Press, 1983), 68–73.

20. Marshall McLuhan, *Understanding Media*, 51.

21. Henry David Thoreau, *Walden*.

22. After Chico MacMurtrie and Rick Sayre, in Sermon, *Der Prix Ars Electronica* (Linz: Veritas, 1991), 126–28.

23. Krueger, *Artificial Reality II*, 89.

24. Quoted by Cynthia Goodman, *Digital Visions*, 141.

25. Krueger, *Artificial Reality II*, 45.

26. Norman White, in *Der Prix Ars Electronica* (Linz: Veritas, 1990), 181.

8

Encapsulated Bodies in Motion: Simulators and the Quest for Total Immersion

Erkki Huhtamo

The quest for "immersion"—even "total immersion"—has become a buzzword in contemporary technoculture. But what does it mean? It has been variously described as "plunging into water," "breaking through the screen (or the mirror)," "leaving (or changing) one's body," "losing oneself in a simulated world" or "navigating in cyberspace." All these metaphors imply a transition, a "passage" from one realm to another, from the immediate physical reality of tangible objects and direct sensory data to *somewhere else*. Technology obviously plays the role of a mediator, but the situation is more complex, because technology itself has become a "somewhere-else land" of our desires. It is an *"obscure* object of desire"—seductive and repulsive at the same time. Many popular texts, including the film *Tron* (1982), in which a computer wizard gets scanned into the not-so-much-like-a-paradise world inside the computer, play on this ambiguity.

The quest for immersion manifests itself both as the product of an experience industry and as discursive formations—dreams, beliefs, desires ,and fears. It has surfaced most sensationally in the discursive formations around virtual reality (VR) technology, but a similar quest has been identified in relation to such diverse phenomena as computer games, CMCSs (computer-mediated communications systems), professional simulators, speciality cinemas, theme park rides, neopsychedelic or "cyberdelic" techno-house parties and drug experiences, the new age interest in "mind machines" and "psychotechnologies," including Eastern philosophies and shamanism, and so on.

Even mainstream cinema is looking for ways to increase audience involvement. The proliferation of "subjective" steady-cam

159

shots, computer-generated "virtual zooms" and "ride" sequences along the depth axis of the image—often combined with their "counter-tropes," objects "flying" *towards* the spectator—is a case in point.[1] They are meant to give the spectator a sensation of plunging straight through the screen into the diegetic world of the film. Renny Harlin, director of *Cliffhanger*, the most recent vehicle for Sylvester Stallone, told an interviewer: "The language of cinema today is like rock 'n' roll, whereas it used to be like classical music. The spectator is out of balance, grabbing his/her fellow spectator in fear. The camera has to absorb him/her all the time. This is a novelty."[2] No wonder parallels have been drawn between the experiences provided by commercial cinema and theme park attractions. *Variety*'s reviewer characterized *Cliffhanger* as "a two-hour roller-coaster ride that never stops from first minute to last."[3]

The quest for immersion as a cultural topos

The quest for technologically induced immersion is by no means a "novelty" that has unexpectedly appeared in the cultural horizon. In the early 1950s a publicity text for *Cinerama*, a new extra-wide screen cinematic spectacle, promised: "You won't be gazing at a movie screen—you'll find yourself swept right into the picture, surrounded by sight and sound."[4] Already in 1944 a text advertising DuMont television sets had promised, "You'll be an armchair Columbus!" adding: "You'll sail with television through vanishing horizons into exciting new worlds."[5] This in turn echoes Oliver Wendell Holmes's classic description (from 1859) of the experience of watching stereographic photographs with a special viewing device, the stereoscope: "I pass, in a moment, from the banks of the Charles to the ford of the Jordan, and leave my outward frame in the armchair at my table, while in spirit I am looking down upon Jerusalem from the Mount of Olives."[6]

As these examples demonstrate, the quest for immersive experience is a cultural topos, which has been activated—and even fabricated—now and again in culturally and ideologically specific circumstances.[7] However, it is hard to pinpoint the logic behind its appearance and reappearance without resorting to "universals," such as mankind's supposed "collective need" to immerse itself in realities other than its immediate physical surroundings, or its innate "quest for naturalism," which in the ideal case will lead to the annihilation of the difference between reality and its representation.

According to this option the ultimate VR would be the perfect simulation of reality, its sensory duplication.

In this discussion I will abstain from such ahistorical explanations and treat immersion as a historical and ideological construction, tracing and comparing some of its manifestations in different times and places as a contribution to the ongoing mapping of the mental topography of the human-machine relationship. As a case in point, the amazing boom that stereography enjoyed among the Victorian bourgeoisie during the second half of the nineteenth century can be related to specific social, cultural, and metapsychological factors.[8] In the Victorian world an increasingly sharp division was created between the public and the private spheres, particularly in the lives of the rising middle class; this division also defined the worlds of the masculine and the feminine. Seen from the safety of the Victorian home, the public space was the realm of stress, increasing speed, and potential threat (symbolized by the industrial proletariat). The colonies and distant lands were, in spite of the development of transportation and reproduction technologies, still beyond the horizon of most people, yet they were strangely present.

Immersing one's eyes into the eyepiece of the stereoscope provided a virtual tunnel, which had the might to transport the Victorian housewife and children (and even the husband in his domestic role) safely through distant lands and cultures, at the same time excluding the disturbing realities of factories, prisons, and slums. As the first domestic "machine of vision" serving as a mass medium, the stereoscope anticipated the role that television as an *instantaneous* "virtual window" would later adopt. Stereography had a predominantly masculine side that coincided with the liberties that the husband could take in his public role: it provided a channel for the forbidden pleasures of voyeurism. As Charles Baudelaire observed, "A thousand hungry eyes were bending over the peep-holes of the stereoscope, as if they were the attic-windows of the infinite. The love of pornography, which is no less deep-rooted in the natural heart of man than the love of himself, was not to let slip so fine an opportunity of self-satisfaction."[9]

Immersion and the dynamics of the media environment

The immersive experience is usually interpreted as an out-of-body experience, and as such it perpetuates the persistent Christian-

Cartesian split between mind and body.[10] But even the wish to leave one's "outward frame" behind and let the "soul" soar into the immaterial realms of the Other, fantasy and desire, should be treated as a historically conditioned phenomenon. Commenting on the virtual reality craze, the critic Vivian Sobchack suggests that the VR motto "reality isn't enough anymore" might be psychoanalytically recast as "reality is too much right now." Sobchack sees in the "anxious rejection of the human body" a reaction to contemporary fears of mortality in the face of AIDS, nuclear annihilation and ecological suicide.[11]

Similarly, the widespread immersion in chemically induced altered states in the 1960s could be partly explained, at least in the United States, as a reaction against the primary (involuntary) immersion in the ubiquitous audiovisual environment of broadcast television. There was a widespread feeling that television did not fulfill its initial promise as a launching station for liberating virtual voyages to anywhere. Instead it filled the screen with mindless pastimes or with assassinated and mutilated bodies, either anonymous (Vietnam) or those of well-known media figures (from JFK to Martin Luther King). This spurred a sense of alienation and collective guilt, which certainly contributed to the urge to leave one's own physical body. Drugs were seen as *a medium*, an alternative communications system, that promised an entry into a less constraining (virtual) environment.[12]

The topic of immersion had been irrevocably linked with the inner dynamics of the media environment since at least the early 1950s. The new triumvirate of television, wide-screen cinema, and Disneyland can in retrospect be seen as a symbolic model for the reorganization of the media-scape of audiovisuality. The new wide-screen spectacles (Cinerama, Cinemascope, Todd-AO and others), as well as 3-D movies, contested television's promise of real-time virtual voyaging "through" the small screen by offering a "new" overwhelming experience of a wraparound image and sound environment.[13] Disneyland involved the audience by inviting it to experience a physical but entirely simulated "universe"; it proposed an alternative to screen practice in that "two-dimensional motion picture stories and spaces were reconstructed in three-dimensional space and transformed into amusement park rides."[14]

All these "new" cultural forms had to do with the metaphor of traveling and the corresponding redefinition and relocation of the traveling body. Disneyland, which became the model for "location-based entertainment" (LBE), offered the most conventional (although enormously successful) solution. By being organized as a simulated and reduced imaginary universe, divided into different "lands" (Frontierland, Adventureland, Fantasyland), it invited the visitor on a "walking tour of the universe," offering out-of-body experiences only intermittently along the way. Cinerama, the most ambitious and spectacular of the wide-screen systems of the 1950s, adopted the travelogue as its principal film genre. The fact that it was organized around a series of "visits" to different locations around the world, instead of following a main narrative story-line, differentiated it from the Hollywood product and brought it closer to the Disney-land product. This was well understood by its inventor, Fred Waller, who stated that Cinerama was "not a child of motion pictures but a brand new form of entertainment."[15]

Significantly, the first Cinerama feature, *This is Cinerama* (1952), opened with a panoramic sequence shot from a roller coaster car. Cinerama publicity emphasized the cinema/amusement park connection by showing the cinema audience as if collectively squeezed on the front seat of the roller coaster. However, it also used photomontages of the spectator in his/her theater seat literally flying or floating inside the virtual world of the film.[16] It is interesting that there is neither a family (as almost always in television publicity at that time),[17] nor even the rest of the audience in the picture. There is just the individual spectator in his/her transformed—or transfigured—body levitating above the audience of La Scala or speeding past the scantily dressed surfers of Cypress Gardens.[18] The voyeristic presence of the spectator inside the diegetic world of the film gives these images an almost metaphysical quality, reminiscent of Antonioni's or Resnais's images of modern alienation—except that here the face of the subject shows a naïve enthusiasm about his/her presence in the "mediatized" mind-scape of modernity.

However immersive and "interactive" at first glance, this fantasy is predominantly passive; the spectator may have become a "participant," but s/he is still an outsider drifting in a brave new world of predetermined meanings. One of them is the role of Cinerama itself as the main attraction; "when you visit Detroit, Cinerama is a must stop."[19] The spectator of *This is Cinerama* visits only secondarily Milan, Venice, Scotland, Spain, Vienna, and several sites in the United States. S/he really flies—and expects to fly even before taking off—straight into the lap of technology as a modern wonder. This "innocent" technological attractiveness accounted partly for

Cinerama's potential as a vehicle for ideological propaganda. John Belton quotes newspaper columnist Hazel Flynn as writing in 1955 that "Cinerama has been entered in the *Congressional Record* as being an important instrument through which the American way of life is illustrated to other nations. It has been presented by the State Department to refute the communists' appeal in other lands."[20]

Towards mapping the psychotopography of audiovisuality

In his discussion of bodies and machines in late-nineteenth and early-twentieth-century culture, Mark Seltzer emphasizes the role of "the radical and intimate *coupling* of bodies and machines" as a way of accounting for the range of "not entirely compatible" notions of the human-machine relationship in American culture during that time. These include the ideas that machines *replace* bodies and persons, that persons are *already* machines, or that technologies *make* bodies and persons.[21] Seltzer draws on a great variety of literary, educational, and medical discourses in his attempt to "map the psychotopography of machine culture."[22] His account works against taking concepts like "the natural" and "the technological" as simple polar opposites and emphasizes their intimate and complex interrelationships.

Seltzer analyzes Jack London's short story "The Apostate," the central character of which is a young factory worker, "the perfect worker and the perfect machine." Suffering from "pathological fatigue" caused by the speed and repetitiveness of the machine work, "the apostate" walks down "a leafy lane beside a railroad track" and climbs in an empty box-car. Seltzer comments: "[I]f machine work makes the apostate turn neurasthenic or hysteric, his 'escape' by entering into the compartment of the train seems less an alternative to either machine work or neurasthenia than another way, like the way of a hysteric, of experiencing one's body (or 'piece of life') set in motion apart from one's own intentions."[23]

Seltzer's ideas can be applied to the analysis of the human-machine relationship in audiovisual systems. All the systems from theme park attractions to cinema and virtual reality can be considered "apparatuses," technological-metapsychological machineries for producing certain cognitive and emotional states of mind (and, arguably, of the body). They evoke not only the notion of "coupling of bodies and machines," but even that of *entering* and being *encap-*

sulated in the machine. The analysis of these apparatuses should be related to the investigation of the general cultural "psychophysics" of our relationships with machines. This becomes especially useful if we relate the discussion of immersive systems to two concepts that underlie machine culture and are often treated as polar opposites: "automation" and "interaction."

An *automaton* is a self-regulating mechanism that performs independently (after being set in motion) a series of predetermined tasks. From the point of view of the audience, a film screening is such an automatic experience, because it unrolls independently of the spectators' mental or physical involvement. But even from the point of view of the projectionist it is at least semiautomatic: his role is restricted to changing the reels and overseeing the screening. An interactive system, on the other hand, requires constant interplay between the user and the machine. The subject is turned from a supervisor into a protagonist on the field defined by the machine's specific functions. His/her actions effect the system, which in turn responds.

The modes of experience elicited by automatic and interactive audiovisual systems are often treated in terms of a polar opposition. The former is labeled as "passive" and the latter as "active." This division has also been genderized, the former representing the feminine (submissiveness, inactivity), the latter the masculine (the quest for mastery, aggressiveness). How does this relate to the immersive tendencies in the media? The polarity seems to reflect itself on the level of cultural discourses. There is a widespread attitude that furnishes immersiveness with negative connotations: losing hold of reality, being pulled into the eye of the storm, or drowning "immersed" in the water. Members of moral majority groups see even watching television and the impact of media in general as immersive, producing passive and alienated subjects.

Yet there is another strong discourse that emphasizes the "natural" bond between immersion and (inter)activity; "the virtual voyager is the one who takes initiative." This kind of discourse is often used by those marketing immersive experiences and technologies, but also by cultural optimists in the McLuhan tradition. New technologies are "extensions" of the human sensory apparatus and ultimately of the nervous system. Immersion into the ever-spreading technosphere provides mankind with new possibilities of contact and mutual understanding, empowering and activating the individual. It also represents a turn towards the mind and the immaterial;

the body is secondary, and may even be an obstacle for the development of a "global consciousness."

To go beyond such generalizations and to "measure" their validity one should consider the specific constellations of the parameters of the human-machine encounter, such as intensity, duration, context, structure, and function. For example, the relationship between immersion and interactivity seems less clear-cut if we move from the level of models to the level of experience. It is still common to mix up "a subject position" (as a feature of the system) and the behavior of an actual subject. A subject position provides a frame, a set of *preferred* codes, but it does not determine the actual readings and experiences. One of the important features of Sherrie Turkle's classic study of the computer user, *The Second Self,* was that she did not try to fit the extreme variety of the users' subjective experiences into such categories as active and passive.[24] The experiences may be induced by encounters with more or less uniform technologies (and interfaces), but they are embedded in personal life histories, which in their turn are embedded in historically, socially, and ideologically specific systems of codification.

The motion simulator as a hybrid form

I would now like to take a closer look at an immersive system that has received very little critical attention in spite of its popular, theoretical, and also historical significance. The case in point is the "motion simulator" or "dynamic cinema" or "leisure simulator" ride. Motion simulator-based attractions can be found today in most major theme parks around the world. In Tokyo they have already entered the new generation game and entertainment centers and also the urban public space as independent attractions ("virtual theaters"). Companies like Iwerks Entertainment and Hughes Rediffusion Simulation have recently introduced mobile, "nomadic" motion simulator units.[25]

The motion simulator is a multiperson leisure attraction that uses a film projection synchronized with the hydraulic movements of either the seats, the floor, or the whole simulator "capsule" to provide a simulated "ride,"—a virtual voyaging experience. Although it appeared in theme parks as late as the 1980s (sure enough, there are many antecedents, such as Disneyland's *Trip to the Moon,* 1955–), the motion simulator can be seen as a hybrid form. It merges features from earlier technological apparatuses, such as mechanical amusement park rides, traditional cinema, and the professional flight simulator.[26] The coexistence of (at least seemingly) discrepant features is one of the things that makes it interesting. The concept is "old-fashioned," yet it owes much to state-of-the-art innovations in digital and hydraulic technologies. It is "non-interactive," but clearly related to interactive systems. It raises interesting questions about the politics of the body—about the relationship between the dematerialization the body and the simultaneous centering of its physicality as the main locus of pleasure production.

"The railway, like the elevator, or like (in its recreational form) the Ferris wheel, puts stilled bodies in motion. What these mobile technologies make possible, in different forms, are the thrill and panic of agency at once extended and suspended," Mark Seltzer writes.[27] The ideas of encapsulating bodies in a "machine" and physically moving them to produce pleasure was already a central feature of the earliest mechanical amusement park attractions in the late nineteenth century, such as water "chutes," Ferris wheels, and roller coasters. Their proliferation was clearly related metapsychologically to the increasing mechanization of man's relationship to his surroundings and to his experience of time and space. Being "bonded" to different technological "prostheses" was as traumatic as liberating, as is proven by Wolfgang Schivelbusch's account of the nineteenth-century "railway neurosis."[28] A more obvious example is provided by the multiple traumas caused by mechanized factory work.

Experiencing an amusement park attraction gave one a momentary outlet from the routine and often stressful relationship to technology in everyday life. The outlet came through its ritualized and modified reenactment of the everyday relationship. The technological bases and even the modes of experience were very similar; only the parameters of the human-machine relationship were changed. A case in point is the curious parallel between the electric chair (introduced in 1888 and since then a very ambiguous discursive object), medical treatment with electricity, and popular arcade machines in which the subject's endurance is tested by leading electricity through his body (the circuit was closed by grabbing two handles). By simply changing the context and controlling the voltage, electricity could be used either for executing, recuperating, or sportively challenging the body.

Roller coasters and other rail-based attractions were "amplified" and yet "reduced" versions of railroads or streetcar networks.[29] Their attractiveness was based on the suppression of functionality and the exaggeration of those features that the railroad and streetcar companies tried to eliminate from their regular services (building *artificial* hills instead of "cutting" lines horizontally through the landscape, emphasizing sudden turns and bumpiness instead of smooth movement). John Kasson has observed that the amusement park "abstracted features from the larger society and presented them in intensified, fantastic forms. Instruments of production and efficiency were transformed into objects of amusement . . . ."[30] Although mechanical thrill rides occasionally had a thematic motivation, their main aim was to supply a pure multisensory delirium. This was based on a double operation. According to Lauren Rabinowitz, "The person surrendered to the machine, which, in turn, liberated the body in some fashion from its normal limitations of placement and movement in daily life."[31]

Phantom bodies in a phantom train

Tony Bennett has described the effect of theme park film shows by saying that "they hurtle the vision through space whilst fixing the body as stationary."[32] This applies also to the cinematic experience. In cinema—the advent of which ran parallel to the creation of the first great electrified amusement parks in the 1890s—the physical movement of the body on a train or a roller coaster was replaced by the virtual sensation of movement, which was created by the interplay of the components of the cinematic apparatus. During the early years of cinema there was even a film genre that explicitly simulated the physical experience of the new transportation technologies; in a sense the cinematic apparatus itself *became* a (virtual) means of transportation, a "surrogate" train or streetcar.

The film 'genre' in question was the "phantom ride" film—it deserves attention here, in part, because it is currently undergoing a revival as the cinematic component of the motion simulator ride. The phantom ride was (technically, in an "ideal" form) a continuous strip of film shot "along the tracks" with a stationary camera placed at the front of a moving train.[33] The unity of the point of view and the continuous movement along the depth axis of the image gave the audience a sense of penetration into the world on the screen. According to an observer, writing in 1897, the spectator of a phantom ride film "was not an outsider watching from safety the rush of the cars. He was a passenger on a phantom train ride that whirled him through space at nearly a mile a minute. There is no smoke, no glimpse of shuddering frame or crushing wheels. There was nothing to indicate motion save that shining vista of tracks that was eaten up irresistibly, rapidly and the disappearing panorama of banks and fences."[34]

The phantom ride film thus positioned the audience as passengers of a phantom train that was simultaneously absent and present. It was an imaginary extension, or a *projection*, of the diegetic space of the screen onto the (psychological) spectatorial space. The darkened "audience space" itself was a prerequisite for, rather than part of, the experience. For the audience, a temporary displacement and reorganization of the sensory apparatus took place; the eyes were foregrounded as a kind of metonymy for the whole sensory-motor complex. The eyes *became* the phantom body seated in the phantom train pushing towards the screen.

Although the "pure" phantom ride film was soon subsumed by the development of the narrative film, it may be considered an *alternative model* for organizing the cinematic spectacle, rather than just a primitive transposition of a familiar experience into a new medium.[35] Tom Gunning has included the phantom ride film in the "cinema of attractions," which he sees as the conception dominating cinema until 1906–7. This kind of film "directly solicits spectator attention, inciting visual curiosity, and supplying pleasure through an exciting spectacle. . . ." It emphasizes "the direct stimulation of shock or surprise at the expense of unfolding a story or creating a diegetic universe"; "its energy moves outward towards an acknowledged spectator. . . ."[36]

In another article Gunning again emphasizes the role of "centering the spectator" in this kind of cinema and uses it to criticize Noel Burch's claim that the "spectatorial identification with a ubiquitous camera" was the linchpin of the classical system of narrative cinema, the forms of which were stabilized years later. According to Gunning, Burch underestimates the central role of narrative strategies (such as the spectator identification with constantly *changing* points of view) in "suturing" the spectator to the fiction in the latter.[37]

In a phantom ride film the centering of the spectator is indeed crucial, even though the energy does not so much "move outward" as help to carry the audience inward.[38] Yet the spectator position is also constrained by the identification with the virtual train; the pleasure production is thus based on the dialectics of simultaneously "empowering" and "disempowering" the spectator. This experience obviously differs from the one described (in connection with the classic narrative cinema) by the Hungarian film aesthete Béla Balázs in the 1920s: "The camera carries my eye. Into the image. I see the things from the point of view of the space in the film. I am surrounded by the personalities of the film and I get mixed up in its action, which I witness from all sides."[39]

Here the phantom vehicle has vanished, and the spectator has been as if released from his/her entrapment. The eye-*cum*-body is carried into the diegetic world of the film smoothly, weightlessly, as in a dream. It has obtained mobile ubiquity. However, this voyeuristic freedom is illusory; it is still constrained by "the camera" (representing the cinematic apparatus), even if this may have been camouflaged by the ideologies of transparency and anthropocentrism. Balázs was without any doubt conscious of this; yet he poetically exaggarates the "pure" immersive potential of traditional cinema (in a way reminiscent of Burch's position mentioned above). He describes a kind of super-experience, which is actually closer to navigating in virtual reality than watching a film.

Balázs's description would be more in place in the context of such cinematic systems as Cinerama or its most important descendants today, Imax and Omnimax, which consciously aim at providing the audience with an immersive experience and simultaneously distance it from traditional narrative suturing.[40] In Imax and Omnimax theaters this is technically achieved by stretching the screen horizontally and vertically to cover the spectator's peripheral vision, by enveloping him/her in a surround-sound environment, and by using very large film frame size to produce ultra-high-definition image quality.[41]

Cinerama in the 1950s and Imax and Omnimax since the early 1970s have actually been attempts to reestablish the "cinema of attractions" as an alternative mode of cinematic experience and also as a new commercial substructure. This means a return to the beginnings, positing both the technology and the filmic experience as an attraction. In the case of Imax and Omnimax, the former goal has been looked for by trademark-(instead of film-) oriented publicity, projection booths with transparent walls, and technological demonstrations to start the show. At the same time everything is done to inscribe the filmic experience itself as "authentic."

This kind of double emphasis on the material and the immaterial (which would have caused problems for the politically inclined theorists of "anti-illusionism" in the 1960s) as a guarantee for a "real" experience seems symptomatic of the development of techno-culture. Technology is gradually becoming a second nature, a terri-tory both external and internalized, and an object of desire. There is no need to make it transparent any longer, simply because it is not felt to be in contradiction to the "authenticity" of the experience. It isn't "either-or" but "both-and," although this position is not without its own contradictions.

Virtual voyaging and physical vertigo

In the motion simulator ride the phantom vehicle is *materialized*. The neutral audience space is turned into a kind of set, a theatrical space, that is a material extension of the virtual space on the screen. Even this was already accomplished around the turn of the cen-tury.[42] One of the forerunners of simulator entertainment, *Hale's Tours and Scenes of the World*, which was first introduced at the St. Louis Exposition of 1904, gave phantom ride films a concrete setting (and renewed the already waning interest in them) by using a simu-lated railway car as the centerpiece of the attraction. The audience sat in the car, and phantom ride films were projected on a screen placed at its open front end. This produced a simulation of actually traveling on rails. Beside vision, other sensory registers were stimu-lated (by rushes of "wind," by artificially produced clacking of the tracks, and by swaying the car).[43]

The motion simulator may be designed as an aircraft, a subma-rine, or a space shuttle; accordingly, the screen is turned into a"windshield." Ride films often depict space wars or underwater cruises.[44] The simulator itself is often framed by a "pre-show," an architectural and theatrical setting; the entrance hall may be turned into a space station, and ticket collectors and guards into fictive staff members in costume, as in Disneyland's classic *Star Tours* ride.[45] The audience may have to visit related spaces by walking and undergo a series of "rites of passage" with thematically motivated waiting time (for "identification," "disinfection," etc.), before it is allowed to enter the motion simulator itself.

For the administration this works as a way to regulate the visitor traffic and to maximize the profits (new groups can be sent in at brief intervals); it also serves to disguise the brevity of the ride itself (usu-ally four to five minutes). This arrangement turns the whole attrac-tion into a kind of huge machine. Visitors are passed through it as on

an invisible assembly line.[46] Their bodies are encapsulated in a tech-
nological-mythical-financial apparatus long before they ultimately
reach the capsule of the motion simulator. In Toronto, the CN-
Tower's pioneering *Tour of the Universe* ride (1984) ends appropriately: the visitors exit from their simulated space adventure through
a hazy tunnel into a combined games arcade and souvenir shop.

For the visitor, the pre-show functions as an initiation to the fictional world of the ride. It creates expectations and raises tension;
even the practical information and warnings about behavior work
towards this goal. The pre-show also helps to produce the immersive
experience by gradually dissolving the border separating the physical world and the virtual world of the screen, even though this takes
place in the sphere of play and the willing suspension of disbelief.
During the ride a *double operation* takes place. Besides the custom-
ary cinematic effect of the dematerialization of the body, the physicality of the body is emphasized. This is mainly the effect of the
moving seats. The synchronized movement of the seats is actually a
physical extention of the virtual movement on the screen, adding to
it a material—even a tactile—dimension. The essence of the motion
simulator experience is based on this double operation, which
merges sheer physical vertigo and virtual voyaging.[47]

Almost a metaphor for this is the *Body Wars* ride at Walt Disney
World. The ride takes place in a miniaturized vehicle traveling
inside the human body [!], leading to a multiple encapsulation: the
body inside the machine inside the body inside . . . The trip is interrupted by an "accident": an infected splinter punctures the host
body's skin and blocks the way. The audience is informed that there
is a doctor aboard; she dons scuba gear and gets out to investigate.
After a while she is seen through the "windscreen" as if swimming
among the cells and blood vessels. This trick makes the case for the
"corporeality" of the virtual world by seemingly transporting a physical body from the vehicle into its realm.

Immersion and interactivity

In spite of its increasing technical sophistication, it can be claimed
that the motion simulator ride in the form described above does not
present anything new. The idea of wrapping the audience within a
"spatialized fiction" was already one of the original ideas of Disneyland, and its basic elements had been described in 1895 by the
British film pioneer Robert W. Paul in his unrealized project based

on H. G. Wells's novel *The Time Machine* (1894).[48] A pre-show is a familiar element from many mechanical thrill rides, such as *Space Mountain* at Disneyland. From this point of view, the motion simulator ride seems almost an object of nostalgia, appealing to the public's taste for conservative experiences in the disguise of contemporary hi-tech.

There is, however a wide agreement among theme park and ride developers that this will not be enough for long. They refer particularly to the current fashion for anything "interactive," which is epitomized by the immense popularity of video and computer games but also seems to be reflected throughout contemporary technoculture.[49] Even though claims about the formation of a "culture of interactivity" may prove to be mere hype, there is unquestionably a wide interest for (to paraphrase Nam June Paik) "doing television with one's own fingers."

Attempts are currently being made to marry immersiveness with interactivity in the field of entertainment. This has meant the activation of another source, the professional simulator. The development of early motion simulator devices, such as *Hale's Tours* in the early twentieth century, ran parallel to that of the development of the professional flight simulator. In spite of the novelty of aviation, according to Ron Reisman there were several professional "flight trainers" already in use by 1910.[50] From the point of view of technical solutions, they were closer to the mechanical amusement park attractions than to the combination of the virtual and the physical achieved in *Hale's Tours*. The Billings Trainer, for instance, was a "non-flying device with wings which was mounted on a column. A rudder bar enabled the machine to be rotated to face the wind and the student operated control surfaces to maintain his equilibrium, somewhat similar to certain present-day surfboard trainers."[51]

The metapsychological motivation behind all these devices— striving for mastery over new technology by submitting to it and releasing the subject from its "natural" spatiotemporal limits—may have been the same, but its manifestations were quite different. The flight simulator was directly concerned with mastering the new aviation technology without taking unnecessary risks. Especially during World War I these "unnecessary risks" ceased to be purely technical and psychological; they became political and ideological as well. Flight simulators became machines for practicing mastery over enemies. The encapsulated body of the pilot was trained to defend its threatened existence by creating a symbiotic and interactive relationship with the machine. The flight simulator became one of the basic models for interactive media, especially after interactive visualization capabilities were added.

In amusement park "thrill" rides the need to master the technology was turned into a ritualized game, a reenactment of the struggle between control and catastrophe; the outcome (except in those rare cases when an actual accident happened) was known in advance. The audience could safely entrust their bodies to technology and surrender to the "white knuckle" rides. This basically passive form of enjoyment was transferred to attractions like *Hale's Tours* and on to the motion simulator rides. The audience gets the impression of being passengers, not being in command of an aircraft or a submarine.[52] The controls are elsewhere, in an imaginary cockpit (curiously equal to the projection booth). Although motion simulators have tried to bridge the gap between the audience space and the virtual world of the screen and to create a more dynamic response from the passengers, they still share a very traditional nineteenth-century conception about the audience. It was encountered in the diorama as well as in the opera or the melodrama theatre.

Interactivity and the collective experience

With the development of real-time computer imaging from the 1960s on, the flight simulators found new ways to combine the exercise of mastery with convincingly simulated scenery. The computer game industry was largely an offspring of this development. Likewise, it stimulated the motion simulator entertainment industry, which was especially impressed by the new possibility to synchronize a state-of-the-art hydraulic platform with computer-controlled moving images.[53] Today companies like Hughes Rediffusion Simulation and Mitsubishi Heavy Industries provide motion platforms for both professional and entertainment use. It is interesting that the *interactive* features, which are an essential element of the professional simulator, have been very underdeveloped in the context of the motion simulator entertainment until recently.

There are obvious reasons, which have to do with sticking to a traditional concept of the audience. If there are tens, even hundreds, of people sitting in the same space, it is difficult to design meaningful modes of interaction that involve them all. This has been proven by the sterility of the systems in which the audience makes a majority decision about how a motion picture will continue by using an electronic voting system.[54] One of the most interesting attempts to marry a multi-user motion simulator with truly interactive capabilities is *Galaxian*, developed by the Japanese games manufacturer NAMCO and introduced at the Osaka Expo in 1990.[55] *Galaxian* accommodates twenty-eight people who sit in a circle in the center of a circular motion platform, facing outwards toward a circular wall that serves as a panoramic 360-degree projection screen. The audience is immersed in a *Star Wars*-like space adventure, in which its members are encouraged to defend the "empire" against hordes of enemy spacecraft; the interface device is a ray gun.

Even though there is no other way to interact beside shooting, *Galaxian* registers and displays both individual and collective successes, which effect the fate of the empire and the length of the session. This seems to increase the concentration and the immersive effect, but in a very different way from traditional motion simulators. There is no time to be passively "carried away by the spectacle," as if meditating on a mandala, or to surrender to the state of relative passivity induced by a motion simulator ride. Instead, there is a near paniclike state of activity, and almost no time to take a breath.

To understand the pleasure provided by this kind of a spectacle, it is instructive to go back to Sherrie Turkle's *Second Self*. Among different groups of computer users, Turkle made observations about executives, accountants, and surgeons as players of video games that can be considered a basic model for immersive *and* interactive technology. Turkle noted the intensive relationship her test people had with the games and concluded: "For people under pressure total concentration is a form of relaxation." Some people mentioned reaching "altered states" as their goal. They emphasized the meditative quality of absorbing oneself totally in the game—"There is no way to think about anything else but the game or it's over. Others emphasized the pleasure they got from goal-oriented activity, of gradually mastering the game—"Unlike in the meditation, when I play games I feel that I've achieved something."[56]

Both types of pleasure can be attained from *Galaxian*. In addition, there is the pleasure of interpersonal competition—beating the rest of the audience from the position of being "alone in the crowd,"—and the physical sensation caused by the hurtling of the body. This kind of intensified and condensed experience seems particularly appropriate for a hypercompetitive, collective media society like Japan. There is a demand for a brief escape from the *logos* of business life to the state of "thinking with one's fingers." There is also a need for reenacting the constant need for self-improvement and competition by raising it on an abstracted and mythologized level. Perhaps even the success of more traditional "passive" motion simulator rides in Japan can be explained this way: the intensity of the experience must increase in direct proportion to the briefness of the time available for the *salariman*, who feels trapped in his/her daily cycle.

From the encapsulation of the body to its de-encapsulation in the net

Such applications as *Galaxian* aside, the *interactive* motion simulator is usually conceptualized as a personal simulator. It may seem to represent the ultimately chapter in the history of encapsulation of bodies in machines. Without even the comforting presence of the fellow audience members, each body—or unit of bodies, usually a couple—is encapsulated separately.[57] A good example is provided by *Commander*, a "two-seater interactive concept leisure simulator" recently introduced by Hughes Rediffusion Simulation. The participant is enclosed in a small capsule and faces a "windscreen" (a computer graphics display) and a smaller "radar monitor." There are a number of controls, including a "panic button"; there is also "a safety exit hatch."[58] —So comforting to know that there still *is* a way back to reality, in case of a sudden burst of nostalgia!

Virtual reality may seem to go even further, because the subject is not only segregated from his/her surroundings; s/he is even segregated from his/her own body. What s/he gets instead is a virtual surrogate body in computer-generated surroundings. The surrogate body is not even subject to the laws that the physical body must obey, but rather to those that are programmed to reign in the virtual world. Simple movements of the (physical) fingers can make the virtual hand replicate itself, as the Australian artist Stelarc recently demonstrated with his creation, *Virtual Arm* (1992). In a way, it is understandable that the VR apologists have located here a major rupture in the politics of the body.

The discourse on the dematerializing effect of VR has often lapsed into exaggerated idealist rhetorics. In its basic form, VR is, like our whole existence, firmly rooted in the physicality of the body; the whole experience is triggered by physical movements and gestures.[59] This was already evident—perhaps unintentionally—in VR-utopian Randal Walser's plans for a "sports and fitness playhouse" utilizing VR equipment (using a rowing machine with HMD to "cross a lake," etc.) or in the silly sexual gymnastics necessitated by love-making in cyberspace in the film *Lawnmower Man*.[60] Actually, one of the most significant achievements of artists working with interactive and virtual technologies, such as Jeffrey Shaw, has been the critical investigation of the *bilocation* brought forth by virtual reality: the simultaneous, interconnected presence of the body in two places, and in two existential forms. The physical and the virtual are complementary, rather than mutually exclusive, realms.

Yet the encapsulation of the body in the simulator capsule may also lead to its de-encapsulation in the net. Even a device like *Commander* can be networked with up to fifteen other capsules, which can be geographically far apart from each other (the signal lag in the network being the limit). These kinds of networked virtual game environments, which are based on the design of virtual military training grounds (such as the BattleTech Center in Chicago), have provided interesting evidence about the ways in which people will socialize and regroup themselves via virtual encounters.[61] They are, however, only the offspring of those "immersed societies" that are developing on-line in the computer-mediated communications networks (CMC), such as the Internet. They point towards new forms of connectivity. Roy Ascott has recently coined the term *Telenoia*, which means "networked consciousness, interactive awareness, thought at a distance, 'mind-at-large,' to use Gregory Bateson's term."[62]

We definitively do not lose our bodies when we meet each other in the Net, but the question about carnal presence, as well as about gender, seems to become more peripheral—at least it becomes more complicated. The aim is not to replace the physicality of our lives but to expand it. The necessity to adapt oneself to the telematic environment, which seems symptomatic of the electronic culture of the late twentieth century, requires one to question old notions of the "audience," of the "masculine" and the "feminine," of the "private" and the "public." It also requires one to establish a new idea about being "alone together"—but not in the same sense as in television culture, where the idea of a "national audience" or an "international audience" is still connected to an abstract, hierarchical, and basically noninteractive way of thinking. Immersion into a telematic environment should be a truly interactive experience, without predetermined technological, economic, and ideological constraints. Although this may never be the case, it is a goal worth striving for.

Notes

1. My understanding about the workings of these "figures," particularly in the context of television but also in that of cinema, has derived much from Margaret Morse's "Television Graphics and the Body: Words on the Move," a paper delivered at the Television and the Body Conference, Society for Cinema Studies, Montreal, 1987. The reason that the immersive tendencies in mainstream cinema today are concentrated on such formal filmic concerns, instead of changing the parameters of the whole apparatus (contrary to the 1950s, when Cinemascope was a real innovation *inside* the prevailing exhibition substructure), has to do with cinema's schizophrenic relationship to the new channels of distribution, such as television and videotape; it does not know where it really wants to be. The innovations that effect the whole cinematic apparatus, such as giant screen and motion simulator rides, take place *outside* the traditional cinematic exhibition circuit—at world fairs, trade shows, games arcades, and ultimately in new substructures, such as Iwerks Entertainment's "Cinetropolis" project.

2. *Ilta-Sanomat* (Finland), 15 March 1993 (in Finnish, translated by the author).

3. Todd McCarthy, "Cliffhanger," *Variety*, 24 May 1993, 44. The reviewer for the *New Musical Express* (26 June 1993, 28), Gavin Martin, called *Cliffhanger* "a sack of shit" and explained: "*Cliffhanger* is not so much a movie, more a staging post between the action adventure genre and the interactive virtual reality movies of tomorrow. This isn't cinema, this is the movie industry making a dry run for its possible future in the games market (director Harlin is in line for the first IMAX feature film). *Cliffhanger* isn't a movie, it's totalitarian leisure fantasy made flesh. A place where the spectator is a prisoner, with no place to think, no room to breathe."

4. Cited in John Belton, *Widescreen Cinema* (Cambridge: Harvard University Press, 1992), 188–89.

5. The advertisement in which a tiny TV spectator sits in front of a huge television screen, both floating in "space," with miragelike scenes (from would-be television programming) "in the clouds" in the background has been reproduced in Cecilia Tichi, *Electronic Hearth: Creating an American Television Culture* (New York: Oxford University Press, 1991), 15.

6. Oliver Wendell Holmes, "The Stereoscope and the Stereograph" (1859), reprinted in *Photography: Essays & Images*, ed. Beaumont Newhall (New York: Museum of Modern Art, 1980), 59.

7. According to Ernst Robert Curtius, topoi or "topics" are commonplace elements, ranging from thematic to stylistic, which are transmitted in literary traditions and in a sense form the basic building material of these traditions. Ernst Robert Curtius, *European Literature and Latin Middle Ages*, translated from the German by Willard R. Trask (1948; London: Routledge

& Kegan Paul, 1979). They can also be considered cultural motifs that emerge and are reinvested with meaning in different discursive formations.

8. There are very few serious cultural and social studies about nineteenth-century stereoscopy. See, however Jonathan Crary, *Techniques of the Observer: On Vision and Modernity in the Nineteenth Century* (Cambridge: MIT Press, 1991), chap. 4, and Rosalind E. Krauss, "Photography's Discursive Spaces," *The Originality of the Avant-Garde and Other Myths* (Cambridge: MIT Press, 1986), 131–50. For the historical facts, see William C. Darrah: *The World of Stereographs*, (Gettysburg, PA: W. C. Darrah, 1977); Wim van Keulen: *3D Imagics: A Stereoscopic Guide to the 3D Past and its Magic Images, 1830–1900* (AA Borger, The Netherlands: 3-D Book Productions, 1990).

9. Charles Baudelaire, "Photography" (1859), translated by Jonathan Mayne, in Newhall (ed.) *Photography. Essays & Images*, 112. For a representative collection of Victorian pornographic stereographs, see Serge Nazarieff, *Der Akt in der Photographie/The Stereoscopic Nude/Le nu stéréoscopique 1850–1930* (Berlin: Benedikt Taschen Verlag, 1990). A treatment of Victorian stereoscopic pornography is strangely missing from Linda Williams's otherwise remarkable *Hard Core: Power, Pleasure, and the "Frenzy of the Visible"* (Berkeley and Los Angeles: University of California Press, 1989).

10. For a historical criticism of this topic, see Simon Penny: "Pre-history of VR," in *Through the Looking Glass: Artists' First Encounters with Virtual Reality*, ed. Janine Cirincione and Brian D'Amato (Jupiter, Fla: Softworlds, 1992), 77–89.

11. Vivian Sobchak: "New Age Mutant Ninja Hackers," *Artforum*, April 1991. Cited from William Boddy, "Electronic Vision: Genealogies and Gendered Technologies," paper presented at the Finnish Society for Cinema Studies Conference, Helsinki, January 1993.

12. Such expressions as "dope is software in the information environment," "dope is a tool" and "the medium of marijuana" were used in the "Bible of the alternative media movement," Michael Shamberg's and Raindance Corporation's *Guerrilla Television* (New York: Holt, Rinehart and Winston, 1971), 17–19.

13. For an account of this development in the context of the history of movie presentation, see Douglas Gomery: *Shared Pleasures: A History of Movie Presentation in the United States* (Madison: University of Wisconsin Press, 1992); for a "reverse angle" from the point of view of 1950s television culture, see Lynn Spiegel, *Make Room for TV: Television and the Family Ideal in Postwar America* (Chicago: University of Chicago Press, 1992).

14. Belton, *Widescreen Cinema*, 79.

15. Cited in ibid., 95.

16. Closest to materializing this fantasy is Imax Corporation's *Imax*

Magic Carpet, which is a specialty theater with two synchronized giant screens, one in front and another deep down under the audience, visible through a transparent dividing floor. The effect is one of being enveloped by the image, especially in flight shots. I have tried the system at the Futuroscope theme park near Poitiers, France. The installation at Futuroscope, inaugurated in 1992, is the first and only permanent Imax Magic Carpet so far.

17. The connection between the family and virtual voyaging figured centrally also in the publicity for View Master, a home-oriented 3-D viewing system fabricated and marketed by Sawyer's Inc. of Portland, Oregon. View Master was very popular pastime during the 1950s (it exists even today, but turned mostly into a children's toy and manufactured by another company). It was, of course, a late development of Victorian stereography. Geographical "virtual voyaging" topics from all over the world figured high on the stock list; subjects from Walt Disney's comics and films as well as from television series became more and more important towards the 1960s, as the marketing focus shifted largely to children. A publicity image from the 1950s shows the globe with View Master picture-reels as "satellites" in orbit. Another image shows the typical family (father, mother, son and daughter) enjoying View Master images together, with the caption "Hours of fun for the whole family." See Wim van Keulen, *3D Past and Present* (AA Borger, The Netherlands: 3D Book Productions, 1986), 16, 18.

18. See the illustrations in John Belton, *Widescreen Cinema,* 97, 98, 190. Publicity images of the audience collectively sitting in the front seat of a roller coaster are on p. 189 and the cover.

19. Ibid., 96.

20. Cited in ibid., 90.

21. Mark Seltzer: *Bodies and Machines* (New York: Routledge, 1992), 12–13.

22. Ibid., 4.

23. Ibid., 17.

24. Sherrie Turkle, *The Second Self: Computers and the Human Spirit* (London: Granada, 1984).

25. There are several companies in the world involved in the field of designing, manufacturing and marketing motion simulator rides. Among the most well-known are the American companies Iwerks Entertainment, Showscan and Omni Films International (Werk bought Omni Films in 1994). Most motion simulators even in Tokyo come from one of these companies. These companies market motion simulators also outside the theme park world. For ride film production, the companies hire the services of special effects and computer graphics houses such as Industrial Light & Magic, Boss Films, Rhythm and Hues, Ex Macchina and Berkshire Ridefilm (now IMAX Ridefilm. Among the most important manufacturers of hydraulic

motion platforms are Hughes Rediffusion Simulation, Intamin AG, and Mitsubishi Heavy Industries. Companies like Lucasfilm have designed major heavy-duty rides for theme parks, pioneered by *Star Tours* at Disneyland. Iwerks Entertainment has recently introduced its *Cinetropolis* concept, which is an attempt to establish a new motion picture exhibition substructure outside the traditional cinema circuits. *Cinetropolis* is a new generation audiovisual entertainment center, consisting of four attractions: a giant screen cinema, a panoramic 360-degree cinema, a motion simulator, and a virtual reality theater; the first *Cinetropolis* was opened in Ledyard, Connecticut, in 1994. Comparable centers—although more arcade game-oriented—function already in Tokyo, for example *Dr. Jeekahn's/MM Land* in Shibuya. (I am indebted to Iwerks Entertainment, Showscan and Omni Films International for providing me with information about their products.)

26. For historical information, see Janine Pourroy, "Through the Proscenium Arch," *Cinefex* 46 (May 1991): 30–45. The article concentrates mainly on the making of *Back to the Future: The Ride* (1991) for Universal Studios Theme Park, Florida.

27. Mark Seltzer, *Bodies and Machines*, 18.

28. Wolfgang Schivelbusch, *Geschichte der Eisenbahn* (1977: Frankfurt am Main: Fischer Taschenbuch Verlag, 1989), chap. 9.

29. Many of the early amusement parks in the United States were founded by streetcar companies as a clever business maneuver. The parks were situated just outside the city at the end of a streetcar line. The visitors thus had to pay for a two-way ticket in addition to the money spent in the park. The parks were also an effective way to use the excess capacity of electricity that the traction companies had at night, on weekends, and during holidays. According to David E. Nye this connection also explains the great number of rides based on streetcar technology. David E. Nye, *Electrifying America: Social Meanings of a New Technology* (Cambridge: MIT Press, 1992) 122–32.

30. John Kasson, *Amusing the Millions: Coney Island at the Turn of the Century* (New York: Hill and Wang, 1978), 73.

31. Lauren Rabinowitz, "Temptations of Pleasure: Nickelodeons, Amusement Parks and the Sights of Female Sexuality," *Camera Obscura* 23 (May 1990): 77.

32. Tony Bennett, "A Thousand and One Troubles: Blackpool Pleasure Beach," *Formations of Pleasure* (London: Routledge & Kegan Paul, 1983), 151.

33. Phantom ride films were produced in great numbers in different film-producing countries during the second half of the 1890s and even later. Like all films during the first few years of the cinema, they were short, usually less than a minute long. However, they were often edited to run one after another. Sometimes they were even combined with views shot laterally

from railway car windows, or from the train's back bridge. This partly shattered the "ideal" formal unity of the spectatorial position of the phantom ride film.

34. August-September 1897, 6, cit. Charles Musser, "The Travel Genre in 1903-04: Moving Toward Fictional Narrative," *Iris* vol. 2, no 1 (1er semestre 1984), 53.

35. The beginnings of the "narrativization" of the phantom ride film can be seen already in the case of G. A. Smith's *A Kiss in the Tunnel* (1899). Smith's idea was to insert within a phantom ride film another shot that was supposed to show what happens when the train is traveling in the darkness of a tunnel. This extra shot, showing a couple kissing in a compartment, was shot from an objective "third-person" point of view. The result was a basic three-shot narrative film, with alternation between subjective and objective point of view. The unity of the subject position created by a phantom ride film was shattered.

36. Tom Gunning, "The Cinema of Attractions: Early Film, Its Spectator and the Avant-Garde," in *Early Cinema: Space, Frame, Narrative*, edited by Thomas Elsaesser and Adam Barker (London: British Film Institute, 1990), 58–59.

In her analysis of television graphics Margaret Morse discusses the "z or depth axis move" as one of the "tropes of motion" on television. Without referring to the role of the phantom ride film, she says "the z-axis moves were developed as special effects in the cinema, where they have the advantage of allowing the viewer to identify all the more with the thrilling kinetic and visual experiences of the hero." It is significant, however, that in the context of the traditional film narrative this trope is always neutralized, "motivated." Morse continues: "The z-axis move in special effects is always recaptured for the fiction by what is essentially a reverse shot of the eye or body of the hero. Thus, these moves which threaten to burst the viewer through the line between fiction and reality are interpreted as safe lateral moves along the line of action which divides the viewer from the fiction." Margaret Morse, "Television Graphics and the Body: Words on the Move" (see note 1), 6. I am grateful for Professor Morse for providing me a copy of her manuscript.

37. Tom Gunning, "Primitive Cinema," in Elsaesser and Barker, *Early Cinema*, 101.

38. It could be claimed that the subject position constituted by a phantom ride film is much more involving than, say, the one constituted by a trick film, which "kept distance," in spite of acknowledging the spectator. Also, the diegetic world of the phantom ride film *does not* acknowledge the spectator. It that sense it already foreshadows the identification mechanisms of narrative cinema. Gunning's description of energy moving "outward towards an acknowledged spectator" brings to mind 3-D cinema, which frequently uses the idea of "throwing things at the audience" as one of its central attractions. Perhaps the most extreme example of such a

"shock attraction" is provided by Cecil Hepworth's film *How It Feels to Be Run Over* (1900). A car runs straight towards the camera, seemingly crashing on it and virtually running over the spectator.

39. Béla Balázs, *Der Geist des Films*, (1930; München, 1983), 9–10 (my translation).

40. The Imax and Omnimax films that I have seen have, almost without an exception, been strange hybrids formally. They are usually "travelogues" and "dramatized documentaries," combining traditional narrative techniques with phantom ride-like sequences, which are normally used only as highlights. In his book *Widescreen Cinema*, John Belton criticizes the theories of spectatorship in the cinema by Stephen Heath, Jean-Louis Baudry and Christian Metz for failing to consider the repositioning of the spectator that took place in the 1950s with the advent of Cinerama and other wide-screen systems. "Participation was no longer a matter of absolute distinctions between active and passive spectatorship. Widescreen cinema had created an entirely new category of participation" (Belton, *Widescreen Cinema*, 192).

41. Imax and Omnimax systems are designed, manufactured and marketed by Imax Corporation, Toronto, Canada. Imax is a motion picture projection system that uses a straight rectangular giant screen. Omnimax, its sister system, uses a dome screen. Imax premiered at Expo '70 in Osaka, Japan. The first permanent Imax theater debuted in Toronto in 1971 and the first Omnimax cinema in San Diego in 1973. The film format for both is the same: 70mm film that runs horizontally. Because of this, the individual frame is ten times larger than a conventional 35mm frame and three times bigger than a standard 70mm frame. The Imax sound, manufactured by Sonics Associates Inc., is a digital, six-channel system. As of July 1993 there were ninety-six permanent Imax or Omnimax theatres operating worldwide. (I am grateful for Imax Corporation for providing me with profuse information in the form of booklets and newspaper clippings, as well as the chance to visit the Imax research and manufacturing plant in Mississauga, Canada, November 1992.) Imax Corporation merged with Douglas Trumbull's Ridefilm Theaters/The Trumbull Company in 1994.

42. The earliest project for motion simulator entertainment utilizing motion pictures must be the British film pioneer Robert W. Paul's unrealized project from 1895, based on H. G. Wells's novel *The Time Machine* (1894). In his patent application Paul described a mechanism that "consists of a platform, or platforms, each of which contain[s] a suitable number of spectators and which may be enclosed at the sides after the spectators have taken their places, leaving a convenient opening towards which the latter face, and which is directed towards a screen upon which the views are presented. In order to create the impression of travelling, each platform may be suspended from cranks in shafts above the platform, which may be driven by an engine or other convenient source of power. These cranks may be so placed as to impart to the platform a gentle rocking motion, and may also be employed to cause the platform to travel bodily forward through a short space. Cited by

Terry Ramsaye in *A Million and One Nights: A History of the Motion Picture Through 1925* (1926; New York: Simon & Schuster, 1986), 155.

43. Raymond Fielding, "Hale's Tours: Ultrarealism in the Pre-1910 Motion Picture," in *Film Before Film*, edited by John L. Fell (Berkeley: University of California Press, 1983), 116–30. Another famous early simulator experience that used film technology was Raoul Grimoin-Sanson's *Cinéorama*, shown at the Paris Universal Exposition in 1900. The audience climbed on an huge platform designed as a simulated hot-air balloon cabin. It watched 360 degree panoramic movies shot from an actual balloon with ten motion picture cameras, placed in a circle. This attraction, which was a further development of the painted panorama, one of the popular public attractions of the nineteenth century, did not have sound or any motion aspect; it did, however, use staff in costume. *Cinéorama* was closed by the authorities after only a couple of screenings, because of bad air-conditioning and the ensuing risk of a fire.

44. The simplest ride films merely reproduce, via camera images, the roller coaster or the driving, flying, or cruising experience. Others are elaborate fantasies realized with miniatures and traditional trick photography (*Back to the Future: The Ride*, at Universal Studios theme park in Florida, by Douglas Trumbull's Berkshire Ridefilm) and increasingly with synthetic 3-D animation (Iwerks Entertainment's *Sub Oceanic Shuttle* by Ex Macchina, Showscan's *Space Race* by ILM, and *The Devil's Mine* by Little Big One).

45. Even these aspects were realized already in the turn-of-the-century spectacles. Grimoin-Sanson tells us about *Cinéorama* : "A peine un nombre suffisant de 'passagers' avait-il pris place que l'ascension commençait. Le capitaine, vêtu d'un costume bleu marine, annonçait solennellement: 'Mesdames et messieurs, nous allons partir du bassin des Tuileries. Lâchez tout!" (Raoul Grimoin-Sanson: *Le Film de ma vie*, cited in Emmanuelle Toulet, *Cinématographe, invention du siècle* [Paris: Gallimard/Réunion des musées nationaux, 1988], 141). Raymond Fielding tells us about *Hale's Tours:* "Often, the front of the theater was made to look like a railroad depot office. Tickets were taken at the door by a uniformed guard who became the conductor and operated the various controls for the car's machinery once the ride was under way." (Fielding, "Hale's Tours," 123).

46. These aspects were dealt with with an almost scientific fervor by turn-of-the-century amusement park managers. They "had to organize the production of these experiences in ways analogous to the way factory managers organized production. To maximize profits, they evaluated attractions in terms of how many patrons they could process in an hour" (Nye, *Electrifying America*, 131).

47. In early accounts of the phantom ride films, the emphasis was often on the sensory delirium instead of the "world seen through the window" aspect. This is understandable, because from a phenomenological point of view the reference point is the roller coaster rather than the train or the

streetcar, where "that shining vista of tracks that was eaten up irresistibly" was usually denied the passengers. Sometimes the virtual voyaging aspect is, however, foregrounded. *The Post-Express* (Rochester, New York) wrote on 4 October 1898: "For three minutes the spectator is permitted to view this panorama, and all is so real that he feels that he is sitting on an observation car pushed by an engine, at the rate of thirty or forty miles an hour, and, with constantly increasing delight, drinking in, with wide open eyes, one of the most fascinating scenes of the world; nature and art being harmoniously blended." Cited in George C. Pratt, *Spellbound in Darkness. A History of the Silent Film* (Greenwich, Conn.: New York Graphic Society, 1973, 21) "An observation car pushed by the engine" was sometimes used to shoot phantom ride films, but it was usually denied normal passengers.

48. See note 42.

49. About mythologizing tendencies and the concept of interactivity, see my "'It is interactive, but is it *art?*'" *Computer Graphics Visual Proceedings: Annual Conference Series, 1993*, ed. Thomas E. Linehan (New York: ACM Siggraph, 1993), 133–35.

50. Reisman, "A Brief Introduction to the Art of Flight Simulation," in *Ars Electronica 1990, Band II: Virtuelle Welten*, herausgegeben von Gottfried Hattinger et al. (Linz: Veritas Verlag, 1990), 159.

51. Ibid.

52. Margaret Morse has made a similar observation about television: "Television graphics have been called a 'real-time flight simulator,' but we are not pilots but passengers supported in thrills of motion by invisible hands" (Morse, "Television Graphics," 16).

53. Douglas Trumbull is usually credited as the key person in making this connection. Trumbull's fame was largely based on his special-effects work on the "Stargate Corridor" sequence of Stanley Kubrick's *2001: A Space Odyssey* (1968). See: Gene Youngblood, *Expanded Cinema* (New York: E. P. Dutton 1970), 151–56. In the midseventies Trumbull's Future General Corporation in conjunction with Paramount Pictures designed a prototype for a motion simulator ride called *Tour of the Universe*. It combined a film using Trumbull's Showscan system (film running at 60 fps.) and a hydraulic motion platform provided by the British company Rediffusion Motion Platforms (today Hughes Rediffusion Simulation). A *Tour of the Universe* ride based on this design was installed only much later, in 1984, at Toronto's CN Tower. This project is considered to be the forerunner for numerous later rides. It inspired, for example, the Disney-Lucasfilm collaboration, *Star Tours*, at Disneyland. Trumbull and his Berkshire Ridefilm Corporation (now Imax Ridefilm) have since designed *Back to the Future: The Ride*, which opened at MCA/Universal Studios theme park in Florida in 1991 (See: Janine Pourroy, "Through the Proscenium Arch") and the major *Secrets of the Luxor Pyramid* attraction at the Luxor Hotel, Las Vegas (1993).

54. An example of such a spectacle is *Cinéautomate* in the French

theme park Futuroscope near Poitiers. The voting is restricted to certain turning points, which are situated to take place between individual film reels. For the viewing experience it is disturbing that there are several different signs to indicate when the voting should start. The film is interrupted, the lights are turned on, and even a live hostess appears to direct the voting. (My own experiences at Futuroscope, June 1992.) A more promising audience interaction system has been designed by Loren Carpenter's Cinematrix, Inc. The audience members hold signal-emitting wands. The signals are detected by sensors in the theater and registered by computers that control a computer-generated game or other application. The system was demonstrated in the USA Siggraph 1991 and 1994, and at Ars Electronica, Linz, Austria, 1994.

55. NAMCO has recently introduced a smaller six-player version of *Galaxian* named *Theater Six*. It is meant to be installed in games arcades. In this version the players are sitting side by side facing the screen, which brings it closer to the traditional motion simulator design. (I am grateful to the NAMCO company and particularly to the general manager of the computer graphics department, Mr. Kazukuni Hiraoka, for inviting me to try *Galaxian* at Namco Wonder Eggs theme park in Tokyo and the prototype of *Theater Six* at the Namco computer graphics department's research facility in Yokohama in November 1992.) A more recent interactive simulator attraction is Werks Entertainment's *Virtual Adventures* (1993), a collaborative underwater adventure.

56. Turkle, *The Second Self*, 77–82.

57. Amusement park attractions traditionally often divide the crowd into units of two, thus reflecting the dominant social ideology based on the (heterosexual) young couple. This can still often be seen in the most thrilling rides, roller coasters, and motion simulators — the motion platform often consists of paired moving seats. These attractions give a "permission" and a motivation to grab the partner.

58. John Vince, "Commander: A Real-time Interactive Leisure Simulator," *Imagina 93: Actes, Proceedings* (Bry-sur-Marne: INA, 1993), 189–98.

59. A very curious and unfortunate element in most VR demonstrations is the necessary role of the very physical helper and guideperson (a kind of Virgil for the "Cyber-Dante"), a constant presence before, during, and after the "virtual voyage."

60. Randal Walser, "Elements of a Cyberspace Playhouse," *Virtual Reality: Theory, Practice, and Promise*, ed. Sandra K. Helsel and Judith Paris Roth (London: Meckler, 1991), 51–64.

61. See Linda Jacobson, "BattleTech's New Beachheads," *Wired* vol 1, no. 3 (July-August 1993), 36.

62. Roy Ascott, "Telenoia," lecture at the "Telecommunication and Art" symposium, Helsinki, 15 April 1993.

9 Image, Language, and Belief in Synthesis

George Legrady

> Toward noon he lay down for a nap.... On awakening, he thought
> that he saw an extraordinary mobile creature next to his face, an
> insect or mollusk which stirred in the shadow of his head. An
> almost terrifying power of life dwelt within that fragile thing. In less
> than an instant, and even before his vision could be formulated in
> thought, Zeno realized that what he was seeing was only his own
> eye reflected and enlarged by the glass, behind which the grass and
> sand formed a backing like that of a mirror.
>
> —Marguerite Yourcenar, *The Abyss*

The sixteenth-century alchemist Zeno, catching himself in the act of
seeing, was shocked by the unusual sight of his own eye mirrored by
a technology: a magnifying glass that he used to examine the plants
he collected. Zeno's startling experience parallels the complex relationship of technology and human consciousness—technology as
an extension of the human body, as a mirror of the self, as a mediation between nature and culture, as a potential discursive medium
or a tool of alienation and control.

All technologies distort. By expanding our abilities to perceive,
they simultaneously diminish us. We experience the world through
the senses and the act of seeing is one of giving meaning, taking
stock of our environment to counterbalance chaos. Technologies
that help us to see shape the way we see, and, in the end, determine
how we see. These inventions have resulted from choices framed by
cultural beliefs to arrive at a particular view of the world that represents not the totality of human experience but a view locked within
the limits of a fluctuating history. In the way that we are born into
language, we also enter an unfolding, socially defined world of

visual continuum. We integrate these conventions unquestionably, recycling them in varying degrees as a means to arrive at the new. As we consider the impact of digital technology on the production and interpretation of images, questions arise about the belief systems that are in place and their development over time.

i

Throughout Western history images have functioned to convey beliefs, becoming authoritative records by making the permanant the transitory. With the introduction of high-resolution still and motion photographic representation, images have maintained their status as the dominant mode of information exchange. Visual documentation is of major importance, for instance, in television news.

Contemporary theoretical discourse has dealt extensively with the subjectivity inherent in photographic representation. It is now generally accepted that even though the photograph represents everything in front of the camera, photography is a symbolic practice in which meaning is determined by beliefs and generated through the connotative strategies of subject selection, framing, and vantage point.

The polemic between photography and painting in the1860s may be a useful reference point regarding the impact of digital processing on the interpretation of images. Photography's mechanical mode of optically recording reflected light onto a light-sensitive surface was initially accepted as a freedom from intervention.

One could visually perceive the resulting differences between the literal mechanical recording of the camera and the coded (stylized) painted work of the same scene.[2] As a result, it exposed the inherent subjectivity in painting and forced painting to recognize its function as a distillation of an experience in perceiving instead of being the objective depiction of a scene.

Digital technology hinders this type of debate as long as the criterion for verisimilitude is based on appearances, since digital processes can simulate existing conventional media to the extent of being visually indistinguishable from them. In the process of converting analog data, such as a continuous-tone image, into digital form, a fundamental transformation takes place. Once the image is stored as numeric data in computer memory, it can be processed in unlimited ways without degradation of information or any trace of change.[2] Given the very high probability that digital filtering of one sort or another could have been used in the transmission process, prior knowledge about an image's history, its source, mode of production, and reproduction have become necessary informational components to accurately understand the full meaning of a digital image.

The media through which cultural images are processed and transmitted are influential components of the visual narratives conveyed. The technological tools of production could not exist outside of institutionalized ideological constructs, since their inventions and utility are socially determined. In digital processing, as in any other form of communication, the technological components of hardware and software are structures that impose a form onto the information they process, but these mediating structures are normally understood as transparent or "value free." In an evaluation of the function of narrative in iconography, the historian Irene J. Winter states that "one must divide the message into at least two components: the actual information conveyed, and the extralinguistic or extravisual referent that is part of the subtext. The ideological message is often built into the structure of how the message is conveyed, rather than what the message contains." In the everyday usage of a tool, as with the everyday acceptance of images and language, little thought is given to their particular ideologically determining functions. In fact, their success in naturalizing the beliefs of a given community depends on the degree to which they remain unknown as independent forms.[3]

The act of seeing in everyday life is taken as a natural event. We generally trust what we see, not questioning why we give importance to certain things and why we sometimes do not recognize visual evidence present in front of us. According to Umberto Eco, one can usually communicate only about those cultural units that a given signification system has made pertinent.[4] Moreover, competence in reading visual imagery is an acquired skill similar to the process of learning language; it is a social activity defined by the norms of a particular culture. Norman Bryson maintains that the reality experienced by human beings is always historically produced. He says it is more accurate to say that realism lies in a coincidence between a representation and that which a particular society proposes and assumes as its reality, a reality involving the complex formation of codes of behavior, law, psychology, social manners, dress, gesture, posture—all those practical norms which govern the stance of human beings toward their particular historical environment.[5]

Photography, digital processing, and social practice

In our image-saturated society, our cultural myths and beliefs are daily reinforced through the numerous photographs we come across in advertising, the news, family vacation snapshots and so forth. Photography's apparent transparency promotes a viewing experience that arouses pleasure without creating any awareness of its act of ideological constructing.[6] It is easily accepted as a window on the world rather than as a highly selective filter, placed there by a specific hand and mind. The photograph is treated so unproblematically as "real" that its grammar of discussions tends to approximate the grammar of face-to-face encounters."[7] "This is Peter Jennings" is a culturally accepted statement whether one is presenting the person or pointing at a shape on a television screen.

Photography depends on the physical world as raw referent resource inasmuch as it requires a subject in front of the camera. Its meaning is culturally defined. Practice and beliefs dictate the image maker's decisions about subject selection, framing, and the moment(s) of exposure. The viewer's understanding and responses are defined in turn by a process involving cultural knowledge that exists nowhere in codified form but remains at a tacit level.[8] As a result, optically recorded visual communication becomes a highly effective rhetorical tool and tends to persuade. Photographic images imply the potential for verification. There is a general presumption that the image must have been dependent to some extent on a real-world event. Concrete information creates belief.

Photographs and video imagery consist of minute, indeterminately arranged components such as the chemically generated grain in film and the variation of light intensities in video. While the digital photograph looks like its conventional counterpart, when examined very closely it reveals itself to be composed of discrete elements called pixels, which are assigned precise numerical values. Each pixel in the image has a determined Cartesian coordinate and a specific color-intensity value. It is this relationship of modular units with definite values that makes it totally controllable. Thus, when we speak of the digital photographic image, we are referring to a simulated photographic representation, achieved through any combination of a mechanical lens, the handheld (electronic) pencil, or filtered mathematical language.

A digital, numeral-based structure is by definition a statistical representation, and the degree of accuracy is dependent on the amount of information that can be processed within a given space and time. The greater the memory, the richer the image's degree of resolution. When the volume of statistical data surpasses the threshold of our physiological capabilities to perceive change, the illusion of total simulation is achieved. A digital image does not represent an optical trace as a photograph does, but provides a logical model of a visual experience. In other words, it describes not the phenomenon of perception but rather the physical laws that govern it, manifesting a sequence of numbers stored in computer memory. Its structure is one of language: logical procedures or algorithms through which data is orchestrated into visual form. Even though both may look the same on the surface, a digital image may be said to differ from its analog counterpart in terms of the verifiable past and the possible future. Because of its dependence on an a priori real-world referent subject, a photograph, by nature, refers to the past. The viewing experience it creates is termed by Roland Barthes the sense of "having-been-there." With the digital image, whose construction could potentially be totally fictive, one can claim at most that the event represented "could possibly be."[9]

The medium of mathematical language

Digital images simulate the real rather then represent it. They can be produced from mathematical algorithms alone and make visible, through the use of computers, concepts and physical phenomena that do not exist in material form. For instance, objects and images that are rotated on television broadcasts exist in virtual space—an environment that is totally fictional. Paul Virilio describes the digital, synthetic image as a tool for seeing things you cannot see in any other manner than by calculation.[10] This displacement of the real by simulation shifts the image's status towards a total representation of concepts. One first conceptualizes one's intentions, then proceeds to realize the imagined through programming.

Computers, which are symbol-manipulating machines, effect a radical rupture with conventional approaches to image making. For artists who create through programming, logical language mediates between intention and the resultant artwork by a process similar to the ways composers create through musical notation. The working method is divorced from sensory experience in that the artist's work becomes one of orchestrating symbolic order through code writing rather than through the physical interaction between material (such as paint) and the senses .[11] It forces the artist to translate events from the real world into complex sequences of rule-based decisions and to previsualize in so precise a manner that even what seems to be chance needs to be determined and coded. Once these logical sequences and commands are stored in memory, any aesthetic and/or logical errors can be reformulated by simply changing the code because computers provide the ability to retrace and undo one's steps.

Some philosophical questions

The processing of digital information depends not on generational reproduction, which would imply data loss, but on the transference of a sequence of numbers by which information can be duplicated ad infinitum. Each individual element of a digital image is readily accessible, and the ability to copy it easily has forced a reevaluation of what constitutes ownership and authorship. For instance, is a change of one pixel in a high-resolution digital image a significant alteration to authorship? In this age of information exchange, where a shift in context results in a shift in meaning, the issue would seem to be one of intention and positioning. Sociologists have voiced concerns about the potential misuse of digital technology in the news media, pointing out that "those who have access to digital image-processing systems have the capacity to alter, reconstruct, or create imagery reflective of the real world that might be passed off as representing accurate data."[12]

While photographs have from the start been doctored or their meaning changed through standard photographic strategies of vantage point, framing, cropping, and retouching, the digital image betrays no surface evidence of alteration. One must first suspect that the image is less than accurate; then one needs a computer with the right program to detect the changes.

ii

The focus of my artistic work in photography during the past fourteen years can be summarized as an investigation of the cultural and syntactical conventions by which photographic images are structured to convey meaning.

Under the Spreading Chestnut Tree, 1984 (see fig. 9.1), examines the coding conventions of corporate iconography. The compositions and body language of group poses in the photographic portraits of the 1980 E. F. Hutton annual report were reconstructed in the tradition of the *nature morte*. The figures were executed to look like wood veneer, a material commonly associated with the corporate body through its use in the architectural and design finishes of corporate boardrooms. These constructions were then photographed by traditional means and printed on metallic gold and silver paper.

I began working with computer programming in 1981, realizing at that time that aesthetic decision-making procedures could be formulated in terms of a sequence of logical conditional statements not unlike rules of language. This structured approach has precedents in the sequential and modular artworks of Sol Lewitt and in the syllogistic propositions of Lawrence Weiner, Doug Huebler, Joseph Kosuth and others associated with the conceptual art movement.[13] The fact that the construction and manipulation of photographic images could take place on a computer screen rather than in front of a camera lens has made computer work an effective alternative.

News Beirut, 1987 (see fig. 9.2), an image from the first series, considers the discursive function of textual labeling in television news imagery. Frames from the news were digitized and segments that contained text were isolated and used to "paint in" the whole image area in a random fashion. These labeling texts—names of cities where the particular news event took place—function in television broadcasts to contextualize images. They impose a meaning that may not necessarily pertain to the original intent of the image. Barthes calls this a strategy of anchorage: "The caption helps me to choose the correct level of perception . . . focusing my understanding. The anchorage is ideological. It remote controls the viewer toward a meaning chosen in advance.[14] By erasing and covering the image with fragments of the text, the text becomes the aesthetic experience, still maintaining a connotative load. We project onto the new image a preconceived idea of what that text refers to. Our perceptions about the world we live in are reinforced by the conventions of representation that inundate us daily, and television's particular mode of defining reality seems to be a dominant conditioning force within the culture. Television becomes an unlimited, real-time image bank when it is linked to an image-processing computer. Appropriating images from this data bank is a means to examine and comment on television's highly ritualized syntax.

"Under The Spreading Chestnut Tree
I sold you and you sold me" -

Fig. 9.1. Studies for Monuments.

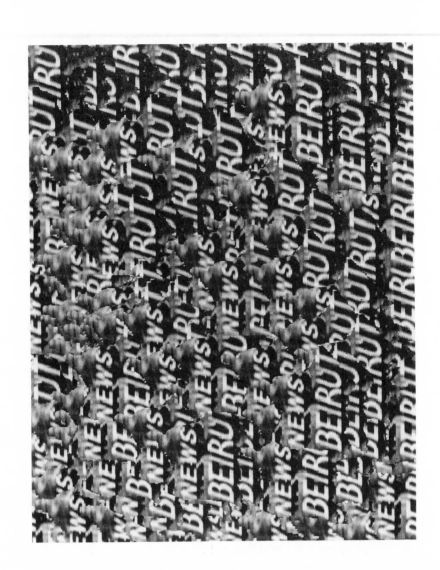

Fig. 9.2. News Beirut

A conceptual starting point for investigating the potential of image-processing software as an arena for conceptual and aesthetic discourse is Claude Shannon's *Information Theory,* which has been labeled as "mathematics turned into philosophy." My approach has been to reverse that sequence, commenting on the semantic discrepancies of information theory, specifically its definitions of language, signal, and noise. (Noise in information theory is defined as random errors within a signal, or unstructured information, distinguishable from signal that is ordered information.) Whereas engineers have invested much energy in filtering out noise from signals to purify communication, my programming activities aim to achieve the opposite; they incorporate into images an order determined through noise and chance. The program *Xerox* (see fig. 9.3) replaces the "inessential" components of an image with a noise pattern, exemplifying one of information theory's dictates: that there is a greater than 50 percent redundancy in language in the form of sounds or letters that are not strictly necessary to convey the message. The resultant image looks as if it had been xeroxed, with over 50 percent of the pixels reduced to black. The actual percentage of "value-free" information (85 percent black in the work illustrated) is calculated at the end of the process.

In *Moral Stories* (see fig. 9.4) a program titled *Smudge* removes image sharpness and photographic depth by a random process of blurring image areas over time. The end result, which resembles water spilled on an ink drawing, looks as if it were hand-painted. When the process is prolonged, it results in the annihilation of the image into a total blur.

Although information theory has revolutionized our culture by demonstrating that information is a quantifiable entity that can be calculated and controlled, thereby providing the theoretical basis for the development of new technologies and modes of information processing, it has also semantically shortchanged our understanding of the value of things communicated. In the bipolar reduction to either signal or noise, the meaning of things—from moral injunctions, philosophical treatises, and love poems to sales messages and parking tickets—all come to be leveled as signal and so too their value. Theodore Roszak comments: "Thanks to the high success of Information Theory, we live in a time of blinding speed; but what people have to say to one another by way of technology shows no comparable development."[15]

A recent project titled *Between East & West* (see fig. 9.5) brings

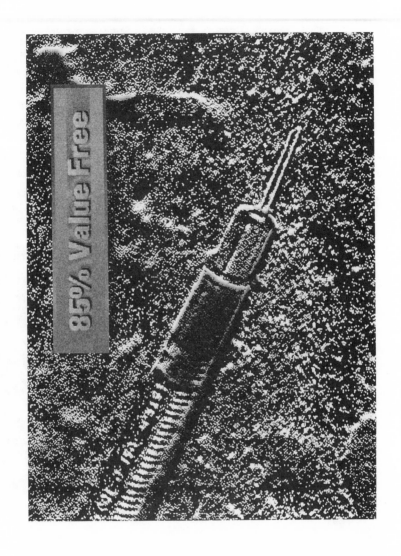

Fig. 9.3. 85% Value Free.

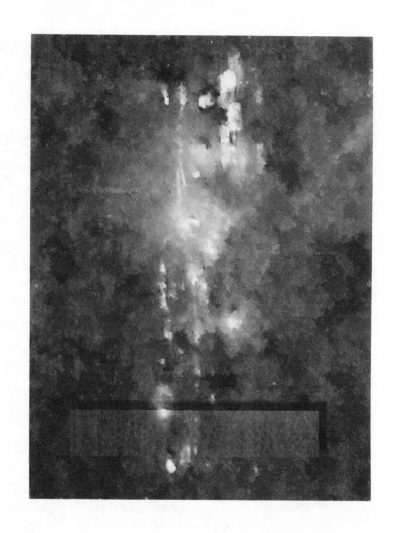

Fig. 9.4. Moral Stories.

together the logistics of software development within a context that is both personal and political. It involves a working dialogue with a scientist from Hungary, where I was born (and which I left in 1956 during a time of political crisis). The project began with an exchange of information: I sent my colleague a mathematical equation to be turned into computer code, a program that would produce images.[16]

After generating a series of random numbers, the equation assigns the average of a "neighborhood" (a cluster of visually adjacent units) of values to each pixel, thereby arriving at a balance between chaos and order. This algorithmic process, derived from image-processing filters, is used to sharpen photographic images. It has particular application in specialized fields where photographic recording provides data documentation, such as the space program, surveillance monitoring, and recently art conservation.[17] Similar digital filters have also been employed to enhance features of the Shroud of Turin, sometimes described as the "first photographic phenomenon in history."

For some time, I had been aware that dialogue in various professional fields had been taking place between the West and the East prior to the recent political changes. Scientists and specialists were communicating on a regular basis, sharing their knowledge and exchanging information. This reality seemed to be in sharp contrast with the official political positions of both sides.

My intention in reenacting this informational exchange had been to make visible the unspoken relationships and to bring attention to the influence of Central European intellectual ideas in Western thought, something that has largely been ignored within the culture at large.

I retrieved the program on a visit to Budapest in August 1989 and expanded it in California to implement color values. These image-enhancement techniques are usually applied by first digitizing images and then filtering them with the algorithmic functions to remove noise and highlight detail. In *East & West* I used the functions instead to generate abstract noise patterns directly from the computer program without employing a referent photograph in the process.

In the center of each textured image was placed a long rectangular panel that looks like a metallic nameplate. Constructed in computer memory through software, it was programmed to have the reflecting properties of chrome, and on it images from a video I made in Budapest were "projected" mathematically.[18] The viewer would

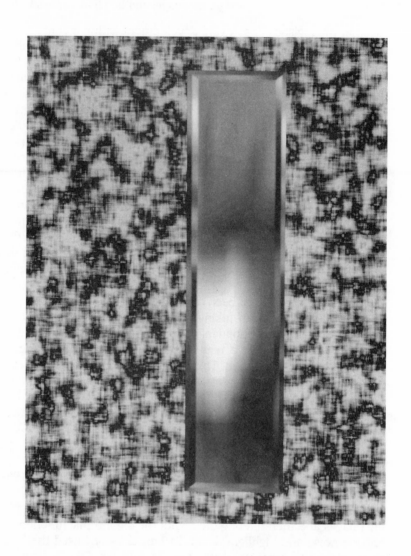

Fig. 9.5. East and West.

not be able to decipher what the plates reflected, but because of our general familiarity with the photographic image, the blurred shapes do read as photographic and therefore maintain the authority associated with photographic representation.

The impetus for this work came out of considering the belief structures we bring to the reading of images. Works of art, like other signs, are initially empty but gain their meaning within a historical context mediated by current social belief systems. In the case of the *East & West* project, where the only existing element in the image is the pattern created by the filter (minus the photograph), the works become similar to the skeletal remains of a stream of punctuation marks after words have been emptied out of a sentence.

In his description of bricolage, Claude Lévi-Strauss makes reference to the artist as someone who constructs through craftsmanship a material object, a symbolic structure that is also an object of knowledge.[19] The act of craftmanship in my work of the last few years has been situated in the programming phase, i.e., the writing of computer code, this being the arena where the relationship of language to image, and the impact of technology on cultural vision, is dealt with. The weight of this activity remains largely invisible, resulting in images that function as outward manifestations of the locus of the work: the software itself. These images serve as residual physical indices to an event that has taken place.

With computer technology, a new twist is introduced to our acceptance of visual evidence: photographic representation can be fabricated through mathematical processing. Computer imaging can simulate and generate any type of imagery or "realities" one chooses. The ideological factor in the digital photograph is exponentionally increased, since the image promotes a form of meaning and value while appearing to merely represent the real.

In my computer-generated works as in my investigations of photography, the intention is to engage the viewer in considering the discrepancy inherent in an image that looks natural on the surface but is in fact mediated, and therefore a challenge to conventional notions of belief in visual representation.

Notes

1. "From this day, painting is dead" is what the French painter Paul DelaRoche reportedly said in 1839 when confronted with photography for the first time. See Nancy Roth's "Art's New Address" in *The Techno/Logical*

Imagination: Machines in the Garden of Art (Minneapolis: Intermedia Arts Minnesota, 1989), 6.

2. Paintings and drawings reproduce only the essential elements determined by the artist. In fact, the drawing process by which an image is created is an act of constituting the significant from the insignificant. Rodin argued that "It is the artist who is truthful and the camera that lies because a photograph is a mechanical representation frozen in time. The photograph is false because in realit   y time does not stop. If the artist can succeed in representing the fluidity of motion in a painting, his [or her] work is much more original than the scientific [photographic] image in which time is abruptly suspended." Paul Virilio, *La Machine de Vision* (Paris: Editions Galilee, 1988), 14–15.

3. Irene J. Winter, "After the Battle is Over: The Stele of the Vultures and the Beginning of Historical Narrative in the Art of the Ancient Near East," in *Studies in the History of Art* (Washington: National Gallery of Art, 1985), 16:28.

4. Norman Bryson, *Vision and Painting* (New Haven: Yale University Press, 1983), 14.

5. Umberto Eco, "How Culture Conditions the Colours We See," in *On Signs* (Baltimore: Johns Hopkins University Press, 1985), 163.

6. Norman Bryson, *Vision and Painting*, 13.

7. Linda Hutcheson, *The Politics of Postmodernism* (London: Routledge, 1989), 123.

8. Michael Shapiro, "The Political Rhetoric of Photography," delivered at the 82nd Annual Meeting of the American Political Science Association, Washington, D.C., 28–31 August 1986.

9. Norman Bryson, *Vision and Painting*, 1.

10. Edmond Couchot, "La Synthèse Numérique de l'Image," in *Traverses/26* (Paris: Centre Georges Pompidou, 1983), 60.

11. From an interview published in "The Work of Art in the Electronic Age," *Block 14* (London: Autumn, 1988), 5. Virilio gives as an example the works of the mathematician Netgrin, whose computer programs pictured Moebius rings turning.

12. Edmond Couchot, "La Synthèse Numérique de l'Image," 58–62.

13. Howard Bossen, "Zone 5, Photojournalism, Ethics and the Electronic Age," *Studies in Visual Communication* (University of Pennsylvania) 11, no. 3 (Summer 1985).

14. "When an artist uses a conceptual form of art it means that all the planning and decisions are made before and the execution is a perfunctory affair. . . .This kind of art is not theoretical or illustrative of theories; it is intuitive, it is involved with all types of mental processes." See Sol Lewitt, *L'Art conceptuel, une perspective* (Paris: Musée d'Art Moderne de la Ville de Paris, 1989), 199.

15. Roland Barthes, "The Rhetoric of the Image," in *Image-Music-Text* (Glasgow: Fontana Collins, 1977), 39.

16. Theodore Roszak, *The Cult of Information* (New York: Patheon Books, 1986), 16.

17. The equation, which I had found in an article titled "From Noise Comes Beauty," was published in the March 1988 issue of *Computer Graphics World* .

18. John F. Asmus, "Digital Image Processing in Art Conservation," *BYTE* 12, no. 3 (1987): 151.

On 18 September 1988 in Budapest I videotaped a public demonstration of about eighty thousand marchers who were protesting the ecologically unsound Nagymaros/Danube hydroelectric works. The project was engineered by the Soviet Union, which contracted with Austrian firms for its construction on Hungarian and Czechoslovak territories. Because of the participation of the Austrian Green Party, this was the first demonstration to be tolerated by the officials in Socialist Hungary.

19. Claude Lévi-Strauss, *The Savage Mind* (Chicago: University of Chicago, 1966), 22.

10 Track Organology

Douglas Kahn

The weight of music

The division between sound and musical sound is negotiated and policed in terms of a traditionally established axis irrelevant to most music. For twentieth-century Western art music theory, however, it is relevant. And for theoretically inspired music impinging upon notions of worldly sound as discursive foil and actual material—music generated in response to changing social conditions of aurality—the implications of this dividing line are as crucial as they are unacknowledged. Music's dominance gained momentum from its complacent valorization as the *sine qua non* of the arts of sound. Its establishment as such has served to stifle the other arts of sound: the blinded ones, the multisensory ones, and the daily experience of aurality in general. Music has, in turn, ironically, weighed upon itself through its imagined mission to model proliferation, chart sublimity, and provide a Dionysian rebuff to constraint. This goal is itself constraining and constrained.

Musical ideas and analogies are constantly employed throughout the nonmusical arts, and the closer their proximity to sound, the more powerful they become as productive aids, circumventions, or impediments. Within the period of modernism and the avant-garde, when many present-day assumptions were generated, music was valued as a model of artistic ambitions for self–containment. Having already thus arrived at what the other arts sought, music failed to question its own representational operations, even though acoustic and electric recording were to offer other possibilities. Thus secured,

musical autoreferentiality did violence to a system of aural signification, whereby the associative characteristics of sounds—their attendant social and imaginative domains—were reduced, trivialized, or
eradicated.

A reading/listening of music from the time of Luigi Russolo's formal introduction of noise in 1913 to John Cage's musically emancipatory postwar endgame demonstrates that the exchange across
these bounds has been performed strategically for the rejuvenation of
musical practice by incorporating ever-expanding realms of hitherto
extramusical sound into the province of music. Russolo, however,
contradicted his profession of a potentially autonomous "art of
noises" in his writings, his compositional and performance practice,
and in the design of his instruments; he diminished a complete play
of the aural signification of worldly sounds to their timbral signatures
in order to engineer "a great renovation of music." From that point
on, Western art music has been consistent in its maintenance of a
unity for music. Varèse battled against noise and imitation to situate
his own "liberation of sound" more securely within the conservative
institutions of Western art music. Stockhausen valorized electronic
sounds over "all instrumental or other auditive associations [, which]
divert the listener's comprehension from the self-evidence of the
sound-world presented to him because he thinks of bells, organs,
birds or faucets."[1] Pierre Schaeffer similarly safeguarded *musique
concrète*, beginning no less than with his first work *Étude aux chemins
de fer* and continuing until recently, when he said:

> You have two sources for sounds: noises, which always
> tell you something—a door cracking, a dog barking, the
> thunder, the storm; and then you have instruments.
> An instrument tells you, la-la-la-la (sings a scale). Music
> has to find a passage between noises and instruments.
> It has to escape. It has to find a compromise and an eva-
> sion at the same time; something that would not be
> dramatic because that has no interest to us, but some-
> thing that would be more interesting than sounds like
> Do-Re-Mi-Fa. . . .[2]

The intrinsic despair of "compromise and evasion" found quick
and sad fruition even more recently in an interview in which Schaeffer dismissed his entire career as having been a futile venture; he
returned to an extremely conservative notion that no music was possible outside of conventional musical sounds. "It took me forty years

to conclude that nothing is possible outside DoReMi . . . ."[3] (When I told Cage of Schaeffer's lament, he replied, "He should have kept going up the scale.") In 1963 the famed musicologist H. H. Stuckenschmidt framed *musique concrète* in terms of feminized mystery of music:

> [The phenomenal power of *musique concrète*] lies in its capacity to change any tone, sound, or noise so that the initial form is no longer recognizable. It is a technique of metamorphosis with results no less astonishing than the ancient metamorphoses of mythology described by Ovid, such as the transformation of a nymph into a laurel tree.[4]

Such negotiation is widespread. It really doesn't matter whether it is Pierre Boulez, Murray Schafer, Trevor Wishart, Chris Cutler, Evan Eisenberg, Marvin Minsky, Throbbing Gristle, Peter Kivy, or Jean-Jacques Nattiez. While its terms may be indispensable in policing musical boundaries, the strategies of proliferation, rhetorical play, and semiotic mobility made familiar through certain theories of postmodernism—let alone workaday attitudes in many of the arts and the daily experience of culture—demand their replacement. It need not occur through any heroics of transgression or reasoned problematization; just to proceed while ignoring the mandates of musicalization would accomplish the same thing. And to call for a "sound art" consisting of what music has historically excluded would simply repeat the same demarcative procedures. But the weight of music has failed to generate even this complaint. One would, of course, expect philosophical delectations à la Roger Scruton to balk at the quotations of Charles Ives, or Claude Lévi-Strauss to pull up short at *musique concrète*. It is a bit surprising to find how rehearsed a Luddite Jacques Attali is in his book *Noise* as he makes the phonograph the wicked steam engine of the undesirable epoch of "repetition" and banishes it from artistic technologies bearing a premonition of the desirable epoch of "composition." It is more ironic to find how pedestrian the champions of deterritorialization—Deleuze and Guattari—are when they walk the line. After celebrating Varèse's composition as the exemplar of a musical machine, "a sound machine (not a machine for reproducing sounds), which molecularizes and atomizes, ionizes sound matter and harnesses a cosmic energy,"[5] and after suggesting the electronic synthesizer might extend to philosophy "like a thought synthesizer functioning to make thought travel, make it mobile, make it a force of the Cosmos (in the same way as one makes sound travel),"[6] they flash the inevitable warning: "Sometimes one overdoes it. . . ."

> The claim is that one is opening music to all events, all irruptions, but one ends up reproducing a scrambling that prevents any event from happening. All one has left is a resonance chamber well on the way to forming a black hole. A material that is too rich remains too "territorialized": on noise sources, on the nature of the objects. . . . (this even applies to Cage's prepared piano).[7]

Of course, the name of Cage leaps instinctually to the lips of most postmodern theorists when required to list a musical name (acid test: do they ever name a tune?) to the patent roster of painters, poets, novelists, theorists, architects, and the like. But Cage's endgame does not depart from Russolo's inaugural strategy for musical rejuvenation. The "lateness" of Cage's modernism is in direct relation to the conservatism of Western art music. He performed the last possible modernist renovation of Western art music and thereby "filled music up." After him there is no dividing line between musical sound and ordinary sound because all sound becomes music. Also, there need not be artistic intention nor any other act of human volition except the willingness to attune to aural phenomena for music to exist. This collapse of sound into a problematic of musical sound betrays an un–Cagean act of imposition at the very center of his philosophy. By saying that sounds not intrinsically human should be thought of as music, he contradicts his anti-anthropomorphism. His suppression of anthropomorphism collides with the politics of ecology, which must begin with an assumption of both the social incursion into nature and the historical determination of the very idea of nature. Cage's subscription to Eastern philosophies—which were constituted prior to the effective capacity for domination of nature, let alone total global ruin—betrays his notion of an idealized separation of nature and society. He promotes an odd transcendence into an already reduced everyday through musical means that entail something of an urban asceticism. Individuals lack or must deny or purge themselves of subjectivity, sociality, and historical situation in order to become empty vessels, receptive of the surround sound as natural and pure as the air they breathe. In fact, it is only because he understands music to be a natural element of the world that his philosophy has not become self-evident; only in this way can his claims for "all sound" run counter to an ecology of aural signification that includes sociality.

The nature of sound

The naturalizing consequences of avant-garde musicalization have run counter to the increasing sociality of sound within the century of sound—the maturation of phonography and telephony, microphony, amplification, sound film, the incidence of radio, television, synthesis, acoustical engineering, virtuality, etc.—where technologies proper are both marked by and the markers of complex relationships among social practices. The early break-up of naturalization began with the rise of communications technologies in the nineteenth century. There arose the technical capacities to see visual sound and visual speech; that began to bring all sound into the primacy, if not conceit, of the text, and to transport over great distances the movements of the finger and the voice. Phonography played a crucial role, for with it came the unique ability to return a person's own voice to his or her own ears, whereas previously the hearing of one's voice was limited to resonance along the throat and on up through the head.[8] The only incidence of a union between audition and utterance, perhaps the most common privatized act performed in the company of others, this self-same voice, a unique sensory organ of centrifugal capacity, was "deboned" by being wrenched from the throat and put into (phonographic) inscription like other auto-affection. This served to represent and technologically manifest the severance of speech from the speaker, the voice from the body, the voice from the soul (especially Bouillaud's and Broca's discovery of a speech center far from of the Cartesian pineal gland) and the voice from the literary voice. The mix of utterance and audition moved from experience to representation, a representation bereft of the resonating chamber of the skull or the reflective landscapes of the echo; but it could move back toward experience, simulating it, in moments of dislocation, composition, relocation, dispersal, and so forth. However, at the turn of the century the mix and mobility ultimately remained fixed in systems of mechanics, scientism, natural philosophy, misanthropies, metaphysics of presence, spiritualism, *Gesamtkunstwerk*, synaesthesia, etc.

The twentieth century of perception actually got underway, according to Henri Lefebvre, with a decline and breakdown of referentials around the years 1905–10.[9] The importance of referentiality did not decrease. Because it was problematized it became more of a concern; from the minute machinations of the sign (this was circa Saussure) to grand cohesions, it suffered its first trenchant critiques and began its desperate celebrations. A contributing factor and consequence of this breakdown was a growth in the complexity of the senses—not a common sense of coming together but an articulation of senses within complex configurations, with listening among them. Ears had not suddenly grown prehensile, but the interpretation of what was listened to and listened for had become increasingly social, cognitive, and self-conscious; perception grew a brain. Furthermore,

> It is not only that the complexity of our senses and of the information they impart has increased; the sense of hearing has acquired a greater aptitude for interpreting visual perceptions and the sense of sight for interpreting auditive ones, so that they signify each other reciprocally. The senses are more highly educated and their theoretical ability has increased; they are becoming "theoreticians"; by discarding immediacy they introduce mediation, and abstraction combines with immediacy to become "concrete." Thus objects, in practice, become signs, and signs objects; and a "second nature" takes the place of the first, the initial layer of perceptible reality.[10]

Within the avant-garde beginning around this time, sound began to be consistently conceived in nonmusical and nonsynaesthetic ways, relating instead in a new way to graphic, textual, spatial, spatial/static, conceptual, and corporeal forms. Important in this respect were Roussel's novels, Duchamp's ideas for conceptual sound, Marinetti's documentary onomatopoeia, several of Apollinaire's writings, the French surrealists' approach to sound and their antipathy to Western art music, and so forth. Some ambitions were keyed to actual phonographic realization: Dziga Vertov's aspirations to develop stenographic audio montage within his Laboratory of Hearing; Moholy-Nagy's plans for a phonographic alphabet of all sounds, his lost drawn-sound film *The Sound of ABC*, and the drawn-sound films of others; certain *Hörspiele* during the Weimar period; and Grigori Alexandrov's direction (debatably in collaboration with Eisenstein) of the ill-fated film *Romance sentimentale*. These ambitions remained isolated and never advanced into anything resembling a practice. Technologically, the greatest promise, whether used in film or radio, resided with optical sound film technology because of its plasticity and its graphic overlap with writing. During the mid-1930s, however, there were more debates about why this promise was never realized than actual attempts at realization.

Starting in the latter half of the 1920s, however, radio and the sound film did change sound in two major ways. They introduced spatial representation and modulation among the auricular and ventricular chambers of minds, bodies, and environments and they introduced on a social scale a pervasive, detailed, and atomized encoding. For the first time, a diapason of worldly sound encompassing and generated by all of its visual, literary, environmental, gestural, and affective context could be displaced, presented, and represented. Worldly sound became worldly. The nature of sound was less natural; the realm of sound expanded and the number of sounds increased, confirming Lefebvre's claim that "The senses are more highly educated. . . ." By the 1950s when, for instance, Cage's influence was beginning to be registered, television was introduced and there had been more than two very active decades where cinema and radio bellowed, often in a mutually parasitic manner. Sound began to be sedimented with multiple allusions and meanings. Music itself began to be inflected with code, even if it was just the code of a famed ephemerality. In a century during which the nature of sound had increasingly become a sociality of sound, the goal of Cage's art, "to imitate nature in the manner of her operation," has become beleaguered and Adorno's axiom that "music rescues name as pure sound—but at the cost of severing it from things" has become wistful several times over.[11]

Social instrumentality

Everyone has already been tutored in the culture of recording, of code, and of space, but few have taken up their instruments. Recent appropriative strategies within Western art music at least acknowledge the phonographic sociality of musical sound, including that which was once noise (following the lead of novelty music, cartoon music/fx, Spike Jones, and others) and have incorporated it on an elemental level. Western music has long covered and quoted other music but this has relied upon appropriations at least as long as a melodic fragment, in which ostensibly neutral elements are organized to invoke a vernacular moment. Now, however, single sounds—say a twangy guitar à la the Ventures, Duane Eddy, Ennio Morricone, spaghetti westerns, Clint Eastwood films, John Zorn arrangements, etc.—have moved from the organizational to the elemental. But no one, to my knowledge, yet composes musically in an ambience of semiosis within which, among other possibilities, the vertical organization of encoded elements strains at the coherence of a passage by way of associative irregularities, chains, and din in the way formerly reserved for dissonance. Nor do I know of anyone composing rhetorically with spatiality: chamber music.

All this would still remain comfortably within the proscribed bounds of music. Composition could go much further once the demarcation was ignored. From the graphic, textual, spatial, conceptual, and corporeal registers of sound, combinatory possibilities suggest the development of numerous transformative rhetorics, whether blinded or with the operations of other perceptions and faculties. To pose a technical example: how could one conceive of a mobility of the voice from a location amid sound teased out of noise by signal and then sustained at a fevered pitch in text with three-part harmony and bleeding off to a space in the body that is racked and choked in puns, and ribbed in allegories, overtones and allusions of choking, and so on. What will be required are notions based on a materiality of sound, beginning with the idea that the ambient medium of sound is not merely air. All the absorption, refraction, reflection, inflection, bifurcation, multitracking, mixing, bodies, voices, writings, spaces, places, noises, communication, and information, all inscriptive, transmissional, dislocative, migratory and reconfigurative strategies of the reproduction and necrosis you've come to expect—these are not merely air.

Instruments are currently pitched phonographically for composition, writing, and accumulation, not for performance, speech, and improvisation. They are laggardly and methodical like a pen, not fast and first draft like a tongue. Writing condenses through the action of the writer's repeated listenings to the artwork-in-formation prior to public audition; a combined listening and utterance is thus stacked amid a detached interlocution. A technical sense of writing has been facilitated by the increased availability of digital audio-recording workstations[12] capable of providing a writing with sound or, rather, a "word processing" with sound. Workstations present a graphic representation alluding to the alphabet of all audible sounds entertained by technologists in the late nineteenth century and by avant-gardists beginning around the 1920s. Workstations can cut-and-paste at subperceptual durations and thereby simulate signifiers, pivot, branch out, detour and flesh out. They can also govern

tedium like any other form of recording. Unlike the musical orientation of samplers, artistic conventions and delimitations have not
been designed into workstations to such a pronounced degree.
Nothing mandates sequencing of reduced units, and conditions are
more conducive to admixture, stretch, continua and transformation
(an imminent art of segue).

Such compositional latitude results from the conflicting industrial exigencies of film/video and music (post-dub and mastering)
being designed into the technology, a conflict that makes it much
easier to defeat conventional protocols. For instance, although subperceptual editing is designed for glitch control, it can be redirected
toward constructing sounds/words from the inside out and toward
semanticizing glitches. Likewise, although macro manipulation at
textual levels is designed to expedite production, it can be redirected
toward intensification. However, idealized efforts to defeat the technology necessarily leave scars; the original never exists but is always
a signal (despite the fact that the terms one hears are either synthesis or recording, either complete artifice or lack of it, but never simulation). Workstations mimic synthesis because the cut-and-paste
editing occurs at such a minute level that it is transformed into a
generative operation independent of its source. The charade is displayed when an elastic independence from the source is amplified
and results in the emblem of the technology: electronic grate and
sheen. There can be no writing from scratch.

The source is always generated with its microphones posed,
spaces modulated, and networks played back, already marked.
Composing with and through it composites code upon code, including codes that can distract and otherwise interfere. The code of the
technology can itself be easily shielded and, although this is what
most people are offered, it can occur in a spirit of masquerade. The
primary dependence upon recorded sources—requiring a working
mode of interpolation that functions better the greater quantity of
material at hand—presents certain limitations in certain situations,
in which the internal logic of an artwork requires material nowhere
at hand. But such limitations are tempered within the daily din of a
society in which recording overflows from instant replays and
archives. The next generation of technology will begin to break free
from such accumulation through analysis and resynthesis, with
capabilities for subtle inflections and gestures, and sophistication
will be gauged by how small a sample is needed to elicit a simulation
of potentially infinite articulation.

The compositional process can begin with the capability to join sonic and phonic events at the level of the signifier and move to and from larger events and to fields between and among them. To date, however, concentration on the auditive signifier has been contained by the urge to anchor an event in physicality, technicism, in utterance and presence, in asocial tropes of nature, in a modeling of events outside of it, and, when it comes to composition with sound conceived at a minute level, in music. Yet the signifier is already somewhere else. It signifies before it exists in its own right. Therefore, it is never an anchor but rather something continually in transit, dispersing movement into other areas.[13] This dispersal could be the figure of echo as allusion, echo as decay into resonance, an allusion to noise; or, it can be modeled on coarticulation, a phonological term for a meshing of adjacent phonemes (especially vowels, glides, nasals, and laterals) such that it becomes extremely difficult, if not impossible, to describe when one ends and the other begins. They are cast in anticipation and recursion, not vertically like simultaneity, although new harmonies and counterpoints could be built vertically. The greatest benefit is the increased probability of encountering "unspoken" nascent or moribund states[14] and the capacity to extend procedures to the coarticulations of ideology. Ideological voices themselves can be ventriloquized, as can any voice, given a proper supply. This paradigmatic practice of generating uncharacteristic candor or untypical intensity is afforded by the ambiguity often attendant upon sound. As site of redirection, amplification, and ambiguation, then, one could explore intricate transitions. There would be certain expectations for the existence of a median between two sounds, including a vocal median between two people, whereas in reality the characteristics would be entirely arbitrary. The gradient between them would provide an occasion for a trail that would always be off-track.

But this is all composition; workstations are still modeled upon the truncation of the desktop, not the full-bodied stage. The instruments are not pitched to speaking and performance. Digital sampling has been generated almost entirely within a framework of music and thus music is burned into its design. Certain limitations can be defeated, but with undue effort for the result. But how would another type of digital recording-based instrument be constructed? An entirely new concept of instrument could, beginning with the simple question, Where and what is the instrument? The sound of a musical instrument is thought to be contained by the instrument itself; the sound of a violin may be directly traced to action upon the physical materials and mechanics of the violin. Recorded sound or radiophonic sound cannot be traced in the same manner but must be splayed and played across locations. Instruments, therefore, are to be constructed as much at the constellated semiotic dislocations invoked by the sound as at the immediate physical site of physiological contact by the performer. This holds true as well for the new generation of "virtual" musical instruments that are played, like a working air guitar, at a similarly fixed locus of body and instrument and with no displacements transforming the materiality of the sound itself. Instruments constructed in and with the medium of semiosis are exceedingly malleable and transformative; they can "fold back" upon themselves like a Klein bottle by incorporating the presumed integrity of the performance itself into a rhetoric constructed dislocatively; they can dissolve any lingering distinctions among instrument, performance, and composition; and they are theoretically infinite or, rather, bound to the innumerable tactics of culture.

The biggest challenge becomes to name the instrument, which may be as delimiting as the name of your best friend, your own name, or that of an encyclopedia or an epoch. Naming cannot be equated with the simple metonymic procedures of sampling, quotation, and appropriation. Metonyms would of course play a large part, not as reductive markers that organize and silence what they exclude, but in propagation as waystations dispersing attention to the elements of what was, could have been, or could never have been excluded, or even as markers of formations constructed within the performance itself. It should be remembered, however, that some very simple musical instruments require years of intense study to master in performance and that instrument building itself can be a extremely meticulous practice; the expediencies usually associated with digital electronics should not mask the possibility of a similarly rigorous practice for this new class of instruments.

The physical attributes of the instrument should be built with aspects overlapping and leading past the writing-oriented model of the digital workstation (perhaps by shorthand?) and the intervalic segmentation of musical samplers should be extended to designs based upon a variety of fluid spaces and on the recursive and "fuzzy" segmentation of a general grammar, or of elements within a constituted rhetoric. It is obvious that the two general areas of construction, in semiosis and physical electronics, would be entirely interdependent. Both aspects of construction are unorthodox and unfamiliar and require equally comprehensive attention; however, the former should be privileged, i.e., the instrument should be named before it is built, not only to hold in check the technicism that plagues all types of design but, more substantively, because it would be presumptuous to build a general physical instrument without it in turn putting undue restrictions upon the field of potential instruments.

The technological area of virtual reality promises a hospitable topos for these types of considerations because of the way spectatorial systems of representation can be at once sensorially coordinated, completed, and then confounded by experiential modes of activity. Composition and performance will have extensive transformative capacity over all elements of the sensorium, including the venue and the corporeality of everyone "present." However, it must be emphasized that the instruments described in this essay are not dependent upon any "new technology" in the physical electronic sense, just in its design, and that there is no guarantee whatsoever that virtual reality will not repeat one more time the inhibitive precepts of modernism, musicalization, and musicalized postmodernism.

Notes

1. Karlheinz Stockhausen, "Electronic and instrumental music," *Die Reihe* (1961): 56–57.

2. John Diliberto, "Pierre Schaeffer and Pierre Henry: Pioneers in Sampling," *Electronic Musician*, December 1986, 56.

3. Interview by Tim Hodgkinson, *Re Records Quarterly Magazine* 2, no. 1 (March 1987): 5. The responses to Schaeffer's interview throughout the magazine fail because they ultimately share the same source that produced his lament.

4. H. H. Stuckenschmidt, "Contemporary Techniques in Music," *Musical Quarterly*, January 1963, 14.

5. Gilles Deleuze and Félix Guattari, *A Thousand Plateaus* (Minneapolis: University of Minnesota Press, 1987), 343.

6. Ibid.

7. Ibid., 344.

8. For more on the deboned voice, please see my "Acoustic Sculpture, Deboned Voices," *Public* 4, no. 5 (1991): 22–34 and "Death in Light of the Phonograph: Raymond Roussel's *Locus Solus*," in *Wireless Imagination*, ed. Douglas Kahn and Gregory Whitehead (Cambridge: MIT Press, 1992), 69–103.

9. Henri Lefebvre, *Everyday Life in the Modern World* (New Brunswick, N. J.: Transaction Books, 1984), 111–14. "A hundred years ago words and sentences in a social context were based on reliable referentials that were linked together, being cohesive if not logically coherent, without however constituting a single system formulated as such. These referentials had a logical or commonsensical unity derived from material perception (euclidean three-dimensional space, clock time), from the concept of nature, historical memory, the city and the environment or from generally accepted ethics and aesthetics" (p. 111).

10. Ibid., 112–13.

11. Theodor Adorno, *Minima Moralia* (London: New Left Books, 1974), 222–23.

12. In a familiar frame, digital audio recording workstations make it easy to migrate between poetry, literature, cinema, theater, journalism, oratory, the ambiences of quotidian speech and sounds, music, etc. Capabilities for synchronization with film, video, installations, theatrical spaces, and so forth, extend this list considerably. Digital workstations are relatively user-friendly and thereby promise some relief from the thick toys-for-boys climate of programming, mathemusic, and electronics that plagues the experimental media arts of sound. Equipped with the desktop and word-processing design, the field should open to all those who write, not just those who solder.

13. Acts of "privileging the signifier," if they truly aspire to this figure, must become mobile. Pregutteral and musicalized speech/sound performed under these auspices would be self-contradictory. Even the musical privileging of pitch over timbre is called into question. It is still argued that musical elements must remain "minimally encoded. . . . highly polished" (Serres) to appeal to universality, to relate "partial to global structures" (Boulez) and to be comprehensible in passages of horizontal or vertical density. The former two ideas should serve well as ambient sounds for watchmakers. Difficulties with timbral and invocatory density should have been addressed long ago by Cagean musical listening and by acknowledging the capacities already practiced in mass media, spectacular viewing/listening (and much not-so-spectacular).

14. For example, Russolo crudely proposed that the acoustic periodicity of conventional musical sound is inscribed in vowels and the aperiodicity of noise is inscribed in consonants. Thus, in someone's speech or in any type of auditive event, there is not only an inscription of one sound upon another, there is a coarticulatory relationship of large categories of sound from one moment to the next.

11 Of Monitors and Men and Other Unsolved Feminist Mysteries: Video Technology and the Feminine

Nell Tenhaaf

Contemporary women artists who work in technological media are faced with a contradiction. The domain in which they are operating has been historically considered masculine, yet women's current access to electronic production tools seems to belie any gender barrier. Indeed, women have benefited by these tools in the last two decades to the extent that the tools have offered some freedom from the sexist art-historical and critical practices associated with more-established media. The philosophy of technology, however, has been articulated entirely from a masculinist perspective in terms that metaphorize and marginalize the feminine.[1] In real social discourse, this claiming of technology has been reinforced by, and has probably encouraged, a male monopoly on technical expertise, diminishing or excluding the historical contributions of women to technological development.[2]

From a feminist point of view, female invisibility in the discourses of technology calls for nothing less than a radical reconstitution of technology, its development, and its uses. While this massive agenda is clearly beyond the purview of feminist cultural practitioners, it is well within our scope to develop images and tropes that are body-based in a way that opens up an affirmative space for the feminine in electronic media practices. My hypothesis

This article was first published in *Parallélogramme* (Toronto), vol. 18, no. 3, 1992–93, as part of the intermagazine publishing project entitled *The Video Issue/Propos Vidéo*, edited by Renee Baert and sponsored by Satellite Video Exhange Society, Vancouver.

is that autobiographical, metaphorical, even mythical feminine enunciations in this domain contribute to an unwriting of the masculine bias in technology.

Willing machines/bachelor machines

The modernist philosophical framework for technology is the discourse of the will, specifically the will to power postulated by Friedrich Nietzsche in the late nineteenth century. Expanded upon by subsequent philosophers, in particular Martin Heidegger, this discourse views technology as the manifestation of an essentially masculine will that is the driving force of the whole modern era. In its language and imagery, the will to power is interwoven with a deeply entrenched and mythic concept of duality that describes commanding (and the power of the machine) as a masculine attribute, while submission (and the rule of feeling) is described as a feminine one. For will commands the body toward ineffable and always predetermined desires. Will, as being, is a kind of machine, necessarily engendering the will to power, which always wants more power. And will has replaced reason as the highest mental faculty, so that the modern thinking ego is characterized by the I-will and, subsequently, the I-can.[3] This characterization has generated a metaphor central to modernity: that of machinelike man, in whom the body—as the domain of affect and source of any sense of authentic desire—is disconnected from and subjugated to the mind, which is configured as pure will.

Will does not stop at commanding the interior life of the male social subject and fueling a cyclical and vicious internal battle in which, according to Nietzsche, pleasure is defined by the conquest of displeasure. The philosophy of the will also constitutes the (male) body as subject to an externalized ruling drive to power—a technological power that is unidirectional and obsessed with the future. Nietzsche writes: "Perhaps the entire evolution of the spirit is a question of the body; it is the history of the development of a higher body that emerges into our sensibility. . . . In the long run, it is not a question of man at all: he is to be overcome."[4] Heidegger, in *The Question Concerning Technology*, reads this forward-looking drive as a progression in which technology, whose very nature is the will to will, would annihilate everything arising from it, an essential and inevitable destructiveness. The fundamental duality of will, its stakes of masculine dominance and feminine submission, may be played out psychologically within any one person, any one body. Or, in contemporary sexual politics, it might shed all gender specificity and be played as a game between consenting adults. But because of its central place in the philosophical legacy of modernism, this duality marks the real technologized world as a battleground characterized by rigid gender differences and a will to power actualized in the form of male-controlled progress through technological growth. This Nietzschean drive, fueled by nineteenth-century man's inner battles, has resulted indeed in a certain amount of destructiveness, through the development of a multitude of technologies that project out into the modern social body in the form of invasive and colonizing tools.

The bachelor machine is an update of Nietzsche's willing machine driven by will and desire. An alluring and obscure figure of the twentieth-century avant-garde, the bachelor machine is constructed around a desire that is equally turned in on itself. This desire is frustrated, and also regenerated, by a nihilistic preponderance of denials focused on celibacy, autoeroticism, and death. The bachelor machine is a literary and theoretical construct taking as its paradigm Marcel Duchamp's *Le Grand Verre: La Mariée mise à nue par ses célibataires, même* (1912–23). Both as representation and as philosophical proposal, it connects a masculine bachelor to a feminine bride in an impossible, eternally suspended, internal coupling of opposites. Depicted by Duchamp as a drawing of simple mechanical elements and recordings of chance events, all caught or "delayed" on a large piece of glass, the bachelor machine has come to mean a self-perpetuating masculine psychic machine. Freud too was very fond of the psychic-machine metaphor, and declared it to be quintessentially masculine: "It is highly probable that all complicated machinery and apparatus occurring in dreams stand for the genitals—and as a rule the male ones."[5]

The bachelor machine exposes desire, that is male desire, as entirely subject to instrumentality. Two terms mediate the bachelor's desire: the machine or technology, present in *Le Grand Verre* as "working parts" that simulate the absent body; and "the feminine," represented as an ethereal cloud or skeleton in the upper half of the work. The bride functions as a conduit for information from another (fourth or n^{th}) dimension and as the desiring impetus that the bachelor below needs for his solitary pursuits. For Duchamp, the bride herself knows a certain limited machine desire, as a "motor with very feeble cylinders: Desire magneto (sparks of constant life)."[6]

Through a multitude of writings that embrace everything from origin myths to alchemy, and that do not overlook psychoanalysis, the bachelor machine has become the signifier for a multiple and layered interpretive strategy that stretches across time like an Einsteinian clock caught in the effects of relativity. In *Le Macchine Celibi*, an exhibition catalog produced in 1975 containing several texts on the bachelor machine, Michel de Certeau calls it a "way of writing" or "writing machine." This machine supplants an older, maternal "way of speaking," that of the seventeenth-century mystical tradition. In this displacement, the loss of the mother leads to "the solitude of speech with itself."[7]

In another of the catalog's texts, Michel Serres situates the bachelor machine within a representational history of the machine, a history that extends from the static model (statues) through a system of the fixed reference point (perspective) into the workings of engines and thermodynamics with God as the motor of meaning. Now, he writes, "the transformational engine of our fathers' days has simply moved on into the informational state."[8] Serres's reading is echoed in Jean-François Lyotard's observation that "the growth of power, and its self-legitimation, are now taking the route of data storage and accessibility, and the operativity of information."[9] The bachelor machine thus outlines a mythical technological framework within which the male nihilistically identifies himself as a point of origin, circumscribing the female, and within representation, playing both masculine and feminine parts: "The bride stripped bare, derealized, is a pretext for producing without her."[10] She is necessary, but she is other than and separate from that dynamo which sustains itself ad infinitum.

The bachelor machine is not the same thing as the willing machine; some of its features are quite different. In particular, the feminine is more present in the bachelor machine and complicates its mechanism. Also, the bachelor machine, as Duchamp posited it, is an ironic, self-conscious, even whimsical construct. But each of these apparatuses proposes representation as male self-representation, and this self-rationalizing strategy is couched in autoerotic fantasy. Nietzsche's willing machine has power over nature, is self-reproducing. The bachelor creates ex nihilo; he needs neither mother nor father because, as an androgyne incorporating the anima and as a celibate priest incarnating God, he himself plays the role of archetypal creator. (He halts evolution, though, and directs it toward self-destruction and the end of the world.) However, in a fundamental way, these psychic machines are not autonomous. Their origin fantasies rely implicitly on a mythical conception of nature as a unified matrix, an assumed but necessarily unarticulated feminine that works as an instrument with which the male, the bachelor, touches and arouses himself.

To become desiring machines that are productive, in the sense employed by Deleuze and Guattari,[11] is to go beyond this desperate dream of original totality toward "pure multiplicity," an affirmation that is not reducible to any sort of unified state. Whatever the desiring machine (literary machine, social machine, celibate machine, etc.) produces, whether it be representation, the body, libido, or madness, this product exists only alongside the separate parts that make it up; it is itself a part. This is how Deleuze and Guattari articulate polyvocality and flux as points of resistance to a unitary history of repressed and repressive desires.

But how to deliver the feminine from its implicit and unspoken function in the machine? The male author is able to speak of his body parts in relation to a whole body or libido from a positive masculine position in the symbolic order, a position of presence as a subject. It is still not as possible for a woman to speak in this way. For a woman, particularly in this era of biotechnologies and their "mechanical reproduction," the body as "object of scopic consumption . . . [is] hyperrealistically overrepresented. . . . [It] remains profoundly absent," Rosi Braidotti says. And in relation to this absence, the feminine is both overinvested within discourse and feared as an essentializing term, so that, as Braidotti clarifies, "it signifies a set of interrelated issues but it is not one notion per se. Not one corpus."[12]

To speak from this fragmentary and fluid feminine place is to see that the strange conjuncture of technological mastery, autoerotic pleasure, and nihilism of the masculine machines might be thought of differently. It might be thought of as a mythical territory to be reclaimed by the desiring bride.

Turn-on

"If machines, even machines of theory, can be aroused all by themselves, may women not do likewise?"[13] So asks Luce Irigaray in a 1974 essay with the enticing title "Volume Fluidity." How do women turn themselves on in the technological order? Irigaray has proposed a kind of feminine autoerotic engine in her theorization of female body parts, specifically the "self-caressing" of the labial lips, indicating a sexuality that is always plural and a psychic economy of "never being simply one."[14] Autoeroticism is a site of empowerment for women, in Irigaray's terms. How is this possible, when the autoerotic in the bachelor machine, corresponding as it does to the loss of the divine commandment of love and procreation written on the woman's body, signifies self-destruction? The bachelor's eroticism is reduced to a mechanism without a soul, while a woman reclaims her soul when she touches herself as, Irigaray says, she always and immediately can. Her autoeroticism can never be reduced—a utopian thought perhaps, but one that at least indicates a sexuality not shattered by the disappearance of laws for procreation and sacred heterosexual union.

Irigaray's emphasis on women's bodies elicits for many of her readers a fear of biological determinism or reductivism, of women's sexuality turned back on itself as defining the essence of being female. This argument against theorizing from the body is valid only if we accept the idea that any aspect of the body is simple or innocent, free of complex and controlling signifying practices. To foreground the body is to confront a set of social meanings already assigned to every one of the body's attributes, including biological sex differences. And it is in fact the persistent, if often invisible, masculinist essentialism in Western philosophy and epistemology that has kept these socially constructed limitations in place. Thus a woman "thinking through the body"[15] and arousing herself is both multiple and complicated, not a reductivist proposition, overturningrather than reinforcing the legacy of dualistic thought.

Irigaray's focus on female autoeroticism is intensely bound up with the pain of living out the textual and sexual instrumentality that the willing/bachelor machine represents. The effects of this instrumentality are lived not just in the psyche by women but in the body as well, and are traditionally called mystery, enigma, or hysteria. Irigaray writes about a possible renewed meaning of mysticism for women.[16] She delineates the historical mystic's path of contact with divinity, which is equally a process of reclaiming her "soul," her identity, from its ethereal state. The blissful and tortuous visit to the mystic of the divine essence, of "God," is registered forever afterward not just on her inner self but also on her body as a wound. The sought-after experience is a searing flame or lightning flash that lights up understanding, and this entails pain: "[T]he wound must come before the flame."[17] But this newly discovered self who has had God as a lover and has fully debased herself (mimetically) to the nothingness that He knows her to be, by this process also reclaims her (auto)eroticism. The mystic's autoeroticism, once it is alight, signifies her coming into herself.

Light my fire

Mythology is both pre- and postmodern, both pre- and postscientific, in its power to metaphorize for primal forces. Different accounts of humankind's introduction to fire are also stories of the acquisition of knowledge, as are the various accounts of mysticism, including Irigaray's reworked version.

Mythology shapes our reception of light, and delineates both its masculine and feminine attributes. Light in the form of raw energy, fire, lightning, the sun, combustion: this light is mythically phallic. But keeping the hearth, harnessing and sustaining pure energy for light and heat, corresponds to matriarchal goddess lore.

Classical Greek mythology operates on a gender duality parallel to the one that structures the philosophy of technology. Theft of fire from the heavens was the birth of technology, and took the form of a man's rebellion against the gods. Prometheus stole energy in the form of fire from the gods and gave it to humans for light, heat, and the ability to transform raw matter—a primal moment of technological enabling. As punishment for his hubris, he was chained to a rock and his liver was consumed each day by a carnivorous bird. Further, in Hesiod's telling of the tale, the gods punished humankind by first having Hephaestus, their artisan, fashion the beautiful Pandora, then sending her to earth with a grain jar full of evil.

In parallel biblical lore, Lucifer offered knowledge (light) to Eve and Adam in the garden. Pandora and Eve, antiheroines of the earliest writing cultures, became figures of the gods' punishment for acquisition and transmission of the light of knowledge.

In prepatriarchal lore the figure of fire guardian or guardian of the hearth is the original keeper of light and heat, embodied in Hestia/Vesta. She was conceived as both the center of the household and the omphaloid center of the earth (the *beth-el* in Hebrew), within a geocentric universe. Her legacy was carried over into the early Christian era, and her priestesses in ancient Rome were the Vestal Virgins, entrusted with keeping alight the perpetual fire at the mystic heart of the empire. As the rise of Christianity wiped out pagan supernatural practices, even as it offered magical revival from death and assumption into heaven for its adherents, and science came to acknowledge heliocentrism as the ordering physical principle of the universe, Vesta was displaced by androcentric figures of power.[18]

These stories break open the philosophical stranglehold of the self-rationalizing will to power by reformulating its strict gender duality and by restoring the sexed body as an active agent in the scene of the unconscious. Further, the multiplicity of mythological lore undermines the primacy of the oedipal story in the modern Western imagination, with its constitution of subjectivity structured on a masculine model.[19]

Threshold

Now turn on the TV. The monitor screen is the threshold of passage from dark into light/life, the cervical opening from a womb that permits a spark of consciousness to come into being. The effect of the monitor screen is a sustained emission of contained light. This is emblematic of birth itself—a coming into light, a harnessing of energy, a materialization from a crossing of electronic codes—arising from two sources, the feminine mystic flame and masculine raw energy. A pattern of light is built on the replication and combination of coded information, a passage between states.

The monitor is a new technological paradigm within the schema of the apparatus. As in cinema, the screen is an interface between a viewing subject and a complex representational apparatus, the camera. But it can also be read alternately, as other than a bachelor machine, because it isn't a mechanical model but an electronic one. Rather than a set of moving parts that go round and round perpetually, it is an instantaneous and ephemeral event, a burst of electrons like a Promethean lightning bolt from within the monitor. The double-sided mirror of the monitor screen focuses light on one side and on the other emits light as it reflects an image. Superseding the mirror effect (the constitution of the spectator as a desiring subject, or the cinematic experience) and the look (the male gaze situating the subject within the dominance of the phallic), even before representation itself (establishing the symbolic order of the phallus), the monitor produces an effect of pure light. The bias of technological progress persuades us to think of video display as postcinematic, but it might also be seen to correspond to a much more primary, generative event: coming into light out of darkness.

Contemporary physics tells us that both the wavelike and particle-like behavior of light are products of our interaction with it, the result of our observations. In this respect, looking at light in display patterns is a confirmation of spectator subjecthood, whatever the apparatus used. But, in one of the paradoxes of quantum mechanics, it is a subjecthood confirmed by computation from probability waves that describe only a tendency to a pattern.[20] Unfixed subjectivity is the embracing condition of our late- twentieth-century technologized world.

The representational fragmentation proliferating in media technologies reiterates this dispersed condition of subjectivity. Digital imaging techniques are particularly prone to hallucinatory visions that scatter the subject's viewing space and identification process: image fragmentation, simulation, virtual realities. Computer-generated imaging proposes thoroughly artificial scenarios and shattered points of view, often in sped-up motion that would be impossible in the physical world. As Paul Virilio says, "That's how we program our definitive absence."[21] Indeed, in this dispersal that we could think of as an electronic overthrow of the will to power, the male subject may be experiencing an evacuated subjectivity that is new to him. But for the female subject, an assertion of corporeality in electronic space is also a struggle against historical absence.

Inside the monitor, in the darkness, is the matrix of electronic matter that generates display. In a cathode ray tube (CRT), the familiar TV or video monitor, electron beams hit a concave surface coated with phosphor. The phosphor glows and produces light. The negatively charged electron beam starts in an electron gun at the back of the tube and is accelerated down a long neck toward the tube face by a large positive voltage. On the outside, the convex side of the screen, the continuous stream of images poses the to-be-looked-at. Irigaray:

> But which "subject" up till now has investigated the fact that a concave mirror concentrates the light and, specifically, that this is not wholly irrelevant to woman's sexuality? Any more than is a man's sexuality to the convex mirror? . . . Not one subject has done so, on pain of tumbling from his ex-sistence. And here again, here too, one will rightly suspect any perspective, however surreptitious, that centers the subject, any autonomous circuit of subjectivity, any systematicity hooked back onto itself, any closure that claims for whatever reason to be

metaphysical—or familial, social, economic even—to have rightfully taken over, fixed, and framed that concave mirror's incandescent hearth.[22]

A refusal of fixed, framed systematicity is a refusal of the rule of the male machine-body.

Body parts

I propose that the early history of video art provides an instance of such a refusal. In the seventies, certain women producers inserted the feminine into video technology in a spontaneous and provisional way, risking essentialist identification with a female machine-body so as to open a space there for the articulation of female desire. Kate Craig's *Delicate Issue* (1979, color, 12 min.) is a powerful tape about relations between the body, technology, and power. A woman's body, the artist's own, is framed by a shaky handheld camera that scans her body at such proximity that the part being looked at is often unidentifiable. As the body goes out of and comes back into focus, its image alternately breaks down into patterns of light or reads as acute detail: creases, hairs, moles, eye, nipple come under the same scrutiny. A voice-over by the artist situates the viewer vis-à-vis issues of closeness and distance, private and public, and how "real" we want the subject to be. The sound of someone breathing accompanies the voice-over, and as the camera travels up the crease of the legs toward the vagina the breathing accelerates. It's never clear whether the breathing is the artist's or the cameraperson's. The credits will tell us later that a man is behind the camera and clearly he is complicit with both Craig's ironic voyeurism and her exposure of her own sexuality. The cameraman shifts between standing in for the imagined viewer, as a trope for Craig's arousal through fantasy, and simply enabling her to fill the visual and auditory space. The camera's gaze lingers on the area around the clitoris, which appears as glistening, pink, vulnerable surfaces folded in on themselves. This is as close as we get, Craig's voice tells us.

The implied autoerotic pleasure mediated by the camera (and the cameraman) in Craig's tape contrasts with the expression of rage as a perverse autoerotic pleasure in *Trop(e)isme* (1980, color, 14 min.), a videotape by marshalore. An artist is again the subject, her face in profile appearing in the foreground of the screen for much of the tape, contorted in a succession of silent screams. Enacting a metaphor for accessing her inner rage, this subject puts her fingers

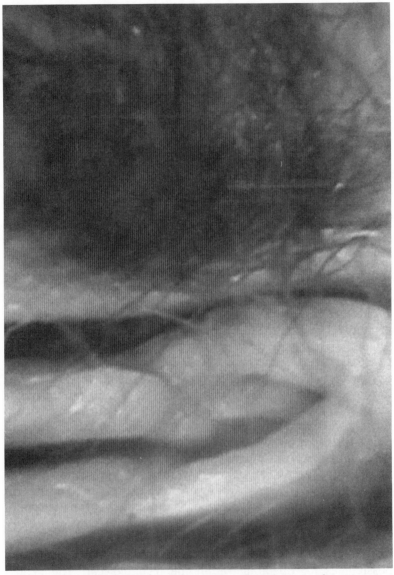

Fig. 11.1. Kate Craig, still from *Delicate Issue*, (1979), 3/4" video, 12:00,
distributed by Video Out, Vancouver.

into her vagina, framed very close, then takes them out covered in menstrual blood and smears the blood across her face. In this intense and cathartic moment that Deleuze and Guattari would characterize as a (schizophrenic) hiatus in the production of the real, excess finds an opening, surfacing as a wounding knowledge akin to the enlightening wound of the mystic. After this disturbing taboo-breaking gesture, the artist takes a long drag on a cigarette, exhaling slowly with sensual satisfaction.

Women's early appropriation of the space of the video monitor can now be seen as a particularly necessary position-taking in the face of the scattered, absent subjectivity that characterizes post-modernism. This issue has been a focal point of women's recent agenda in the domain of technology and its media, where women have been doing much of the important work in both theory and practice. Much of it has been psychoanalytically based deconstructive work, particularly in the domain of cinema, but this work also parallels contemporary feminist projects in language in its proposal of a female subject-in-process.[23]

There are complications in proposing a language of technological media as a language of the body, in particular the female body. In the all-encompassing embrace of the technological apparatus, any declaration of the body is suspect. On the one hand, assertions of bodily integrity are swept up into an ideology of the (always unattainable) idealized body, to be striven for as a commodity like so many others. On the other, the body fragmentation of the decentered subject feeds the metal-flesh interpolation that is postulated as irreversible in the technological dynamo (the automaton, the bionic body, half metal/half flesh). These processes reflect the ideological underpinnings of a society that has come to be controlled by its technological media: a denatured "natural," one that is artificially constructed, plays a critical reaffirming role, and technology itself is naturalized. This ideological premise seems to reconfigure a reductivist reading of the body: what was previously determined by "life cycle," the biological, will now be circumscribed in the biotechnological, the body enhanced through designer body parts.

The problem thereby posed is, how can women speak from an interior knowing to arrive at a transformative language that opens up possibilities for operating within the technological? The heated debates around essentialist practices in the past decade imposed constraints on naïve representations of the feminine, but did not adequately address women's deeply felt need to assert difference, and not only deconstruct it. This lacuna was necessarily reformulated as women of color called attention to specifics of difference, breaking down the monolithic construction of gender difference held by white Western feminists. It remains pertinent to the many feminisms now being formulated to develop theories and strategies for female self-representation that both assert identity and challenge any form of fixed labeling. Especially in convergence with technological or electronic media, self-representation is key to affirmation, visibility, and strategies for changing consciousness that can take into account the whole range of technological intervention in identity formation.

I've looked at certain body-based video works by Canadian women producers that are representations of self made prior to these debates. Although they were formulated outside of any feminist theoretical construction and address difference from only a gender standpoint, they can be seen as not just refusing the long-standing representational codes of male control over women's bodies, but also transgressing the theoretical limits of the philosophical discourse on technology. I've looked at these works because they articulate in electronic technology a metonymical correspondence between the body, implicitly problematized by the probing eye of the camera, and the video-viewing apparatus itself: body parts become the very substance of the monitor, become its shifting incandescent feminine insides. These works are historical moments, and are emblematic of women's practices in relation to the philosophical and historical framework that I have delineated.

These are not the only instances of genital imaging in women's video history (a quiet closeup in *Facing South*, Lisa Steele, 1975; and later, a digital drawing overlay of vaginal forms in *Hot Chicks on TV*, Liz Vander Zaag, 1986). Such images are an immediate challenge to the persistent figure of the feminine in philosophy—of idea, truth, morality, nature, etc. More to the point, now, at a time when there is no possible "imagined organic body"[24] resistant to the effects of technology, women are turned into techno-tropes anyway, without their complicity, let alone their control. In popular cultural imagery, women are represented as powerful yet docile sex-robots or androids (as in the film *Blade Runner*). Our bodies are taken over, hybridized. The developers of technology seek out metaphors, such as the metaphor that DNA replication produces "daughter" strands from the mother, that a voice recognition cellular phone is named "Sally," and so forth. These trendy tropes reiterate the familiar figure of woman as nature, biology, matter, or extension of man.

The video screen is a threshold of possibilities, the place at which a stimulus is of sufficient intensity to begin to produce an effect. The screen is a site of agency, of an event brought about through intention and action. Through strategic self-representation, certain video works by women producers have documented the feminist project of freeing the female body from its status as a reflection to be looked upon. The video screen is a two-way reflection, and is thus a threshold of something from nothing. Its implications of the body through elusive, mutating images, parallel to our own complex interior knowing through our bodies, constitute a site of the feminine in technology.

Notes

1. My terminology includes the whole gamut of gender-difference identifiers: woman and man, female and male, feminine and masculine, feminist and masculinist. These are not used interchangeably, but certainly they overlap. My intention is to emphasize that even the biological terms *male* and *female* have to be seen as socially constructed. I use the term *the feminine* in the sense that it has been proposed by the French feminists, especially Luce Irigaray.

2. See, for example, Joan Rothschild, ed., *Machina Ex Dea: Feminist Perspectives on Technology* (New York: Pergamon Press, 1983) and Maureen McNeil, ed., *Gender and Expertise* (London: Free Association Books, 1987).

3. Hannah Arendt, *The Life of the Mind: Willing* (New York: Harcourt Brace Jovanovich, 1978), 20.

4. Friedrich Nietzsche, *The Will to Power*, trans. Walter Kaufmann and R. J. Hollingdale (New York: Vintage Books, 1968), 358.

5. Cited in Constance Penley, "Feminism, Film Theory and the Bachelor Machines," *m/f* 10 (1985): 49.

6. Paul Matisse, *Marcel Duchamp: Notes* (Boston: G. K. Hall & Company, 1983). This is from Note 155.

7. Michel de Certeau, "Arts of dying / Anti-mystical writing," in Jean Clair and Harold Szeemann, eds., *Le Macchine Celibi/The Bachelor Machine* (Venice: Alfieri, edizioni d'arte, 1975), 88.

8. Michel Serres, "It was before the (world-) Exhibition," in ibid., 68.

9. Jean-François Lyotard, *The Postmodern Condition: A Report on Knowledge*, trans. Geoff Bennington and Brian Massumi (Minneapolis: University of Minnesota Press, 1984), 47.

10. De Certeau, "Arts of dying," 92. Constance Penley calls attention to another apparatus that links the individual psyche, technology, and the

social body, "one that can offer impeccable credentials with respect to the bachelor machine's strict requirements for perpetual motion, the reversibility of time, mechanicalness, electrification, animation and voyeurism: the cinema." Penley, "Feminism," 39–40.

11. Gilles Deleuze and Felix Guattari, *Anti-Oedipus* (Minneapolis: University of Minnesota Press, 1983), 33–43. Deleuze and Guattari describe the desiring-machine as producing repression, its own antiproduction, which is then integrated into the desire-production process, in the way that interruptions or breakdowns in the functioning of the technical machine are integral to its operations. Likewise, schizophrenia is a break in the flow of the real, in its production, which permits that flow to continue outside of the constraints of (oedipal) social production. The interest of Deleuze and Guattari's machines is precisely their productivity, in contrast to bachelor nihilism.

12. Rosi Braidotti, "Organs Without Bodies," *Differences* 1 (1988): 52. See also Donna Haraway, "A Manifesto for Cyborgs: Science, Technology, and Socialist Feminism in the 1980's,"*Socialist Review* 80 (1985).

13. Luce Irigaray, *Speculum of the Other Woman*, trans. Gillian C. Gill (Ithaca, N. Y.: Cornell University Press, 1985), 232.

14. Luce Irigaray, *This Sex Which Is Not One*, trans. Catherine Porter (Ithaca, N. Y.: Cornell University Press, 1985), 31.

15. See Jane Gallop, *Thinking Through the Body* (New York: Columbia University Press, 1989).

16. Luce Irigaray, "La mystérique," in *Speculum of the Other Woman*, 191.

17. Ibid., 193.

18. Ginette Paris, *Pagan Meditations*, trans. Gwendolyn Moore (Dallas, Tex.: Spring Publications, 1986), 176.

19. See Jessica Benjamin, *The Bonds of Love: Psychoanalysis, Feminism, and the Problem of Domination* (New York: Pantheon Books, 1988), 133–81, and Deleuze and Guattari, *Anti-Oedipus*.

20. Gary Zukav, *The Dancing Wu Li Masters* (Toronto: Bantam Books, 1980), 65–66.

21. Chris Dercon, "An Interview with Paul Virilio," *Impulse* 12, no. 4 (Summer 1986): 36.

22. Irigaray, *Speculum of the Other Woman*, 144.

23. This is a central concern of the writers identified with French feminism, writers who engage in a specifically feminine practice of writing or "écriture feminine": Luce Irigaray, Julia Kristeva, Helène Cixous, Michele Montrelay. Another important issue is that in video practices, it is especially women's narrative video that has characteristically refused narrative closure and sought to subvert rather than confirm a potentially unified subject and spectator. See Dot Tuer, "Video in Drag: Trans-sexing the Feminine," in *Parallélogramme* 12, no. 3 (Feb./Mar. 1988): 26–28.

24. See Haraway, "A Manifesto for Cyborgs."

12

The Irresistible Interface: Video's Unknown Forces and Fire-Lit Waves

David Tafler

At a time of overpropagation, the begetting of ever more sophisticated communication tools helps to shrink remaining notions of intermittent space. Global differences diminish rapidly on the television. Identity and community acquire new meaning along the electronic highway. Ubiquitous and inconspicuous, television continually plays on the individual, on the group, and on our changing relationship with the changing environment.

On the television screen, a plethora of multichannel video environments stretch out to viewer bodies through remote buttons. Each new television channel offers the hope of new attractions. The spectrum could promise a limitless horizon. Unfortunately, the expanding electromagnetic palette seems to cultivate a controlled array of mostly repetitive forms of mediation.

On the reception side, the growing use of remotes by viewers to fragment narrative events into short clips and bites slowly destabilizes the residual formats shaping individual experience. While certain things like storytelling endure, their traditional formats succumb to increased segmentation. As the formulaic staples of character identification and plot intrigue decline proportionately, the often spontaneous and not-so-subtle linkages constituting a linear experience begin to form the crucial taxonomy of the text. As the form of a text becomes its content, the viewer spends considerably more time playing with the frame supporting the sensory play of the image than in assessing and critically engaging its meaning. In essence, the viewer's investigation gets caught up in the structuring process.

This evolving new reflexive process may ultimately do no more than restructure old viewer-text encounters. New transitional strategies may simply reposition the viewers' fascination. More disturbing, this overt self-referential structuring may just provide one more method of viewer accommodation, thereby contributing to the already discomforting mystification, manipulation, and opacity of mass media.

Nevertheless, new technological advances do bring to market new tools, which in turn disrupt whatever settling down has occurred between users and their old tools. Something in the overall interface between the individual and technology shifts with each new electronic instrument, and each new tool offers new manipulative pleasure. Unfortunately, most tools manipulate the viewer-user even when the viewer-user seems to manipulate his or her new improved environment.

Within a contemporary environment of interactive games, information screens, and automatic teller machines, programmed self-guided experiences have appeared in myriad locations in schools, corporate displays, and shopping malls, not to mention video arcades. Most represent the lowest form of stimulus-response activity, useful only for training, simulation, and escapist entertainment.

Though mainstream operant conditioning will continue to define video arcades, more marginal programming efforts open up new ground for exploring the cybernetic interface or "cyberface." Occasionally, a novel system transforms the operation and significance of the electronic experience, though it may be limited at first to the privileged confines of a gallery or museum. With repercussions that extend beyond its immediate parameters, certain electronic installations can ignite and agitate the conditions governing individual involvement. If successful, these disruptions can set in place forces that will overhaul the framing operations of mainstream supporting structures, even host institutions.

The fundamental nature of the installation becomes crucial. Most installations will not stretch the parameters of viewer involvement. An interactive project that does must exceed the individual's cognitive capacity to fully process the event. It must remain open-ended.

Equally important, in an environment loaded with many more fixed attractions than any single individual or group could ever possibly absorb, a single kinetic-electronic installation's explicit and hierarchical assemblage of impressions must compete much more intensively for a share of that individual or group's total time and attention. Physically moving through an urban environment already compresses the borders and parameters highlighting any single encounter or installation. For one such event to make time demands at the expense of another, it must interfere with more traditional patterns of programmed reception.

As part of this upheaval, other transitions will remain uncertain. Linkages unifying the text will metamorphize into their own kinetic language, often unrecognizable. Grammatical cues binding the producer/designer's implicit intent with the work's explicit array of sounds and images will split and fracture along multiple tracks. Reconstructing that iconic, more often hieroglyphic, assemblage of symbols and signs, an individual actively engaging the brave new work reforms its sounds and images into an abstract coherence. Movement within the piece stretches the conventions of structural, perhaps narrative, coherence while introducing new expressive paradigms.

The question looms, What form will this so-called open-ended (electronic) installation assume? An open-ended confrontation resists a detailed textual projection and challenges its own analysis. Too many openings and competing events cloud the horizon and make a linear projection and subsequent reading of its complex grid difficult, if not impossible. Nevertheless, the relatively short-lived presence of a novel shadow/sound structure provides several junctures for just such an examination.

The play of the interface—its zone of operation—lies between projection and reflection, communication and introspection. To clarify this condition, I would like to call attention to one such installation, a piece by Peter Rose called *Siren*,[1] that engages its participants by disturbing the membrane harboring their affective equilibrium. Once committed to entering its portentous interior, an individual gropes unexpectedly with a difficult, unavoidable, and yet irresistible challenge.

At the outset, the individual crosses a simple threshold, moving through curtains on either side of a stark white pavilion, and enters a dark theater. Inside a chamber approximately ten feet wide by five feet deep is a bench, situated between the entranceways, and three visible screens. Two video monitors face the respective entrances. They seem to float, somewhere, almost halfway between the opaque dark floor and the equally opaque dark ceiling. Mounted at eye level on narrow, lateral, inwardly directed proscenium walls, the monitors bracket a third rear-projected screen, centrally located within a recessed center. Hidden within the unseen periphery of that central recess, two additional monitors cast their television light and lure the more curious and adventurous individuals or groups. Each inner monitor presents a continuous view of the outer entrance to the installation corresponding to its side of the pavilion.

When entering the chamber, an individual immediately confronts the proscenium monitors. If unoccupied, the bench against the wall permits the viewer an out-of-the-way place to sit between the two curtained portals. An omnipresent sound system fills the ambiguous gap by spilling out, marking, and selectively defining the interior space. Between the walls, the room meanders toward the inner recess.

Violating classical viewing operations, the separation of the three screens shatters the unified viewing field. Architecturally in rhythm with the surrounding space, the lateral monitors herald the central screen by bracketing its structural and thematic contours; the monitors point like signifying arrows toward the open gap, the more distant image. Unexpectedly, that interior image only intermittently appears, more often embodying a spectacle of its own absence.

Depending on the variables governing individual experience—the size of the crowd, the length of an individual's stay, the overall movement of individuals and/or groups in and out of the pavilion, and the temporal point of the individual's entry and departure within the cyclical sequence—an individual or group may or may not move inward. If they do, they disappear from view.

The installation's theatrical configuration complicates this passage by setting up false cues. The bench becomes the privileged vantage point. Within this given space, such a fixed platform compounds congestion and maneuvering. Wanderers crossing into the interior risk disturbing the spectacle for others. *Siren's* bench provides an esoteric station for framing a larger coherence. Perhaps, it symbolizes the contradiction and captures the complexity of unifying film/theatrical determinants with open-ended video-oriented installations.

Immediately upon entering, the viewer-participant's decision-making begins. In the first chamber, he or she must alternately engage the lateral monitors and/or the recessed screen. By redirecting his or her foveal attention, or dwelling somewhere along the horizontal/peripheral axis, the individual moves.

Even on the bench, the individual lacks a privileged position. The very intermittent duration of the central image destabilizes a privileged point of view. The long pauses separating the screen's abbreviated play deflect the attention of all but the most steadfast viewer. When the viewer shifts his or her attention back and forth from side to side, the rapid firing of multiple-layered images structurally assures that the spatial distance between screens provides a temporal lapse in the continuity of the sequence.

Though the side monitors project the same channel at all times, their decentered position entices this back-and-forth engagement. While trying to affirm the congruity of both screen images, the viewer, in fact, matches the projected events with the contextual play of people entering and/or leaving the chamber. The frequency of distraction and the temporal and spatial parameters of the viewer's shifting activity shape the lapses and determine the effects of those saccades or interruptions on the composite experience. Meanwhile, the complexity of the respective images inhibits their comparison.

Throughout literary history, similar models abound.[2] In elaborating the cave metaphor, Plato describes the scene around the fire:

> [Imagine] men who have been prisoners there since they were children, their legs and necks being so fastened that they can only look straight ahead of them and cannot turn their heads. Behind them and above them a fire is burning, and between the fire and the prisoners runs a road, in front of which a curtain-wall has been built, like a screen at puppet shows between the operators and their audience, above which they show their puppets.[3]

The fire burns in the background of the interactive installation and projects a silhouetted panorama on the opposing walls.

Within the dark interior of the metacave, light comes from behind the respective screens. Sound emanates from the surrounding walls. The composite environment promises renewed life.

> And if the wall of their prison opposite them reflected sound, don't you think that they would suppose, whenever one of the passers-by on the road spoke, that the voice belonged to the shadow passing before them?[4]

No human shadow passes before the screen. A series of clues, traces, and linguistic intersections builds an illusive puzzle that coheres in some other cognitive region. The viewer-participant enters as the shadow marked within the illuminated image.

Through an anabiotic mirror, the imaginary plays itself out.[5] Something of spectator experience reveals itself as the individual watches those traces and shadows. The individual coalesces with the knowledge of himself or herself standing on the threshold just before any symbolic meaning takes over. The movement of the people in the installation-cave forges indexical relationships with the vestiges of those movements captured by the shadows oscillating in the flickering light.

> Then think what would naturally happen to them if they were released from their bonds and cured of their delusions. Suppose one of them were let loose, and suddenly compelled to stand up and turn his head and look and walk towards the fire; all these actions would be painful and he would be too dazzled to see properly the objects of which he used to see the shadows. So if he was told that what he used to see was mere illusion and that he was now nearer reality and seeing more correctly, because he was turned towards objects that were more real, and if on top of that he were compelled to say what each of the passing objects was when it was pointed out to him, don't you think he would be at a loss, and think that what he used to see was more real than the objects now being pointed out to him?[6]

From the dying embers in the fireplace, the shadows on the wall gradually fade, revealing in their absence an existential window on the future.[7] As the silhouettes of figures rise and fall with the fluctuating flames, appear and disappear in the alternating light, time defines the first cinematic event. When the firelight fades, the inhabitants step out from the chamber of shadows out into a world of ambient light. On that horizon, the internal projections continue indefinitely, forever changed and changing.

Moving through a shrouded entrance into a dark chamber, in and of itself, covers no new ground. When the enclosed space resembles the cave and its derivative mysteries or odysseys, the event of moving into this space simply becomes a variation on a theme. It becomes one in a number of similar codified experiences or representations.

Over and over again, popular interests have appropriated this fascination. For example, the Coca-Cola Company refabricated the cave along the image contours of corporate America. At the 1964–65 New York World's Fair, Coca-Cola constructed a winding trans-oceanic passageway for its pavilion. On that spatial/temporal platform, the self-engaged viewer wandered along a path from habitat to habitat, chamber to chamber, across continents, en route to a configured, often anticipated final climactic realization of his or her desire. The promise of the eventual satiation of that configured desire, the ultimate sign of that desire, always the same, a bottle of Coke accompanied by the cola syrup's sweet aroma, marked each arrival prior to that last destination. At the end of the corridor, the wanderer emerged from the darkness and came into an outdoor courtyard, a fountain of Coca-Cola products in the hub of twentieth century civilization.

In the technologically sophisticated but persistently simple social environment, the interactive installation can reconstruct that seminal moment when the individual successfully steps out of his or her preconfigured context, where every image reaffirms a sense of historic unity wrapped in bourgeois ideology, where everything belongs, guided by some absolute universal order. On the one hand, the spectator momentarily enters the cave for what becomes yet another cycle in the historic evolution of performance art. On the other hand, each cycle embodies its own profound change to the language of the cave.

In particular, the corporeality of the sound makes the cave into a body. Within that interiority, the spectator lies in the belly of the piece, both inside and outside time and space. As the force that drives the spectator's condition, aural traditions and auditory signals govern the crucial junctures.

Hidden, insubstantial, and ephemeral, sound situates the spectator within the installation's hierarchical arena. Marlowe, of Joseph Conrad's *Heart of Darkness*, during a passage through the jungle, recapitulates sound's peripatetic experience:

> We penetrated deeper and deeper into the heart of darkness. It was very quiet there. At night sometimes the roll of drums behind the curtain of trees would run up the river and remain sustained faintly, as if hovering in the air high over our head, till the first break of day. Whether it meant war, peace, or prayer we could not tell. The dawns were heralded by the descent of a chill stillness; the woodcutters slept, their fires burned low; the snapping of a twig would make you start. We were wanderers on a prehistoric earth, on an earth that wore the aspect of an unknown planet.[8]

In *Siren*, sound events define the landscape, motivate its architecture, and regulate its interior design, including the positioning of the bench. Music and effects link and buttress the entire infrastructure of the piece.

Greater than any visual lure, the score cements the viewer to the itinerant continuity. In *Heart of Darkness*, asynchronous relationships direct the viewer/reader:

> I had been dimly aware for some time of a worrying noise, and when I lifted my eyes I saw the wood-pile was gone, and the manager, aided by all the pilgrims, was shouting at me from the river-side.[9]

In *Siren*, the emergence of a voice, in effect, becomes the metasubject of the narration. The quoted text describes itself:

> [T]he evening uproar of the howling monkeys burst out, and after three or four minutes ceased. The after silence was pierced at intervals by screams. . . .[10]

By its sometimes synchronous and other times asynchronous timing with the image(s), the soundtrack reveals the play of its own narration.

The combination of voices enunciates/enumerates the text. Once the "viewer" focuses on the track, the track disassembles the viewer's attention. It eludes precise meaning by becoming a score. Screams, screeches, and unexpected utterances form a prominent component of that score. They grab at the viewer's emotional threads.

At the same time, the screens project messages that shape the viewer's reception of the score. Words fluctuate on the screen, abstracting the moans, whispers, and screeches. The flora mediating the camera's movement match the multilayered sheaths of sound. Sound once more becomes the principal structuring device. It provides the clues, traces, fragments of the landscape from which the viewer marks his or her status and position within the maze.[11] Passages, such as "After that tempest of motion and confused noises, the silence of the forest seemed. . ." direct attention by resembling oral narration. Oral text, however, becomes written text. That written text decomposes into assorted fragments, waves, phonemes—imprints, fossils, sticks, and leaves. Voices form antisymbolic visual or graphic perambulations; they emanate from the center of those screens surrounding the spectator on the left, right, and center. Inevitably, narrative forks in the path lead to a dead end.

Another fork materializes. Metaphorically, it leads to a bridge, but only to the under side of that bridge. Moving into the vacuum predicated by an absent center, the bridge replenishes the totemic vision and shapes it into a spiritual force. Here, too, tensions and contradictions prevail. The under side of the bridge, the walls and ceiling of the cathedral, connotes a vulva. A sense of uncertainty, of hidden meanings, eludes a deliberate move toward a fixed interpretation.

Conscious of its own temporality, the voice speaks without certainty. The auditory accompaniment supports what the track describes as a "a tender spiritual music, a language without words" that bathes and embraces and promises some sort of aesthetic harbor.

WHAT FEELING & FANCIES,
WHAT TURNS OF EXPRESSION,
UNFAMILIAR TO MY MIND
WERE CONTAINED IN THOSE SWEET, WASTED,
INARTICULATE SOUNDS.

Following a spiritual fork in the path, however, ultimately leads to another interpretive dead end. Uncertainty prevails. From the cathedral, the ongoing cycle eventually returns the viewer to the mystery of the text.

Throughout that cycle, pauses punctuate the continuity. Those "intervals of silence," the gaps in the text, transcend their musical counterparts, the notes and the rests. Each pause blocks the walkway and builds the uncertainty. As the connections between segments fall away, the lapses between sections form self-contained cells. They never quite hinge together.

Pauses mark the pathways through which the spectator passes. Like signs, they construct a cohesive position from which to formulate meaning. Nevertheless, despite this punctuation, the installation endures as an enigmatic odyssey.

AND IF I OBEYED
TO WHAT DELIGHTFUL discoveries or frightful
dangers might it lead?

Visually, the piece climaxes with the viewer's arrival at the center of a maze. Marked by an icon of Icarus and a mirror, the center represents closure. The installation, however, never ends. The curtains never close. When the proscribed image goes out, the radiant light of the interior monitors suddenly becomes visible; it beckons the viewer inward. When the proscribed image goes out, external crowd sounds transform the interior of the installation. From that of a tunnel, the ambience shifts to that of a larger chamber, decompressing the interior to match the ambient space in the gallery outside.

Slowly, the spectators begin making their way back or forward, depending on the point of reference. Some disappear. Disparate thoughts occupy the landscape. On the threshold of discovery, some can be heard:

> "Why don't they turn on the lights?"
> "Is this supposed to be funny?"

These outcries mask other ruminations.

> It was the farthest point of navigation and the culminating point of my experience. It seemed somehow to throw a kind of light on everything about me—and into my thoughts. (Marlowe in Conrad's *Heart of Darkness*)[12]

Responses form a language without words. Words, fluttering back and forth, resemble thoughts breaking apart dialectically, fleeting, faltering at the forks in the maze.

Within the cycle, the center screen projects movement through particular sections of the maze. Gradually, the camera comes upon a fork in the path. As the camera approaches that fork, the side monitors project the following graphic message:

> *The Same Voice*
> *BUT*
> *Not the Same Song*
> *Not the Same Phrase* [13]

By the seventh section, the speakers announce:

> *There were pauses*
> *intervals of silence*
> *(squeaky high pitched voices)*

Over and over again, the role of the image as the principal narrator continues to fluctuate.

The eternal fascination with sound from the sightless womb of prenatal experience moves quickly to the dark side of human cognition, where spoken and written language blocks, disrupts, problematizes human experience. Here lies the frontier. At this crossing, the habitual Sisyphean insufficiency of language looms mischievously. The ordeal of transcending rational thinking begins. Once again, by abstracting familiar communication systems, the artist tries to transcend simple denotative structures. Narrative yields to unmitigated experiential traces. When the historical distance and the underlying support of a prevailing format disappears, the interactive project treads a deliberate but uncertain path. Appropriately, the underlying stress and tension appear on the screen and implicitly inhabit the architecture of the installation.

As in the cave, images come and go. Unlike the cave, the flickering images do not reflect back the ambient light surrounding the spectator. Instead, the screens project an explicit, direct light that comes and goes. It comes and goes as mysteriously and unpredictably as the embers in the fire casting their last shadows. Without any extraordinary moments marking its passage, time passes despite the narrative fissures, spatial crevasses, and cracks in continuity. Only within these gaps, measures, and passageways will the spectator actually discover the clues buttressing the installation's underlying structure.

The interior of an interactive psychic cavern forms both a finite juncture and a figurative circle without a clear-cut destination. In its deepest recesses, an unanticipated vision awaits the viewer. Discovering the hidden, nested monitors, the spectator unexpectedly finds himself or herself outside the cave, implicated in a circular loop whereby he or she must reenter the installation in order to return to the outside world.

In the beginning, before penetrating the electronic depths, an individual must make the first decision, the decision to enter the cave. No longer a theatrical marquee, this threshold promises a dark, more intimate chamber of unknowing experience. Crossing it immediately challenges institutionalized, passive, spectatorial complacency.

The individual, with or without the group, passes through the curtains. Moving out of the well-lit gallery into the dark interior reveals a mock theater framing the inevitable performance/spectacle. Accordingly, the spectator awaits the onset of anticipated event(s).

Crossing the threshold, however, promises nothing. The individual's mere physical presence in the darkened space does not guarantee closure. The assemblage of events may not cohere, nor will it necessarily produce anything more than a superficial reading. For an incisive encounter, the individual must engage the impulse of the presentation. A reconstructed maze must come to exist in the abstract field represented by the multiple layers and folds of the mind. No signs, guides, or legends mark this path.

The play begins. It cycles through its carefully scripted format. Unlike the atemporality of a painting, or an installation that remains hierarchically equal at every moment, *Siren*'s thirteen- to fourteen-minute continuity begins on the quarter hour, builds toward a climax, and concludes. Unlike many installations, it remains committed to a linear structure. Nevertheless, a sense of cycle pervades the piece. Narrative linearity is offset by intermittent movements on the screen through the two respective mazes as individuals go in and out of the installation chamber. The alternating presence and absence of image and sound traces forms constellations of clues, waves of information to be processed and reprocessed as if reliving the daytime/nighttime, conscious/unconscious twenty-four-hour clock cycle of awakening, sleeping, and then reawakening. The open format makes stepping over the threshold at any other time equal to engaging the piece at its incipient moment, for the layers never form a set sequence. Simply made up of these layers, and not of shots or scenes, the continuity provides no direct passageway through the piece.

Complementing the oceanic score, the physical design of the installation handicaps traditional point-of-view operations. Tempering the totemic structure of the image by decentering the viewer's fascination, *Siren*'s interior design raises many issues that may carry over to other installations replicating the conditions of the cave. Its central screen, though larger and historically more privileged than its smaller, lateral counterparts, remains dark for long stretches of time. When activated, the central screen often merely echoes the activity on the side monitors. Viewer attention, therefore, oscillates back and forth between the peripheral active stimulation sites. By dispersing the contact points, the installation dislocates and diffuses its central regulating stimulus.

In her 1977 book titled *This Sex Which Is Not One,* Luce Irigaray's discussion of female sexuality brackets this marginalization of experience.

> [W]oman's autoeroticism is very different from man's. In order to touch himself, man needs an instrument: his hand, a woman's body, language. And this self-caressing requires at least a minimum of activity. As for woman, she touches herself in and of herself without any need for mediations, and before there is any way to distinguish activity from passivity. Woman "touches herself" all the time, and moreover no one can forbid her to do so, for her genitals are formed of two lips in continuous contact. Thus, within herself, she is already two—but not divisible into one(s)—that caress each other.[14]

The electronic installation performs along that threshold. Both impulsive and calculated, sublime and relentless, it constrains the imaginary yet liberates the intellect.

> Perhaps it is time to return to that repressed entity, the female imaginary. So woman does not have a sex organ? She has at least two of them, but they are not identifiable as ones. Indeed, she has many more. Her sexuality, always at least double, goes even further: it is plural. Is this the way culture is seeking to characterize itself now? Is this the way texts write themselves/are written now?[15]

The split interior and semantic obliquity on one level corresponds to that dualism suggested by Irigaray's description.

On the other hand, the lips do not meet, do not form closure and identity. Rather, they remain open, leading into that psychodynamic orifice that forever represents the unknown, fear, and uncertainty for the uninitiated.

> This autoeroticism is disrupted by a violent break-in: the brutal separation of the two lips by a violating penis, an intrusion that distracts and deflects the woman from this "self-caressing" she needs if she is not to incur the disappearance of her own pleasure in sexual relations.[16]

The spectator operates within that space. After the intrusion, the spectator seeks to satiate his (or her) appetite by completing the form/structure of the experience. Once satiated, exploration falls off dramatically. The spectator moves on.[17]

If an individual takes pleasure in the vertical rather than the narrative thrust of the piece, interest in the installation endures. Satisfaction comes from more than a simple in and out.

Regardless of specific spectator experience, the installation represents a body open to penetration. The individual's gaze and passage implies the penetration. Appropriately, the earliest image seen on the center screen forms an orange, burning mouth pronouncing the words that beckon the viewer into the maze. Seductively, the oral orifice opens a passageway into the spiritual, an opaque domain of poetic language and thought. As a cavity, it remains close to that play on desire, fornication, the communication of inexplicable feeling, and, at least for the male, the drive to enter the unknown, a potentially threatening but wonderful temporary world.

On the screen(s), the cinematography through the respective mazes complements the structure of the installation, and, at the very least, embodies this adventurous play. No single conduit of pleasure, however, marks the entrance into this experience. No central viewing angle channels the viewer's attention. The decentered focus suggests a different spectrum of pleasure.

Multiple screens fill the gap. The diverse locations, the manner in which the screens inhibit a privileged angle among the limited viewing positions, breaks the scopic-erotic, voyeuristic foothold. In his article "Ideological Effects of the Basic Cinematographic Apparatus," Jean-Louis Baudry describes the origins of the privileged center.

> It is the perspective construction of the Renaissance which originally served as model. . . . The center of this space coincides with the eye which Jean Pellerin Viator will so justly call the "subject.". . . Contrary to Chinese and Japanese painting, Western easel painting, presenting as it does a motionless and continuous whole, elaborates a total vision which corresponds to the idealist conception of the fullness and homogeneity of "being. . . ."[18]

In contrast to the model of Japanese and Chinese painting's different totalizing vision, Western displacement, according to Irigaray, becomes promulgated in a culture in which sexual relations are impracticable because man's desire and woman's are strangers to each other . . . in which the two desires have to try to meet through indirect means, whether the archaic one of a sense-relation to the mother's body, or the present one of active or passive extension of the law of the father.[19]

Decentering the image suspends the immobility of the spectator. It liberates the viewer to wander visually, physically, and cognitively through the reconstituted space, "to take pleasure more from touching than from looking."[20]

As the piece proceeds and people move about the installation interior, a smaller number of viewers risk blocking the central screen. They cross the second threshold and pass into the interior chamber(s). On the inside, now visible on the side walls on a trajectory similar to the inclination of the two outer monitors, the two smaller monitors appear. The inner monitors replay the other side of the closed-circuit divide, the outside of the cave.

In essence, within the deepest recesses of the installation lie the most distant reaches of the experience. When the viewer tries to look back on the entrance into the pavilion, on his or her own shadow entering the cave, the image of that entrance has disappeared. There is a schism in time and space. The viewer looks into the future and observes the next viewer(s) entering the cave. Moreover, the viewer sees his or her future exit and its inevitable re-presentation to the new viewer. The unknowing tread the now-known path toward the interior of the pavilion. As the locus of forces converge, the new entrants, however, may never make it as far as the silent observers of their entrance into the outer chamber.

This existential odyssey marks the beginning of language. It crystallizes with the viewer's passage into the deepest recesses of space and marks the primal opening through which time replays the viewer's experience of the piece. The loop or temporal warp does not end there. Upon exiting the pavilion, the viewer reappears on that chimerical screen, perhaps to be viewed by someone else.

This inside-out perversion of time and space represents the ultimate play of any installation. Does the falling tree in a deserted forest make no sound? What does it mean when nobody views the viewer entering or leaving the pavilion, the installation, the cave? Must an individual know that he or she becomes implicated as part of the spectacle for the synaptic sparks to fly? Though this mystery remains fleeting, each installation undertakes its investigation.

In the maze, in the cave, in the cognitive recess, the installation lacks an absolute form. In the context of the times, it opens up a larger number of sensuous platforms. If none lingers, the environment forces the stalker to shift attention. Darkness prevails. As the wanderer retreats to the auditory spectrum, traces of visual information break through the opaque underbrush. The visual text, another physical voice speaking its own kinetic language, inverts the collective experience. The individual experience remains one. In the end, the individual's presence equals his or her absence, while the events' emotive and signifying status goes on.

Notes

1. Installed in the Spring of 1990 at the Philadelphia Museum of Art.

2. All secondary references to the text of the installation should not be confused with the artist's intent; they originate with this writing.

3. Plato, *The Republic*, trans. H. D. P. Lee (Baltimore: Penguin Books, 1955), 278–79.

4. Ibid., 279.

5. "In relation to meaning, the Imaginary is that in which perceptual features like resemblance operate. . . . For Lacan, the Imaginary relationship, of whatever kind, is also that of a lure, a trap. In a sense, he is close to the normal usage of the word "imaginary" to describe something we believe to be something else." Anthony Wilden, "Lacan and the Discourse of the Other," in *Jacques Lacan: Speech and Language in Psychoanalysis*, trans. Anthony Wilden (Baltimore: Johns Hopkins University Press, 1968), 175.

6. Plato, *Republic*, 279–80.

7. Existence before essence.

8. Joseph Conrad, *The Heart of Darkness* (New York: W. W. Norton, 1963), 35–36.

9. Ibid., 39.

10. The text is derived from W. H. Hudson's *Green Mansions*.

11. *Siren* represented two mazes: a landscaped field on Block Island, Rhode Island, and a fabricated brick circular concourse construction in the Catskill Mountains of New York State.

12. Conrad, *Heart of Darkness*, 7.

13. The textual score of *Siren*.

14. Luce Irigaray, *This Sex Which Is Not One*, trans. Catherine Porter (Ithaca, N.Y.: Cornell University Press, 1985), 24.

15. Ibid., 28.

16. Ibid., 24.

17. The metaphor of the spectator should not be taken at face value, but rather as a starting point for examining this installation in light of the reference to female sexuality and autonomous pleasure. In short, the visitor should not be read as a violating penis.

18. Jean-Louis Baudry, "Ideological Effects of the Basic Cinemato-graphic Apparatus," *Film Quarterly* 28, no. 2 (Winter 1974–75): 41–42.

19. Irigaray, *This Sex*, 27.

20. Ibid., 26.

One Video Theory
(some assembly required)

Gregory Ulmer

Against explanation

People have become concerned about "totalization" in all of its forms, one of which is explanation. Explanation, perhaps because it shares so many features with narrative (teleology, closure, the truth effect), has become suspect. It is little more than "secondary elaboration," suturing the gaps of ignorance, reasoning by enthymemes, imposing a causality that derives more from syntax than from the object of study. Explanations lend a false unity, homogeneity, universality, to a heterogeneous body of materials, ignoring or sublating real differences in the interest of an artificial verisimilitude of plausibility.

At its worst, this argument against explanation is a rejection of theory by those who would deny the fictional, speculative dimension of academic writing. At its best, this suspicion of totalization supports the increasing interest in collage/montage, allegory, and associative reasoning that is evident in poststructuralist textualism and deconstructive art (Brian Wallis, *Art After Modernism*). I want to take advantage of this situation in order to work through a theory of video, in pieces, providing an inventory of materials that might constitute the basis for a general account. The collection makes no claims to completeness, but the sequence is not random. Each item of the set will be described in an order created not by a goal (for that is unknown) but by associations, which is to say that the final principle of classification is not argumentative or expository, but poetic.

The act of unification, then, is shifted to the side of reading, partly to leave more room for the process of inference that is involved in understanding any written text, and partly to invite additions to the sequence, to enrich the chain of associations in order to give the theory greater complexity. The question is how to distribute thoughts on video. My assumption is that a theory of video, to be adequate, must adapt itself to the cognitive style of the electronic apparatus, regardless of the medium in which it is deployed.

The television set

The problem of electronic cognition poses the question of how information is to be organized in the medium of video. If the computer as a technology supports algorithmic order, then video may be said to be the technology of heuristics (heuresis, heuretics). To the degree that the two technologies converge institutionally as well as technically, a theory of video will have to be a theory of computers as well. For now it is possible to leave the mathematics of sets on the side of algorithms in order to explore the supplement to artificial intelligence programming available in the artificial nonsense (or stupidity) of television programs: the television set (or Poste).

There is a television set in my living room, incredible as that may seem. The fact that more homes have television sets than have indoor plumbing should not detract from the unusualness of each instance.

Growing up in Montana, I did not have an opportunity to see very much television (technical and economic factors delayed the wiring of the high frontier). I have no recollection of my family owning a TV set at all. I am skeptical even of the photograph my mother produced showing me (as a senior in high school) standing next to a set in our living room. Photographs can be doctored. Certainly I would have remembered that set, which was in style something between a portable and a console, resting on four splayed legs in the corner next to the picture window. I have repressed the memory of that initiation into television in the 1950s that has become American memory itself. It should seem odd that the conventions of this unrealistic genre would be internalized by viewers as a yardstick for "life" itself. As John Waters recalls, "When I was a kid, you were raised to believe that your family should be like *Leave It to Beaver* or *Father Knows Best*. . . . I was raised to think that *Father Knows Best* was the Way It Was" (Graham, 113). In fact, it was that way (at least as far as I can remember). In memory, the 1950s is to America what the Eiffel Tower is to Paris.

In graduate school I never thought about television, except when I watched the evening news to keep track of Vietnam. The tube on this twelve-inch set (purchased used) was going bad, so that the picture was squeezed into an ever narrowing band. Finally there was just a two-inch strip of image across the middle of the screen. I remember Lyndon Johnson's face, pressed into this strip as if in a fun-house mirror, announcing that it would not run for reelection.

The first year my wife and I were in Gainesville we were invited to participate, on a trial basis, in a "Gourmet Club." Eight couples showed up at the home of the host, each with an elaborately prepared dish. In keeping with the character of the times, a huge argument broke out about Nixon. The men yelled at one another, gobbling their food without tasting it, while the women frowned at them and only picked at their plates. On the way out (having flunked the trial) I noticed a large color television console in the host's living room. "Are you sure that set's big enough?" I asked, sarcastically. "Or are you just keeping this for the neighborhood?" "After you've been in Gainesville a little longer," he replied, "you'll have one of these too." His defense of Nixon was wrong, but not his prediction about my TV set.

"Believe it or not"

The host is Jack Palance. He explains how a Martian came to be buried in a small Texas town, adding, in a voice that makes your hair stand on end, "Believe it–or not!" Palance handles all the tales from the far side. The hostess is Marie Osmond (just as scary as Palance in her own way). As if reading for a part in the junior class play, Osmond explains the origins of Dadaism in the Zurich of 1916. She is taped standing in the Dada museum, recalling in a bemused tone (and in her own words) Hugo Ball's account of his performance. "I wore a special costume designed by Janco and myself. My legs were encased in a tight-fitting cylindrical pillar of shiny blue cardboard which reached to my hips so that I looked like an obelisk. Above this I wore a huge cardboard coat-collar, scarlet inside and gold outside, which was fastened at the neck in such a way that I could flap it like a pair of wings by moving my elbows. I also wore a high, cylindrical, blue and white striped witch doctor's hat" (Melzer, "The Dada Actor," 40). Then Marie Osmond reads the text (I don't remember exactly which one, but it goes something like this): "Gadji beri

bimba glandridl laula lonni cadori gadjamma gramma berida bim-
bala glandri galassassa laulitalomini gadji beri bin blassa glassala
laula lonni cadorsu sassala bim gadjama tufim izimzalla binban gi
gia wowolima bin ber ban." "Believe it–or not!" Hugo Ball's audience is said to have laughed, screamed, applauded. Or, as in the
usual account of a French avant-garde event, "a fist-fight ensued."
What was the effect in the living rooms of America of Marie Osmond
meeting Hugo Ball on this program, as uncanny a congruence as
finding a sewing machine on an operating table? Michael Taussig
reminds us of the original intent of such performances, that the
wordlessness of words is more than words, that gurgling of frogs in
the millennial mud of the jungle of the throat of mankind that cures
in Putumayo, that too was taken up as a weapon in the confrontation with the bad new times. As the German Dadaist poet Hugo Ball
wrote in his diary on 5 March 1917, planning an event for the
Cabaret Voltaire in Zurich: "The next step is for poetry to discard
language as painting discarded the object, and for similar reasons.
Nothing like this has ever existed before" (Taussig, 29). What has
existed before, however, is the likes of television, one of whose pre-
cursors, as the *Ripley's* show makes clear, is the "dime museum" of
P. T. Barnum, where he presented "freaks, variety acts, and other
attractions in his 'lecture room' to augment the appeal of his inanimate exhibits." All were designed to convey a moral lesson acceptable to the middle class (Allen, *Channels of Discourse*, 62–63).

What is the relationship between the "monster" and its frame?
One theory claims that this mediated monster is received homeo-
pathically as an "inoculation."

Mythologies

Taussig's *Shamanism, Colonialism, and the Wild Man* is not an
explanation but an experiment in cultural hybridization, tapping the
surrealism of the colonial unconscious formed out of the mixing of
European literacy and Indian orality. At stake is a program for making socially effective images. In his theoretical collage, Taussig
applies Walter Benjamin's philosophy of history to the problem of
ethnography, putting into practice the lesson Benjamin drew from
the catastrophe of his own epoch: the political image mixes history
and myth, the old and the new at once, dreams and science.
"Another way of putting this is to point out that [Benjamin] didn't
place much faith in facts and information in winning arguments, let

alone class struggle, and that it was in the less conscious image realm and in the dream world of the popular imagination that he saw it necessary to act" (Taussig, *Shamanism*, 69). Not concepts, but images, images in which might be concentrated extensive quantities of cultural information, could penetrate thought impermeable to logic.

The province of popular media is mythmaking, just as properly as it is the function of discipline discourse to make science. Events are the raw materials for both, but historiography and journalism make different uses of them. As Taussig points out, there are always, and from the beginning, several stories available for any set of events. Science tends to select the one in the style of nonfiction treatise. Journalism tends to pick the one with the best fit to an extant narrative formula. At the time of Custer's last stand, for example, two interpretations were available—one fairly close to the version prevalent today (anticolonialist) and the other in the form of heroic legend. Richard Slotkin has shown how the Eastern newspapers of the day, principally James Gordon Bennett's *Herald*, selected the latter to form a metaphor, in the guise of news, for the threat posed to the status quo by blacks and the working class (Slotkin). The myth of Albert Einstein, associating the pure scientist with the nuclear holocaust, is similarly traced to a cover of Time magazine juxtaposing Einstein's face with his famous formula and a picture of a nuclear explosion (Friedman and Donley). In fact Einstein's involvement with the development of the bomb was belatedly political and not technical.

It is not a question of a confrontation between scholars and journalists, with one constantly trying to hold the other to the literal facts, but of a complementary collaboration in which history and myth interact. For in the age of information, history is a product of the accounts made during the unfolding of an event, as in the "social drama" of terrorism. In the case of the kidnapping of Aldo Moro, for example, the full range of literate, oral, and electronic media were engaged in an attempt, in the public sphere, to control the meaning of the event, with the various protagonists constructing their own stories and deconstructing those of their antagonists (Wagner-Pacifici). The modes of this hermeneutic struggle (a version of Bakhtin's heterological word), Wagner-Pacifici stresses, are dependent in part on aesthetic imperatives that shape the "rhetorical surround" guiding the representation and reception of information. The organizing idea of her analysis of Moro's social drama is that "good theater encourages good politics, that bad theater encourages bad politics, and that the theatrical aspects of politics can similarly be good or bad depending on the theatrical paradigms (going back to Turner and Marx) called forth (12). In this instance melodrama triumphed over tragic emplotment, with negative political and social consequences. That melodrama and not tragedy is the dominant mode of popular media does not bode well, in this view, for an electronic democracy. Why limit the choice to these two options? Journalism is ready for the avant-garde process (for the break with realism–a trail blazed by the *National Enquirer*).

The public sphere

John Forester edited a collection, *Critical Theory and Public Life*, intended to be an applied version of Habermas's critical communications theory. Taking up the question of social construction and management of political consent, the authors address specific instances of the colonialization of the life world by instrumental reason, and the decline of the public sphere mediating private experience and the state, thus permitting direct, unmediated penetration of commodification into individual desire. The problem as stated could be compared to the hole in the ozone that has appeared over the South Pole, indicating the decay of the atmosphere mediating earth's relationship with the sun. What happens to the process of legitimation by rational consensus in an age of informational capitalism, in which the invention, distribution, and application of information replaces the industrial manufacture of goods and the provision of services as the predominant economic force in society? Forester and his colleagues still operate according to the grand explanatory metanarrative of emancipation. Habermas's reformulation of relations of power in terms of life-world colonization or penetration suggests a far wider range of sites of resistance, including not only workplaces but also homes, schools, the public sphere, the state, and cultural institutions. Thus the praxis that these essays may inform combines purpose with a vision of freedom from illegitimate power. Resistance to illegitimate power is itself social action, itself interpretive and contingent, itself an offering to others to act together, to learn together, to make possible life in a community. Resistance here does not mean the pursuit of ideal speech; it does mean organizing to make democratic politics a reality (Forester, *Critical Theory*, xv). Few could disagree with the values expressed in this goal. The question rather concerns the model of the subject upon which the strategy of "resistance" depends. It is the subject as reader, autonomous, unified, self-aware, capable of rational analysis of information in the privacy of the home, free from the passions and prejudices of emotion. It is a subject formed in the apparatus of literacy, dependent on a specific historical configuration of technology, institutional practices (a written model of knowledge and law and the behaviors of selfhood (the humanistic ideology of individualism). Is this apparatus still in place? The debate about the constructed nature of the human subject among humanists, Marxists, and deconstructors is one symptom that things are changing. The institutions organized by the apparatus of literacy express a nearly universal condemnation of a new institution whose organization reflects a new apparatus–television, representing the electronic apparatus (different technology, institutional practices, and personal behaviors). The recent presidential election campaigns in general, and George Bush's use of television in particular, indicate what happens when a literate institutionalization of democracy is conducted by a technology alien to that apparatus. There is a fundamental confusion of realms, which calls for a major commitment to applied research in order to avoid the political equivalent of organ rejection in transplant operations. Two political phenomena fundamental to American existence—democracy and the nation-state–are based on literacy. Are they transferable to an electronic apparatus?

What needs to be thought is the other of literacy. The positivistic ideology of literacy excluded the magic of oral culture from the discourses of knowledge, but now a cooperation between literacy and orality is possible through a technology with features of both apparatuses (written and spoken). The electronic epoch does not come after literacy, but between, bringing literacy and orality into a potentially supportive rather than exclusionary relationship for the first time in history.

Is the concept of the public sphere adequate to the requirements of mediation in an electronic world, or does mediation itself have to be reinvented within the electronic apparatus?

"Differences between positions blur, resulting in unavoidable fusion and confusion. Deprived of objective limits, the architectonic element begins to drift, to float in an electronic ether devoid of spatial dimensions yet inscribed in the single temporality of an instantaneous diffusion. From this moment on, no one can be considered as separated by physical obstacles or by significant "time distances." With the interfacade of monitors and control screens, "elsewhere" begins here and vice versa. Constructed space now occurs within an electronic topology, where the framing of the point of view and the scan lines of digital images give new form to the practice of urban mapping. Replacing the old distinctions between public and private and "habitation" and "circulation" is an overexposure in which the gap between "micro" and "macro" disappears through electronic microscope scanning" (Virillo, "The Overexposed City," 18).

How shall we think about information in an electronic apparatus? Haven't we all seen some version of the statistics? Ninety-five percent of the knowledge amassed in the year 2020 will have been created after 1980; knowledge is expanding at a rate of 100 trillion bits per year; to be as adequate to knowledge in 2020 as Diderot's encyclopedia was to knowledge in the eighteenth century would require 200 million volumes of the Britannica. By the time an American child reaches the age of eighteen, he/she has spent as much time watching television as attending school. In short, a new behavior has been invented—the daily contemplation of a multitude of dramatized murders and car crashes—whose function is a mystery to the literate mind.

Grammatology

Literate intellectuals, beginning in the Enlightenment, took up the task of inventing the "other," a project that may be understood best by analogy with the project that preceded it–the invention of the "self." The extraordinary preoccupation with every manner of otherness, defined negatively at first by its opposition to the dominant ideology of the subject in Western civilization (now characterized as "patriarchal"), may be recognized as a part of the transformation process associated with the change in apparatus from literacy to electronics. In terms of the apparatus (a social machine), the "self" is as much an invention as the technology associated with it (alphabetic writing). It is useful, in attempting to formulate a theory of video, to work by analogy with the scholarship available on the origins of literacy.

In *The Muse Learns to Write*, Eric Havelock reviews his career as a grammatologist, summarizing the insights of a movement whose coherence became apparent with the nearly simultaneous publication (in a period of less than twelve months, ending in the spring of

1963) of five studies: *The Savage Mind* (Lévi-Strauss), *The Conse-quences of Literacy* (Goody and Watt); *The Gutenberg Galaxy* (McLuhan), *Animal Species and Evolution* (Mayr); and *Preface to Plato* (Havelock) (Havelock, *The Muse*, 25). Publications by Walter Ong and Jacques Derrida (among others) in this decade established the continuing vitality of grammatology. The key insight of this movement, for Havelock, "involves the proposition that the way we use our senses and the way we think are connected, and that in the transition from Greek orality to Greek literacy the terms of this con-nection were altered also, and have remained altered, as compared with the mentality of oralism, ever since" (98). Havelock stresses that conceptual thinking had to be invented. It emerged gradually, extracted from the works of Homer and Hesiod, among others, as a new way to connect materials. In an oral culture, information is held in memory and thus made available for thought in two principal ways—by verse rhythms and by narrative. With the advent of liter-acy, this combination of patterns was replaced with a new manner of connections, following not the actions of a specific example but the definition of types; it reflected not doing but being. There was intelligent thought before the alphabet, obviously, but it was not log-ical in the way that we understand the term. The transitional step is manifest in Hesiod's innovative decision to devote a formal discus-sion not to a person but to a topic—*dike*, or "justice." "Having made his choice, Hesiod could not conjure the required discourse out of thin air. We could easily manage it today, because we inherit two thousand years of literate habit. He, on the contrary, had to resort to the oral word as already known—the only preserved word that was known. He had to build his own semiconnected discourse out of dis-connected bits and pieces contained in oral discourse, either some pieces in which the term happened for whatever reason to occur or others in which incidents occurred that he felt were appropriate to connect with the word. His decision was compositional (rather than ideological), or perhaps we should say recompositional" (102). Hes-iod did not yet have the syntax of propositional definition, but his efforts were a major part of the invention of conceptual language that culminated in Plato's dialogues. He made do with a collage pro-cedure, revealing the extent to which the Greek invention was a hybrid of oral and literate qualities.

The other element of this invention process of special impor-tance for our analogy with the similar process underway in the appa-ratus of electronics is, as noted previously, the association of the invention of conceptual discourse with the invention of "self." "The "self" was a Socratic discovery or, perhaps we should say, an invention of the Socratic vocabulary. The linguistic method used to identify it and examine it was originally oral, so far as Socrates was concerned. Later it was "textualized" by Plato. But though oral, the Socratic dialectic depended upon the previous isolation of language in its written form as something separate from the person who uttered it. The person who used the language but was now separated from it became the "personality" who could now discover its existence. The language so discovered became that level of theoretic discourse denoted by logos" (114). The symbol of this selfhood, Havelock adds, became the psyche, the ghost of oral epic now internalized, and called "the ghost in me." A corollary of the subject formation called psyche was the invention of the institutional practice of dialectics, or reasoned argumentation, whose reception among the orally oriented citizens we may figure in Nietzsche's terms: "The dialectician leaves it to his opponent to prove that he is no idiot—he makes one furious and helpless at the same time. The dialectician renders the intellect of his opponent powerless. Indeed? Is dialectic only a form of revenge in Socrates?" (Nietzsche, *Will to Power*, 476).

What is the analogy, then ? How does it direct our attention and research, as we work to formulate a theory of video? Nietzsche's sympathy with the "noble" values of oral civilization against those of literacy marks the paradigm shift that is the analogical basis for grammatology. His attack on concepts signals the beginning of postliterate thinking, and clears a space negatively for a positive invention of electronic reasoning, perhaps a hybrid of action and abstraction. The first point to make about this process is that any theory of video will be literate, a product of the thought invented out of the introduction of the alphabet into an oral culture. Thus it will be to video thinking as a kind of hymn to writing. At best it can be useful in reviewing the activities of theorization as they come up against an obstacle and are blocked by the limits of memory organized conceptually (or, as Nietzsche said, "turned into mummies"[479]).

What of this process of emergence, the gradual invention of an alternative cognition? It is happening now between us and our sets—TVs and monitors—interacting with literacy. The ghost is changing its relation to the body again. It is no longer in us entirely, but escaping out of the crypt known as "ego." At the level of writing, the same process described by Havelock of isolating and extracting a signifier out of the flow of speech (revealing a pattern of *dike* around the stories of the heroes) is happening again as video artists play Hesiod to the Homer of the television. The prototypical example is Dara Birnbaum's *Kiss the Girls: Make Them Cry*, in which she isolates a unit of meaning, a "syntagm" such as the whirl that transforms Wonder Woman. TV shows "break down into recognizable syntagms (syntagm means here: gestures, articles of clothing, identifying shots that repeat weekly, like rules of habit in a story vocabulary). That is why they are so easy to appropriate in video art" (Klein, "Audience Culture," 584). What is being isolated in the few seconds of each syntagm, Klein suggests, is audience memory: "Body language and familiar apparel refer literally to audience memories; in short, the eras of consumerism and fashions are indexed as audience history. Bits of forties and fifties nostalgia compete in hat styles: a porkpie hat for Mike Hammer, a slouched hat for Indiana Jones" (386).

Meanwhile, all we talk about is the "other," which must be the name of an electronic resubjectivation. And who is the electronic Socrates (who today is the one most denounced)? Wouldn't it have to be a subject that is not one?

The subject of television

In its classic formulations, the concept of the "apparatus" took account of the role of ideology in the invention process. The cinema "machine," for example, was said to include the mind of the audience (ideology and practices). In this perspective it is never a question of technological determinism. The camera comes into practical existence (after a long historical evolution) as a function of a certain individualism, a tendency that continues in the design and distribution of electronic devices. In classic Hollywood films, which were dominated by a single mode of narrative form (continuity editing) and the aesthetics of realism, the assumption is "that the action will spring primarily from *individual characters as causal agents*" (Bordwell, *Film Art*, 98). That this emphasis on the individual is not merely political in a narrow sense may be seen in the rejection in Soviet cinema of Eisenstein's attempts to develop an alternative to Hollywood narrative by creating a narrative based on a collective subject.

The dominant mode of film theory has focused on this individual subject, if only to show the extent to which that subject is positioned by collective cultural systems and operations beyond the grasp of an individual. A convenient transition from film theory to a theorization of video is available in a collection of essays edited by Robert C. Allen, *Channels of Discourse*, in which a group of academics explore the applicability of film theory to television. Although treating a wide range of critical schools, the group is unified in its politics, taking the explanatory metanarrative of emancipation as the legitimation for its critique.

It is the problem of critique and the public sphere. On one hand, the scholars manifest all the assumptions of the apparatus of literacy, including the subject of conceptual knowledge; on the other hand, they are uniformly skeptical about the applicability of current film theory to television, even if the notion of the subject at work in that theory is psychoanalytic (recognizing a split, discontinuous subject, that differs from the self of Enlightenment rationality). Thus cinema might be a transitional apparatus, part literacy, part video, designing a new mode of information in accord with an extant literate being of the "self." After all, what is cinema but novels (literate form) translated into film—the equivalent of inscribing the *Iliad*. Television is a different matter. "From these examples it should be clear that the classical cinema's unified form contrasts with the fragmentation at the heart of the televised daytime drama. Both film and television have specific systems of enunciation that structure relations of vision and identification in different ways. These produce a different type of spectator, a different subject-effect for each mode of meaning-production. I have tried to show by this example how virtually every psychoanalytic process in the cinematic apparatus is deconstructed by the complex strategies of enunciation in the soap opera (as a prime example of the TV apparatus)" (Flitterman-Lewis, "Psychoanalysis, Film," 203).

It is not simply a question of a different technology (video instead of film), but of a different institutionalization as well, and different practices of viewing that occur in the home, in the family that uses television. There are also the different forms and genres emerging in television that distinguish it from cinema. It is the question of posthumanism—the obstacle of the subject to any further thought. Yet we know from the analogy with the invention of conceptual language that the "self" is subject to change. Michel Foucault took the technologies of self as his problematic and attempted to think them through without the story of emancipation. Even Foucault, however, at the moment of stating the project at its most radical, could not escape the ubiquity of this metanarrative of liberation. "The conclusion would be that the political, ethical, social, philosophical problem of our day is not to try to liberate the individual from the state and from the state's institutions, but to liberate us both from the state and from the type of individualization that is linked to the state. We have to promote new forms of subjectivity through the refusal of this kind of individuality, which has been imposed on us for several centuries" (Foucault, 424). Jean Baudrillard, in the same collection of essays (representing postmodernism), indicates more specifically the association of Foucault's program with the electronic media. "Power can have no hold on persons in a media environment, because ideology as legitimation, as the manipulation of consent, depends upon a distinction between reality and copies. But in the confusion of the simulated and the real effected by the electronic apparatus, the critique of institutions based on subject positioning (the essence of film theory) loses its relevance" (Baudrillard, 268). The logic governing discourse in this view is that of the "precession of the simulacra," in which the map does not refer to the territory but precedes and generates it (the map as heuretic rather than hermeneutic).

If the behaviors of self were invented, as Havelock describes it, with the help of a freeze–frame arresting of the word out of an acoustic flow, they are disappearing again, adapting to a different flow of information. If the subject of film was still positioned by its relation to the look, to the gaze (somehow in the family of Hesiod's *dike*), television is no longer consumed as a spectacle. The convergence of home computer, television, and telephone lines as the nexus of a new social machinery testifies to an undoing of the spectacular consumption of the commodity. It is a reversal of the process indicated by Debord, in which the seeming self-sufficiency of the commodity was a "congealment" of forces that were essentially mobile and dynamic. Now, however, with pure flux itself a commodity, a spectacular and "contemplative" relation to objects is undermined and supplanted by new kinds of investments (Crary, *Techniques of the Observer*, 287). Crary uses *General Hospital*, a soap opera, to exemplify the new logic available in this apparatus, in which referentiality and representation are replaced (as they were in Hesiod) with an abstract invention. "In its construction and effects, *General Hospital* announces the disappearance of the visual and narrative space that might seem to have authorized it and points toward a fully programmable calculus of continually switching syntheses of figural and narrative units. More and more the so-called "content" of television shifts in this direction: it is not at all a question of the replication of life, but of its reduction to abstract and manipulatable elements ready to be harmonized with a plethora of other electronic flows" (289). Television is repeating, with an entirely different look, the construction of a new power of generalization, in other words, comparable to the one built out of narrative action with the advent of literacy. The *Theogony, Works and Days*, and *General Hospital* should be compared more systematically, in the interests of the analogy of apparatuses. And the alliance of television with other electronic networks, creating new social arrangements, contributes, Crary says, to the formation of a new subject, such that the site of greatest instability, of volatile disequilibrium, in our culture now (with no guarantees of either emancipatory or fascist control) is the connection of body to keyboard, to video tube.

Alienation

Fredric Jameson shows one way to put these pieces together in "Reading Without Interpretation: Post-Modernism and the Video-Text." Jameson identifies the primary obstacle to a theory of video—the assumption of critical distance. Or rather, he suggests that video is a medium in which not only is critical distance not involved (critical distance is a feature of literacy, and not of orality or electronics), but (and this is much more surprising) neither is memory. The virtue of his approach is to come to the discussion of video without—as nearly as this is possible in written form—the assumptions and expectations of literacy. That is, it is possible to imagine that critical distance is no more necessary for electronic memory than singing is for nuclear physics. He also tried to clear his mind of "explanatory temptations," meaning finally the entire machinery of film theory. Presuming, rather than trying to prove, that the dominant force in our culture now is video ("in its twin manifestations as commercial television and as experimental video"), Jameson excludes film theory from any account of the new apparatus. "The very richness of film theory today makes this decision and this warning unavoidable. If the experience of the movie screen and its mesmerizing images is distinct, and fundamentally different, from the experience of the television monitor, then the very maturity and sophistication of film conceptualities will necessarily obscure the originality of film's cousin, whose specific features demand to be reconstructed afresh and empty-handed, without imported and extrapolated categories" (Jameson, 201).

To help him think from the side of the video paradigm, Jameson selects a "tutor video" that exemplifies the qualities of "flow" (in it can still be recognized, however, a "collage" style, or compilation). The text is entitled alieNATION (available from Video Data Bank in Chicago). "It includes experimental mice, voice-overed by various pseudoscientific reports and therapeutic programs (how to deal with stress, beauty care, hypnosis for weight loss, etc.); then s. f. footage (including monster music and camp dialogue), mostly drawn from a Japanese film, *Godzilla vs. Monster Zero* (1966); optical children's blocks and erector sets, reproductions of classical paintings, as well as mannequins, advertising images, computer printouts, textbook illustrations of all kinds, cartoon figures rising and falling, including a wonderful Magritte hat slowly sinking into Lake Michigan; sheet lightning; a woman lying down and possibly under hypnosis . . ." (210). Jameson's strategy is to delay as long as possible his alphabetic response to this text—his ability to recognize its associative organization by means of juxtapositions and repetitions of images and sounds, and to relate these patterns to a hermeneutic frame (translating the video into a literate discourse). He finally compromises by producing a singular reading, selecting from the flow of images a very few items on the basis of contingent associations of his own: he identifies, in short, what could be called the "secret" of the text (its ghost). He supplies, that is, a motivation from the referential realm for the unmotivated scenes of the laboratory experiments on Twinkies, and the milk carton with the hole in it (identified as a bullet hole). "For the American media public the combination of the two elements—milk and Hostess Twinkie—is too peculiar to be unmotivated. In fact, on 27 November 1978 (the year immediately before the production of this particular videotape), the San Francisco supervisor Harvey Milk was shot to death by a former supervisor, who entered the unforgettable plea of not guilty by reason of insanity precipitated by the excessive consumption of Hostess Twinkies" (220). Having produced this link, Jameson doesn't know what to do with it, except to relate the implausibility of anyone noticing this association to the crisis of the referent in poststructuralism and postmodernism. (He missed, perhaps, the installment of "American Justice" on the Arts and Entertainment channel devoted to the "Twinkie defense.") He is reluctant to take responsibility for his own status as switch, joining the play of signifiers (the "logic of postmodernism" as opposed to the monumentality of modernism) with the historically real. The opening sequence of "alieNATION," in fact, is a didactic piece on how to make a circuit, complete with wiring, a switch (upon which a laboratory mouse is crawling) and an explanation of "conduction." "Conduction" is the name of the logic that the tape (representing video in general) is teaching us to think. I described conduction at length in *Teletheory and Heuretics*, so I will not go into it again, except to say that it is an electronic supplement to the established modes of reasoning, including induction and deduction in empirical and rationalist science, and abduction in hermeneutic pragmatics. If the circuit of reasoning moves from things to rules by means of abduction, from rules to cases by deduction, and cases to things by induction (see Eco and Sebeok), then reasoning moves directly from thing to thing in the real by means of conduction. Conduction concerns a logic of invention or of making, and is to heuretics what abduction is to hermeneutics. A tape such as "alieNATION" can be treated hermeneutically as an object of study for a reading, for a literate subject of knowledge, but that is not the kind of thinking organizing the tape itself. Jameson shows us, albeit reluctantly, how to think conductively, by joining the Twinkie and milk scenes into an evocation of the story of Harvey Milk. What remains to be imagined is what to do with that kind of reasoning, leaping from one bit of information to another on the basis of the weakest motivation possible. Its value is certainly not interpretive, even if Jameson thought he was behaving hermeneutically when he produced this circuit. It is, rather, as the analogy of the apparatuses suggests, an alternative means of gathering information into sets, for the purpose not of proving or testing an idea, but of having a thought, of inventing both in the rhetorical sense of finding something to say and in the creative sense of innovation.

Memory television

Jameson's observation of the absence of memory from the event of television provides a frame for a theory of video. "If anything like critical distance is still possible in film, indeed, it is surely bound up with memory itself. But memory seems to play no role in television, commercial or otherwise (or, I am tempted to say, in postmodernism generally). Nothing here haunts the mind or leaves it afterimages in the manner of the great moments of film. A description of the structural exclusion of memory, then, and of "critical distance," might well lead on into the impossible, namely a theory of video itself: how the thing blocks its own theorization, becoming a theory in its own right" (Jameson, 202). Is it that video technology is exuded from memory, or only that Jameson's preference for modernism inhibits his access to it? Jameson is a modernist ethnographer in the land of postmodernism, doing his best to bracket his science in order to describe the domains of native cognition. One of Jameson's contributions to the theorization of video, then, is just this identification of "memory" as the fundamental element distinguishing video from film (and film theory): "If the contrast here with the memory-structures of Hollywood-type fiction films is stark and obvious, one has the feeling—more difficult to document or to argue—that the gap between this temporal experience and that of experimental film is no less great" (209–10). His negative intuitions are sharp—perceiving, for example, that the concepts of "work" and "author" do not apply easily to the flow of video textuality. But he leaves us on our own for a positive account of the cultural operation of the technology.

A starting point for such an account would be to restate the relation of video to memory, saying not that memory is absent from television, but that television is pure memory—mnemonics without portfolio. The age of modernism was an era of specialization, whose dynamics in everything from art to industry led to purification, to division according to what was proper and specific to a form or an activity. Habermas represents this dynamic when he objects to the postmodernist mixing of genres (confusing philosophy and literature) and types of discourse (confusing the realms of expert culture and the everyday world) (Habermas, *Philosophical Discourse*, 207). In this context, the "implosion" identified by Baudrillard as the feature characterizing postmodernism may be seen as a reversal of the extended drive for separation that characterized modernism ("what modernism put asunder . . ."). A more positive version of "implosion" notable in the technological register of the electronic apparatus is Stewart Brand's observation that all technologies are now converging (computer, video, telephone), a phenomenon aided by digitalization. "With digitalization all of the media become translatable into each other. Computer bits migrate merrily, and they escape from their traditional means of transmission. A movie, phone call, letter, or magazine article may be sent digitally via phone line, coaxial cable, fiber optic cable, microwave, satellite, the broadcast air, or a physical storage medium such as tape or disk. If that's not revolution enough, consider this: with digitalization the content becomes totally plastic—any message, sound, or image may be edited from anything to anything else" (Brand, *The Media Lab*, 18).

A theorization of video requires an understanding of and speculation about this convergence in terms of video and computers as social machines (the electronic apparatus), recognizing that whatever the interest of the current use of video in the mode of leisure, as part of the entertainment industry, that restriction is superficial, a consequence of the modernist tendency to separate out one practice from another, and is not the final or necessary institutionalization for this invention. The question must be: What are the equivalents at the level of institutional practices and personal behaviors of the convergence of electronic technologies? These practices and behaviors must be invented and do not follow automatically from the nature of the equipment.

The suggestion that television is pure memory is based on the grammatological analogy with the invention of other information-storage technologies, such as writing or print, which constitute prostheses for memory. The history of writing shows that print favored a style of logical representation that finally replaced and exceeded the hermetic tradition of the memory theater—the mnemonics of places and active (strong) images derived from ancient rhetoric. What began in ancient oratorical training as a method for memorizing quantities of information by associating it in the imagination with a series of striking images distributed through the rooms of one's home, or along the street of one's community, had evolved by the time of the Renaissance into a theater, a building, designed as an encyclopedia of total knowledge. Such was the Memory Theater of Giuilo Camillo, of which one model was actually built. It was made of wood, large enough for two people to enter, and "marked with many images, and full of little boxes." As one of Camillo's contemporaries explained: "He pretends that all things that the human mind can conceive and which we cannot see with the corporeal eye, after being collected together by diligent meditation may be expressed by certain corporeal signs in such a way that the beholder may at once perceive with his eyes everything that is otherwise hidden in the depths of the human mind. And it is because of this corporeal looking that he calls it a theater" (Frances Yates, *Art of Memory*, 151–52).

Yates notes that the combinatorial systems of the memory theaters subsist in the "mind machines" of today (225). Indeed, the individual who did the most to transform the function of the dynamic mnemonic theater from religious meditation to the scientific exploration of the natural world—Leibniz—is also a major figure in the genealogy of computing. The spinning wheel in the disk drive of computer hardware is the heir of the turning wheels of the hermetic art of memory. From our vantage point, we can see that Camilio's theater has much in common with hypermedia.

Print, and the Ramist method of dialectical outlines, abstract tree diagrams, drove the memory systems out of rhetoric; both were part of the growing predominance of mathematics over images in science. There was simply no way to write and calculate in the image systems, a fact that must be understood as a problem of technology, and not as some inherent incapacity of images to support reasoning. In the era of print, formalized logic replaced associational reasoning. The artificial memory systems were rejected on the following grounds: "The animation of the images, which is the key of memory, is impious because it calls up absurd thoughts—insolent, prodigious, and the like—that stimulate and light up depraved carnal affections. It burdens the mind and memory because it imposes a triple talk on memory instead of one; first (the remembering of) the places; then of the images; then of the thing to be spoken of" (277). Mnemonics was a hog of organic memory; a more efficient method was possible, due to the visualization capacities of the printed page. The flow of programs on television now may be seen as solving the problem of storage in that the images and places of mnemonics need no longer be held in living memory, in the head, but are given over to the machine.

The absurdity and carnality of mnemonics and of television are similar (as testified to by the continuing complaints from various groups monitoring the content of television). The only thing lacking from television, in fact, to make it a full technologization of the memory theater is the expert knowledge associated with the places and images in the mnemonist's imagination. When an audience listened to a public oration—perhaps a sermon on the virtues and vices, or a learned discourse on any order of knowledge—they did not experience the walk through the places filled with grotesque or surreal scenes that was running through the speaker's mind. The experience of television today is just the opposite: the public receives only the stream of absurdities delivered into their living rooms, but none of the expert knowledge (due to the segregation of functions and discourses effected by modernism). The task of a video theory, then, is to show how to reason and calculate with the artificial memory of television, putting in place the one dimension of the new cognition missing from the operation—the knowledge content, that about which one is reasoning by means of these violent, absurd, carnal images. Television producers show us scenes of love and death for the same reason that orators used such scenes as active images in their places of memory—because they are memorable. It is just that we forgot what memorable images are for, or how they might function towards some end other than that of spectacle. With the convergence of video and computers in on-line multimedia stations, soap operas meet disciplinary discourse.

How can one restate the present moment, full of talk about information infrastructure and universal fiber-optic wiring of the American nation, in terms of the apparatus? The technology is hypermedia. The institutional practices (just now being invented) will be some hybrid of education and entertainment. And the new subjectivation? Postliterate people, viewed from this side of the paradigm, appear to be monsters (a term that has more than one meaning).

Out of the fly-bottle

Frances Yates suggests that we have forgotten the mnemonic motivation for the imagery of many an obscure medieval or Renaissance text. In the mnemonic tradition the work of knowledge generated the scene of memory. "What scope for the imagination would be offered in memorizing Boethius's *Consolation of Philosophy*, as advised in a fifteenth-century manuscript! Would the Lady Philosophy have come to life during this attempt, and begun to wander, like some animated Prudence, through the palaces of memory?" (Yates, *Art of Memory*, 123). We have preserved the work of learning, but not the practice of artificial memory that might have been used to operate it, although Dante's *Commedia* offers a glimpse of the possibilities. "That Dante's *Inferno* could be regarded as a kind of memory system for memorizing Hell and its punishments with striking images on orders of places will come as a great shock. . . . In this interpretation, the principles of artificial memory, as understood in the Middle Ages, would stimulate the intense visualization of many similitudes in the intense effort to hold in memory the scheme of salvation, and the complex network of virtues and vices and their rewards and punishments. . . . The *Divine Comedy* would thus become the supreme example of the conversion of an abstract summa into a summa of similitudes with Memory as the converting power, the bridge between the abstraction and the image"(Yates, *Art of Memory*, 95–96). Television puts us in just the opposite relation to knowledge. We have the artificial memory, but none of the works of learning that these scenes might represent. What if the Lady Philosophy were put on *General Hospital*? Aren't the soaps our own *Commedia*, in any case, formulating in concrete terms the abstractions of our own prudence?

A glance at almost any critical commentary on television bears out the possibility that television is not simply "pure" memory, but is in fact remembering something specific—our ideology. "In order to make sense of the *Hart to Hart* segment, the viewer is encouraged to identity with white, male Americans, family-oriented (the Harts are a close married couple, the villain and villains a divided pair), in the prime of life (which is a mix of high physical and sexual attractiveness together with a degree of experience, maturity, and wisdom). These abstract social values or agencies are given concrete representation in the program, and together produce a unified subject position that the reader is invited to occupy in order to make easy, obvious sense of the text. The unity of this subject position is what makes it so acceptable in an individual ideology" (Fiske, *Television Culture*, 50–51). In its separated, entertainment institutionalization as television, video remembers ideology; its flow is a round-the-clock, updated reminder of our collective identity. What happens when this memory converges with the computer? The theory was already noted that the subject positions constructed by the ideology were open to occupation by any member of society regardless of race, ethnicity, gender, sex or class (anyone may be a WASP). What is happening on-line, when the rote memorization of television is made dynamic by telephone and computer, is that individuals are breaking out of the confines of literate selfhood to write with identity. Watch "cyberspace" for the formation of electronic subjectivation. In the MUDs and MOOs of the on-line universe the conventions of this new behavior (replacing literate selfhood) are already being worked out (how many "bodies" one may have, how many anonymous identities, whether or not killing is permitted). The outcome of these experiments eventually will be codified in the primers of whatever replaces the composition courses now required in the universities, in order to learn the procedures for storing and retrieving electronic information (for these behaviors will have to be taught, just as are the behaviors of literacy).

Thinking these thoughts, and others like them, I was watching one evening on my research television set the remake of *The Fly*, again. I wondered if this film could be the *inventio* for a hybrid text on the history of criticism, joining Nietzsche and Wittgenstein with science fiction. Wasn't Wittgenstein trying to relieve philosophy of its metaphysical illusion in the manner of showing a fly the way out of the fly-bottle? In the search for an electronic writing, such metaphors are to philosophy (that practice invented out of literacy) what *dike* was to the actions of Agamemnon. Could this monster fly be Wittgenstein's philosophical insect? Wouldn't Nietzsche's Zarathustra, who philosophized with a hammer, account for the otherwise weakly motivated presence of an anvil near the teleportation machine? If I assigned mnemonically a Nietzschean value to the anvil and a Wittgensteinian value to the fly, would I then have the outline of an abstract argument dramatized in the scene in which the girlfriend's colleague saves her from genetic merger by throwing the anvil into the teleportation machine, leading to the destruction of the scientist?

With video it is not that this story simply makes concrete a system already formulated in the abstract (in the manner of Yates's Dante), but that the story and the abstraction generate a new thought, in the manner of a metaphor (the oral scenario and the literate categories become one).

I recognize through this frame that what crawls out of the machine—part anvil, part insect, part human—is a hieroglyph, a syntagm, in an allegory of prudence. What is it trying to say? Is it the story of television trying to protect the purity of its memory, to ward off the coming merger of social machines that might result in its own disappearance, and even the mutation not only of entertainment but of all institutions in their separateness—school, work, fame? The theory suggests a different response, less hermeneutic, more heuretic: something other, something to do, not something to know or to say.

BIBLIOGRAPHY

Adorno, Theodor. *Minima Moralia*. London: New Left Books, 1973.

Allen, Robert, ed. *Channels of Discourse: Television and Contemporary Criticism*. London: Routledge, 1987.

Anderson, Benedict. *Imagined Communities*. London: Verso, 1983.

Angus, I., and S. Jhally, eds. *Cultural Politics in Contemporary America*. New York: Routledge, 1989.

Apollonio, Umbro, ed. *Futurist Manifestos*. London: Thames and Hudson, 1971

Armes, Roy. *On Video*. London: Routledge, 1988.

Augitus, Daina, and Dan Lander, eds. *Radio Rethink*. Banff, Alberta: Walter Phillips Gallery, Banff Centre of the Arts. Forthcoming.

Balazs, Bela. *Der Geist des Films*. 1930. Reprint, Munich, 1983.

Banham, Reyner. *Theory and Design in the First Machine Age*. Cambridge: MIT Press, 1980.

Barthes, Roland. "The Rhetoric of the Image." In *Image-Music-Text*. Glasgow: Fontana Collins. New York: Hill and Wang, 1977.

Baudelaire, Charles. "Photography" (1859), translated by Jonathan Mayne. In *Photography: Essays & Images*, edited by Beaumont Newhall. New York: Museum of Modern Art, 1980.

Baudrillard, Jean. *Simulations*. New York: Semiotext(e), 1983.

———, Jean. *The Mirror of Production*. St. Louis: Telos Press, 1975.

Baudry, Jean-Louis. "Ideological Effects of the Basic Cinematographic Apparatus." *Film Quarterly* 28, no. 2 (Winter 1974–75).

Bazin, André. *What is Cinema?* Vol. 1. Berkeley: University of California Press, 1967.

Belton, John. *Widescreen Cinema*. Cambridge: Harvard University Press, 1992.

Benedikt, Michael, ed. *Cyberspace: First Steps*. Cambridge: MIT Press, 1991.

Benjamin, Jessica. *The Bonds of Love: Psychoanalysis, Feminism, and the Problem of Domination*. New York: Pantheon Books, 1988.

Bennett, Tony. "A Thousand and One Troubles: Blackpool Pleasure Beach." In *Formations of Pleasure*. London: Routledge & Kegan Paul, 1983.

Bennington, Geoffrey. *Jacques Derrida*. Chicago: University of Chicago Press, 1993.

Binder, Carl. "Hypertext Design Issues." *Performance Improvement Quarterly* 2, no. 3 (1985).

Bolter, David. *Turing's Man: Western Culture in the Computer Age*. Harmondsworth: Penguin, 1986.

Book for the Unstable Media. s-Hertogenbosch: Stichting V2, 1992.

Bordwell, David, and Kristin Thompson. *Film Art: An Introduction*. New York: Knopf, 1986.

Bossen, Howard. "Zone 5, Photojournalism, Ethics and the Electronic Age." *Studies in Visual Communication* (University of Pennsylvania) 11, no. 3 (Summer 1985).

Braidotti, Rosi. "Organs Without Bodies." In *Differences*, 1988.

Brand, Stewart. *The Media Lab: Inventing the Future at MIT*. New York: Penguin, 1988.

Broughton, John. "Computers in the Fantasies of Young Adults." In *Individual, Society, and Communication*, edited by Robert Reiber. New York: Cambridge University Press, 1989.

Bryson, Norman. *Vision and Painting*. New Haven: Yale University Press, 1983.

Bukatman, Scott. *Terminal Identity: The Virtual Subject in Postmodern Science Fiction*. Durham, N.C.: Duke University Press, 1993.

Bürger, Peter. *Theory of the Avant-Garde*. Translated by Michael Shaw. Minneapolis: University of Minnesota Press, 1984.

Burroughs, William, and Brion Gysin. "The Cut-up Method of Brion Gysin." In *The Third Mind*. New York: Viking Press, 1978.

Cage, John. *Silence*. Middletown, Conn.: Wesleyan University Press, 1973.

———, ed. *Richard Kostelanetz*. New York: Praeger, 1968.

Carey, James. "Technology and Ideology: The Case of the Telegraph." In *Communication as Culture*. Boston: Unwin, Hyman, 1989.

Castells, Manuel. *The Informational City*. Cambridge: Basil Blackwell, 1989.

Catano, James V. "Poetry and Computers: Experimenting with the Communal Text." *Computers and the Humanities* 13 (1979).

Cavalaro, A., R. Harley, L. Wallace, and M. Wark, editors. *Cultural Diversity in the Global Village: the Third Intrnational Symposium on Electronic Art*. Australian Network for Art & Technology, Adelaide, 1992.

Cha, Theresa Hak Kyung, ed. *Apparatus*. New York: Tanam, 1980.

Contemporary Sound Arts. *Essays in Sound* (Sydney) 1 (Fall 1992).

Cooley, Mike. *Architect or Bee? The Human Price of Technology.* London: Hogarth Press, 1987.

Couchot, Edmond. "La Synthèse Numérique de l'Image," In *Traverses/26.* Paris: Centre Georges Pompidou, 1983.

Crary, Jonathan. *Techniques of the Observer: On Vision and Modernity in the Nineteenth Century.* Cambridge: MIT Press 1992.

Crary, Jonathan, and Sanford Kwinter, eds. *Incorporations.* New York: Zone Books, 1992.

Critical Art Ensemble. "Plagiarism is Necessary." *Real Life Magazine* 20 (Spring 1990).

Cubitt, Sean. *Timeshift: On Video Culture.* London: Routledge, 1991.

Cumings, Bruce. *War and Television.* New York: Verso, 1992.

Darrah, William C. *The World of Stereographs.* Gettysburg, Pa.: W.C. Darrah, 1977.

Davis, Mike. *City of Quartz.* London: Verso, 1991.

Debord, Guy. *Society of the Spectacle.* Detroit: Black and Red, 1983.

de Certeau, Michel. "Arts of dying/Anti-mystical writing." In *Le Macchine Celebi/The Bachelor Machine,* edited by Jean Clair and Harald Szeemann. Venice: Alfieri, edizioni d'arte, 1975.

———, *Heterologies: Discourse on the Other.* Minneapolis: University of Minnesota Press, 1986.

de Jonge, Alex. *Nightmare Culture: Lautréamont and "Les Chants de Maldoror."* New York: St. Martin's Press, 1973..

Delanda, Manuel. *War in the Age of Intelligent Machines.* New York: Swerve Editions, Zone Books, MIT Press, 1991.

Deleuze, Gilles, and Felix Guattari. *Nomadology: The War Machine.* New York: Semiotext(e), 1986.

———. *Anti-Oedipus: Capitalism and Schizophrenia.* Minneapolis: University of Minnesota Press, 1983. London, Athlone Press, 1984.

Derrida, Jacques. *Margins of Philosophy.* Chicago: University of Chicago Press, 1982.

Diliberto, John. "Pierre Schaeffer and Pierre Henry: Pioneers in Sampling." *Electronic Musician,* December 1986.

Douglas, Susan. "Amateur Operators and American Broadcasting: Shaping the Future of Radio." In *Imagining Tomorrow,* edited by Joseph J. Corn. Cambridge: MIT Press, 1987.

Dreyfus, Hubert. *What Computers Still Can't Do: A Critique of Artificial Reason.* Cambridge: MIT Press, 1992.

Duchamp, Marcel. *Marcel Duchamp.* Edited by Anne d'Harnoncourt and Kynaston McShine. New York: Museum of Modern Art, 1973.

Dunn, Douglas, ed. *Eigenwelt der Apparate-Welt/Pioneers of Electronic Art.* Linz, Austria: Ars Electronica, 1992.

Dyson, Frances. "Circuits of the Voice." *MusicWorks Journal* 53.

Eco, Umberto, and Thomas A. Sebeok, eds. *The Sign of Three: Dupin, Holmes, Peirce.* Bloomington: Indiana University Press, 1983.

Elsaesser, Thomas, and Adam Baker, eds. *Early Cinema: Space, Frame, Narrative.* London: British Film Institute, 1990.

Feyerabend, Paul. *Against Method.* London: Verso, 1975-80.

Fielding, Raymond. "Hale's Tours: Ultrarealism in the Pre-1910 Motion Picture." In *Film Before Film*, edited by John L. Fell. Berkeley: University of California Press, 1983.

Fiske, John. *Television Culture.* London: Methuen, 1987.

Flamm, Kenneth. *Creating the Computer: Government, Industry and High Technology.* Washington, D.C.: Brookings Institute, 1988.

———. *Targeting the Computer: Government Support and International Competition.* Washington, D.C.: Brookings Institute, 1988.

Flitterman-Lewis, Sandy. "Psychoanalysis, Film, and Television." In *Channels of Discourse*, edited by Robert C. Allen. Chapel Hill N.C., 1987.

Forester, John, ed. *Critical Theory and Public Life.* Cambridge: MIT Press, 1985.

Foss, Paul. "Theatrum Nondum Cogitorum." In *The Foreign Bodies Papers.* Local Consumption Series 1. Sydney, 1981.

Foster, Hal, ed. *Vision and Visuality.* Seattle: Pub Bay Press, 1988.

Foucault, Michel. *Discipline and Punish.* Harmondsworth: Penguin Books, 1977.

Foucault, Michel. "What is an Author?" In *Critical Theory Since 1965*, edited by Hazard Adams and Leroy Searle. Tallahassee: Florida State University Press, 1988.

Friedman, Alan J., and Carol C. Donley. *Einstein as Myth and Muse.* Cambridge: Cambridge University Press, 1985.

Gallop, Jane. *Thinking Through the Body.* New York: Columbia University Press, 1989.

Gibson, Ross. *South of the West.* Bloomington: Indiana University Press, 1992.

Gomery, Douglas. *Shared Pleasures: A History of Movie Presentation in the United States.* Madison: University of Wisconsin Press, 1992.

Goodman, Cynthia. *Digital Visions.* New York: Harry N. Abrams, 1987.

Graham, Allison. "Journey to the Center of the Fifties: The Cult of Banality." In *The Cult Film Experience: Beyond All Reason*, edited by J. P. Telotte. Austin: Texas Press, 1991.

Gramsci, Antonio. *Selections from the Prison Notebooks.* New York: International Publishers, 1973.

Gray, Chris H. "The Cyborg Soldier." In *Cyborg Worlds*, edited by Les Levidow and Kevin Robins. London: Free Association Books, 1989.

Grossberg, L., C. Nelson, and P. Treichler, eds. *Cultural Studies*. New York: Routledge,1992.

Grossberg, Lawrence. *We Gotta Get Out of This Place: Popular Conservatism and Postmodern Culture*. New York: Routledge, 1992.

Habermas, Jürgen. *The Philosophical Discourse of Modernity: Twelve Lectures*. Translated by Frederick Lawrence. Cambridge: Polity Press, 1987.

Hall, Doug, and Sally Jo Fifer, eds. *Illuminating Video: An Essential Guide to Video Art*. New York: Aperture, n.d.

Hall, Stuart. "Cultural Studies and its Theoretical Legacies." In *Cultural Studies*, edited by Lawrence Grossberg et al. New York: Routledge, 1992.

Hanhardt, John G., ed. *Video Culture: A Critical Investigation*. Rochester, N.Y.: Visual Studies Workshop, 1986.

Haraway, Donna J. "A Manifesto for Cyborgs: Science, Technology, and Socialist Feminism in the 1980's." *Socialist Review* 80 (1985).

———. *Simians, Cyborgs, and Women: The Reinvention of Nature*. New York: Routledge, 1991.

Harley, Ross, ed. *Art and Cyberculture*. Special issue of *Media Information Australia* 69 (August 1993).

Havelock, Eric A. *The Muse Learns to Write: Reflections on Orality and Literacy from Antiquity to the Present*. New Haven: Yale University Press, 1986.

Hayles, Katherine. *Chaos Bound*. Ithaca: Cornell University Press, 1990.

Hayward, Philip, and Tana Wollen, eds. *Future Visions: New Technologies of the Screen*. London: British Film Institute, 1993.

Hayward, Philip, ed. *Culture, Technology and Creativity*. London: John Libbey, 1990.

Hegel, G. W. F. *The Philosophy of History*. Buffalo, N.Y.: Prometheus Books, 1991.

Heim, Michael. *The Metaphysics of Virtual Reality*. New York: Oxford University Press, 1993.

Hodgkinson, Tim. Interview with Pierre Schaeffer. *Re Records Quarterly Magazine* 2, no. 1 (March 1987).

Holmes, Oliver Wendell. "The Stereoscope and the Stereograph" (1859). Reprinted in *Photography: Essays & Images*, edited by Beaumont Newhall. New York: Museum of Modern Art, 1980.

Huhtamo, Erkki. "It is interactive, but is it art?" In *Machine Culture*, edited by Simon Penny. Visual Proceedings, ACM Siggraph 1993.

Hutcheon, Linda. *The Politics of Postmodernism*. London: Routledge, 1989.

IDEA (International Directory of Electronic Arts). *Chaos*. Paris, 1992.

Ihde, Don. *Technology and the Lifeworld: From Garden to Earth.* Bloomington: Indiana University Press, 1990.

Innes, Harold. *The Bias of Communication.* Toronto: Toronto University Press, 1992.

Irigaray, Luce. *Speculum of the Other Woman.* Translated by Gillian C. Gill. Ithaca: Cornell University Press, 1985.

———. *This Sex Which is Not One.* Translated by Catherine Porter. Ithaca: Cornell University Press, 1985.

Jacka, Elizabeth, ed. *Continental Shift: Globalisation and Culture,* Local Consumption Publications. Sydney, 1993.

Jacobson, Linda. "BattleTech's New Beachheads." *Wired* 1, no. 3(July–August 1993).

Jameson, Fredric. "Reading Without Interpretation: Post Modernism and the Video-Text." In *The Linguistics of Writing: Arguments Between Language and Literature,* edited by Nigel Fabb et al. New York: Methuen, 1987.

Jonassen, David, and Brent G. Wilson. "Hypertext and Instructional Design: Some Preliminary Guidelines." *Performance Improvement Quarterly* 2, no. 3 (1989).

Kahn, Douglas, and Gregory Whitehead, eds. *Wireless Imagination: Sound Radio and the Avant-Garde.* Cambridge: MIT Press, 1992.

Kahn, Douglas, and Gregory Whitehead, eds. "Acoustic Sculpture, Deboned Voices." *Public* 4, no. 5 (1991).

Kasson, John. *Amusing the Millions: Coney Island at the Turn of the Century.* New York: Hill and Wang, 1978.

Keulen, Wim van. *3D Imagics: A Stereoscopic Guide to the 3D Past and its Magic Images,1838–1900.* AA Borger, The Netherlands: 3-D Book Productions, 1990.

Klein, Norman M. "Audience Culture and the Video Screen." In Hall and Fifer, *Illuminating Video: An Essential Guide to Video Art.* New York: Aperture, n.d.

Knabb, Ken, ed. *Situationist International Anthology.* Berkeley, Calif.: Bureau of Public Secrets,1981.

Krauss, Rosalind E. *The Originality of the Avant-Garde and Other Myths.* Cambridge: MIT Press, 1986.

Krupnick, Mark, ed. *Displacement: Derrida and After.* Bloomington: Indiana University Press, 1987.

Lander, Dan, and Micah Lexier, eds. *Sound by Artists.* Toronto: Art Metropole, 1990.

Lander, Dan, ed. "Radiophonies and Other Phonies." *Musicworks* (Toronto) 53 (Fall 1992).

Landow, George P. "Changing Texts, Changing Readers: Hypertext in Literary Education, Criticism, and Scholarship." In *Reorientations: Critical Theo-*

ries & Pedagogies, edited by Bruce Henrickson and Thais E. Morgan. Urbana and Chicago: University of Illinois Press, 1990.

Landow, George. *Hypertext: The Convergence of Contemporary Critical Theory and Technology.* Baltimore: Johns Hopkins University Press, 1992.

Laurel, Brenda, ed. *The Art of Human-Computer Interface Design.* Edited by Brenda Laurel. Reading, Mass.: Addison Wesley, 1990.

Lefebvre, Henri. *Everyday Life in the Modern World.* New Brunswick, N.J.: Transaction Books, 1984.

Lovejoy, Margot. *Postmodern Currents: Art and Artists in the Age of Electronic Media.* Ann Arbor, Mich.: UMI Research, 1989.

Lutembi. "Contribution á une étude des sources de la Cantatrice Chauve." *Cahiers du Pataphysique,* 1953.

Lyotard, Jean-François. *The Postmodern Condition: A Report on Knowledge.* Translated by Geoff Bennington and Brian Massumi. Minneapolis: University of Minnesota Press, 1984.

Marcus, Greil. *Dead Elvis: A Chronicle of a Cultural Obsession.* New York: Doubleday, 1991.

Marvin, Carolyn. *When Old Technologies Were New.* Oxford: Oxford University Press, 1988

Mattelart, A., and M. Mattelart. *Rethinking Media Theory: Signposts and New Directions.* Minneapolis: University of Minnesota Press, 1992.

Mattelart, Armand, and Hector Schmucler. *Communication and Information Technologies: Freedom of Choice for Latin America?* Translated from the French by David Buxton. Norwood, N.J.: Ablex, 1985.

McCaffery, Larry, ed. *Storming the Reality Studio: A Casebook of Cyberpunk and Postmodern Fiction.* Durham, N.C.: Duke University Press, 1991.

McLuhan, Marshall, and Quentin Fiore. *The Medium is the Message.* New York: Bantam, 1967.

McNeil, Maureen, ed. *Gender and Expertise.* London: Free Association Books, 1987.

Mellencamp, Patricia. *Indiscretions: Avant-Garde Film, Video, and Feminism.* Bloomington: Indiana University Press, 1990.

Melzer, Annabelle Henkin. "The Dada Actor and Performance Theory." In *The Art of Performance: A Critical Anthology.* New York: Dutton, 1984.

Meyrowitz, Joshua. *No Sense of Place: The Impact of Electronic Media on Social Behaviour.* New York: Oxford University Press, 1985.

Michaels, Eric. *For a Cultural Future: Francis Jupurrurla Makes TV at Yuendumu.* Artspace Art & Criticism Monograph Series. Sydney, 1987.

Morison, Elting. *Men, Machines, and Modern Times.* Cambridge: MIT Press, 1984.

Morris, Meaghan. *The Pirate's Fiancée.* London: Verso, 1988.

Morse, Margaret. "Television Graphics and the Body: Words on the Move."

Paper delivered at the meeting "Television and the Body," Society for Cinema Studies, Montreal, 1987.

Mowlana, Hamid. *The Passing of Modernity: Communication and the Transformation of Society.* New York: Longman, 1990.

Nietzsche, Friedrich. *The Will to Power.* Translated by Walter Kaufmann and R. J. Hollingdale. New York: Vintage Books, 1968.

———. "Twilight of the Idols." In *The Portable Nietzsche*, edited and translated by Walter Kaufmann. New York: Viking, 1968.

Nye, David E. *Electrifying America. Social Meanings of a New Technology.* Cambridge: MIT Press, 1992.

O'Brien, Flann. *The Third Policeman.* 1940. New York: New American Library, 1976.

Olalquiaga, Celeste. *Megalopolis: Contemporary Cultural Sensibilities.* Minneapolis: University of Minnesota Press, 1992.

Penley, Constance, and Andrew Ross, eds. *TechnoCulture.* Minneapolis: University of Minnesota Press, 1991.

Penley, Constance. "Feminism, Film Theory and the Bachelor Machines." *m/f* 10 (1985).

Penny, Simon."Virtual Bodybuilding." *Media Information Australia* 69 (August 1993).

———. "Kinetics, Cybernetics, Art Practice in the Age of the Thinking Machine."In *Irrelevant Ethics: Notes on Art Practice in a Technological Context*, edited by Simon Penny. Sydney: Virtual Object, 1988.

———. "The Intelligent Machine as Anti-Christ." in *SISEA 1990 Proceedings.* Groningen, Netherlands, 1990.

———. "Pre-history of VR." In *Through the Looking Glass: Artists' First Encounter with Virtual Reality*, edited by Janine Cirincione and Brian D'Amato. Jupiter, Fla.: Softworlds, 1992.

Poster, Mark. *The Mode of Information: Poststructuralism and Social Context.* Chicago: University of Chicago Press,1990.

Pourroy, Janine. "Through the Proscenium Arch." *Cinefex* 46 (May 1991).

Pratt, George C. *Spellbound in Darkness: A History of the Silent Film*, Greenwich, Conn.: New York Graphic Society, 1973.

Public (Toronto) 4/5 (1990/91).

Rabinowitz, Lauren. "Temptations of Pleasure: Nickelodeons, Amusement Parks and the Sights of Female Sexuality." *Camera Obscura* 23 (May 1990).

Ramsaye, Terry. *A Million and One Nights: A History of the Motion Picture Through 1925.* 1926 New York: Simon & Schuster, 1986.

Ray, Robert B. *A Certain Tendency of the Hollywood Cinema: 1930–1980.* Princeton: Princeton University Press, 1985.

Reisman, Ron. "A Brief Introduction to the Art of Flight Simulation." In *Ars*

Electronica 1990, Band II: *Virtuelle Welten*. Herausgegeben von Gottfried Hattinger et al. Linz, Austria: Veritas-Verlag, 1990.

Richards, Catherine, and Nell Tenhaaf, eds. *Virtual Seminar on the BioApparatus* (Banff, Alberta: The Banff Centre, 1991).

Robertson, Roland. *Globalisation: Social Theory and Global Culture*. London: Sage Books, 1992.

Rogers, Paul. "The Myth of the Clean War." In *Incorporations*, Zone 6, edited by Jonathan Crary and Sanford Kwinter. New York: Urzone, 1992.

Rosenthal, Pam. "Jacked In: Fordism, Cyberpunk, Marxism." *Socialist Review*, January-March 1991.

Ross, Andrew. *Strange Weather: Culture, Science and Technology in the Age of Limits*. London: Verso, 1991.

Rossi, Paolo. *Philosophy, Technology and the Arts in the Early Modern Era*. New York: Harper Torchbooks, 1970.

Roszak, Theodore. *The Cult of Information*. New York: Patheon Books, 1986.

Roth, Nancy. "Art's New Address." *The Techno/Logical Imagination: Machines in the Garden of Art*. Minneapolis: Intermedia Arts Minnesota, 1989.

Rötzer, Florian. "Observers and pictures of the first, second and n-th order." In *Die Welt von Innen: Endo und Nano*, edited by Karl Gerbel and Peter Weibel. Linz: Ars Electronica '92 / PVS Verlager, 1992.

Rothschild, Joan, ed., *Machina Ex Dea: Feminist Perspectives on Technology*. New York: Pergamon Press, 1983.

Sakane, Itsuo. *Catalogue: Wonderland of Science-Art*. Committee for Kanagawa International Art & Science Exhibition, 1989.

Schivelbusch, Wolfgang. *Geschichte der Eisenbahn*. 1977 Frankfurt am Main: Fischer Taschenbuch Verlag, 1989.

———. *The Railway Journey: The Industrialisation of Time and Space in the Nineteenth Century*. Hamburg: Berg, 1986.

Schodt, Fredrik. *Inside the Robot Kingdom: Japan, Mechatronics and the Coming Robotopia*. Tokyo: Kodansha International, 1986.

Science as Culture. Free Association Books, London

Seltzer, Mark. *Bodies and Machines*. New York: Routledge, 1992.

Shamberg, Michael, and Raindance Corporation. *Guerrilla Television*. New York: Holt, Rinehart and Winston, 1971.

Shaw, Jeffrey. *The Legible City*. Amsterdam: Colophon, 1990.

Slotkin, Richard. *The Fatal Environment: The Myth of the Frontier in the Age of Industrialization*. Middletown, Conn.: Wesleyan University Press, 1985.

Snow, C.P. *The Two Cultures*. N.p., Cambridge University Press, 1959.

———. *The Two Cultures: A Second Look*. New York: Mentor, 1963.

Sobchack, Vivian. "New Age Mutant Ninja Hackers." *Artforum*, April 1991.

Spiegel, Lynn. *Make Room for TV: Television and the Family Ideal in Postwar*

America. Chicago: University of Chicago Press, 1992.

Sterne, Laurence. *The Life and Opinions of Tristram Shandy*. Hammondsworth: Penguin Books, 1986.

Stockhausen, Karlheinz. "Electronic and instrumental music." *Die Reihe*, 1961.

Stone, Allucquere Roseanne. "Virtual Systems." In *Incorporations*, Zone 6., edited by Jonathan Crary & Sanford Kwinter. New York: Urzone, 1992.

Taussig, Michael. *Mimesis and Alterity: A Particular History of the Senses*. New York: Routledge, 1993.

————. *Shamanism, Colonialism, and the Wild Man: A Study in Terror and Healing*. Chicago: University of Chicago Press, 1987.

Thoreau, H. D. *Walden*. Edited by Owen Thomas. New York: Norton, 1966.

Tichi, Cecelia. *Electronic Hearth: Creating an American Television Culture*. New York: Oxford University Press, 1991.

Toulet, Emmanuelle: *Cinematographe, invention du siècle*. Paris: Gallimard/Reunion des musées nationaux, 1988.

Trinh, T. Minh-ha. *Women, Native, Other: Writing Postcoloniality and Feminism*. Bloomington: Indiana University Press, 1989.

Tuer, Dot. "Video in Drag: Trans-sexing the Feminine." *Parrallégram* 12, no. 3 (February/March 1988).

Turim, Maureen. *Flashbacks In Film: Memory and History*. New York: Routledge, 1989.

Turkle, Sherry. *The Second Self: Computers and the Human Spirit*. London: Granada, 1984.

Vince, John. "Commander: A Real-time Interactive Leisure Simulator." *Imagina 93: Actes, Proceedings*. Bry-sur-Marne: INA, 1993.

Virillo, Paul. "The Overexposed City." *Zone 1/2*, n.d.

————. *War and Cinema*.

"VNS Manifesto." *Art & Text* 42 (May 1992).

Wallace, Michele. *Black Macho and the Myth of the Superwoman*. London: Verso, 1990.

Wallis, Brian, ed. *Art After Modernism: Rethinking Representation*. Boston: Godine, 1984.

Wark, McKenzie. "From Fordism to Sonyism: Perverse Readings of the New World Order." *New Formations* 16 (1992).

————. "Japan, Postmodernism and Beyond." *Tension* 22 (August 1990).

————. "News Bites: War TV in the Gulf." *Meanjin* 50 (1991).

————. "On Technological Time: Cruising Virilio's Overexposed City." *Arena* 83 (1988).

————. "Speaking Trajectories: Meaghan Morris, Antipodean Theory and Australian Cultural Studies." *Cultural Studies* 6, no. 3 (October 1992).

Wark, McKenzie. "The Logistics of Perception." *Meanjin* 49, 1 (Autumn 1990).

———. "Vectors of Memory... Seeds of Fire: The Western Media and the Beijing Demonstration." *New Formations* 10 (Spring 1990).

———. *Virtual Geography: Living with Global Media Events.* Bloomington: Indiana University Press, 1994. (Forthcoming.

Wilden, Anthony. "Lacan and the Discourse of the Other." In *Jacques Lacan. Speech and Language In Psychoanalysis* translated by Anthony Wilden. Baltimore: Johns Hopkins University Press, 1968.

Williams, Linda. *Hard Core: Power, Pleasure, and the "Frenzy of the Visible."* Berkeley and Los Angeles: University of California Press, 1989.

Williams, Raymond. *Problems in Materialism and Culture.* London: Verso, 1980.

———. *Television: Technology and Cultural Form.* London: Fontana, 1974.

Winner, Langdon. *Autonomous Technology: Technics-Out-of-Control as a Theme in Political Thought.* Cambridge: MIT Press, 1978.

Wollen, Peter . "Bitter Victory: The Art and Politics of the Situationist International." In *On The Passage of a Few People through a Brief Moment in Time: The Situationist International 1957-1972*, edited by Elizabeth Sussman. Cambridge: MIT Press,1989.

Yates, Frances A. *The Art of Memory.* Chicago: University of Chicago Press, 1966.

Youngblood, Gene. *Expanded Cinema*, New York: E. P. Dutton 1970.

Yourcenar, Marguerite. *The Abyss.* New York: Farrar, Straus, and Giroux, 1981.

Zelizer, Barbie. *Covering the Body: The Kennedy Assassination, the Media, and the Shaping of Collective Memory.* Chicago: University of Chicago Press, 1992.

Zukav, Gary. "Towards a Genealogy of the Radio Voice." In *Radio Rethink.* Banff: Walter Phillips Gallery. Forthcoming.

———. "Transmitter Bodies: Aurality, Corporeality, Cuts and Signals." In *New Music Articles 8*, edited by F. Dyson. Melbourne: NMA Publications.

CONTRIBUTORS

Critical Art Ensemble

Critical Art Ensemble (CAE) is a collective of six artists of various specializations who are committed to the exploration and examination of the intersections between art, critical theory, and technology. CAE was formed in the decentralized zone in 1987.

Frances Dyson

Frances Dyson is an Australian media artist and writer based in Arizona, U.S.A., who specializes in audio art and the emerging field of sound theory. She has taught media production and theory at universities in Australia and the United States and has a Ph.D in Humanities from the University of Technology, Sydney. Her radio artworks, sound installations, and theoretical writings have been broadcast, exhibited, and published in Australia, Europe, North America, and Japan. They include *Telesthesia* (installation: Walter McBean Gallery, San Francisco); *Golf Wash* (installation: Kawasaki Museum, Tokyo); "The Ear that Would Hear Sounds in Themselves: John Cage, 1935–65" (in *Wireless Imagination: Sound, Radio and the Avant Garde*, edited by Douglas Kahn, MIT Press); "Romancing the Signal: Virtual Sound in the Tropology of Virtual Realities" (in *Immersed in Technology*, Walter Phillips Gallery and MIT Press). Currently she is publishing her doctoral dissertation, entitled "The Silencing of Sound: Philosophy, Technology, Media," and coediting an anthology on women and cyberspace.

Erkki Huhtamo

Erkki Huhtamo, born in Helsinki in 1958, received his M.A. from the University of Turku, Finland. He is currently acting as professor of media studies, University of Lapland, Rovaniemi, Finland. He lectures about the history of audiovisuality at the University of Art and Design, Helsinki, and elsewhere. He has edited more than ten books and written extensively about the cultural history of audiovisuality and about interactive media and art. His writings have been published in ten languages. He has also curated three international exhibitions of interactive art as part of the MuuMedia Festival (Helsinki and Espoo, Finland). He was in the "Machine Culture: The Virtual Frontier" exhibition committee (Siggraph 1993) and contributed an essay to the "Machine Culture" catalog. Currently he is involved with organizing the Fifth International Symposium on Electronic Arts (ISEA 94), Helsinki, Finland.

Douglas Kahn

Douglas Kahn, artist, writer, and Associate Professor of Media Arts at Arizona State University West, Phoenix. His essays on the history and theory of sound in the arts have appeared in the journals *October* (New York), *Art & Test* (Sydney), *Public* (Toronto), *Musicworks* (Toronto), and *Music Today Biannual* (Tokyo) and in the books *Sound by Artists* (Toronto: Art Metropole, 1990), *In the Spirit of Fluxus* (Minneapolis: Walker Art Center, 1993) and *Radio Rethink* (Banff: Walter Phillips Gallery, 1994). He has lectured internationally. He is coeditor of *Wireless Imagination: Sound, Radio and the Avant-garde* (Cambridge: MIT Press, 1992) and author of *John Heartfield: Art & Mass Media* (New York: Tanam Press, 1985). He has recently collaborated on the installations *Telesthesia* (San Francisco, 1991), *The Call (of the Product)* (Phoenix, 1993) and *Golf Wash* (Tokyo, 1993). He has been Media Arts Resident at the Banff Centre for the Arts (Summer 1993).

George Legrady

George Legrady was born in Budapest in 1950 and immigrated to Montreal in 1956. He attended Loyola College (Montreal) and Goddard College, and received an M.F.A. from the San Francisco Art Institute in 1976. He is Associate Professor in Information Arts/Conceptual Design in the Department of Art at San Francisco State University, an art program that integrates cultural theory and advanced applications in digital technology within the contexts of conceptual art and contemporary art practice. His previous full-time appointments include those at the University of Southern California, Cal Arts, and the University of Western Ontario. Legrady has received the USC Innovative Teaching Award; Prix Ars Electronica, Austria, and numerous awards from the Canada Council. Legrady's research and artwork began in a conceptual approach to photographic representation. Since the mid-eighties, his projects have focused on the cultural and theoretical implications of digital computer media and its impact on our belief in the image.

Simon Penny

Simon Penny has worked in electronic media arts as an artist, writer, and teacher for over ten years, and has lectured, published, and exhibited widely in Australia, Europe, the U.S.A., and elsewhere. His art practice takes the form of electronically controlled interactive machine and media installations that simultaneously utilize and critique emerging technologies. Current projects include the construction of robotic art works with voice recognition and voice synthesis capabilities, and a development proposal for the world's first virtual tourist attraction, using virtual reality technologies. He curated the "Machine Culture," a survey exhibition of interactive art, for Siggraph '93 in Anaheim in August 1993. He studied sculpture at the South Australian School of Art and Sydney College of the Arts, Australia, and was awarded an International Studio at PS1, New York, for the year of 1983–84. After coming to Carnegie Mellon University in Pittsburgh in 1989 to take up a visiting artist position, he spent three years at the University of Florida establishing a new program called Electronic Intermedia. In August 1993 he joined the faculty at Carnegie Mellon as Associate Professor of Art and Robotics, a joint position between the Department of Art and the School of Computer Science.

David Rokeby

David Rokeby is an interactive installation artist based in Toronto, Canada. He evolved his interactive sound installations as a way of integrating his disparate interests in visual art, dance, music, electronics, and philosophy. His work has been exhibited in shows across Canada, the United States, Europe, and Japan, including the Venice Biennale in 1986, Festival des Arts Electroniques (France) in 1988, the Siggraph '88 Art Show (USA), Kunst und Electronik

(Germany) in 1989, the Kanagawa International Arts Festival (Japan) in 1990, and Ars Electronica (Austria) in 1991. He was awarded the first Petro-Canada Award for Media Arts in 1988 and Prix Ars Electronica Award of Distinction for Interactive Art (Austria) in 1991. He collaborated with German theater director Martin Politowski, creating interactive acoustic stage settings for a provocative staging of *Ein Sommernachtstraum* (*A Midsummer Night's Dream*) in Munich. He recently created a large interactive video installation, *Silicon Remembers Carbon*, for the central exhibition of the Mediale in Hamburg. He is currently working on a new installation entitled *The Giver of Names*.

Florian Rötzer

Florian Rötzer, born 1953, studied philosophy and lives as a freelance writer, journalist, and editor in Munich, Germany. He has written many articles about art and media theory, is a member of the jury of the Prix Ars Electronica for interactive art, Linz, and for the Medienkunstpreis, Center of Art and Media Technology, Karlsruhe. He is a regular contributor to *Kunstforum International*, Cologne. He designed the concept and organization for several conferences: "Strategies of Fiction," Frankfurt 1990; "Cyberspace—On the way to the Digital Gesamtkunstwerk," Munich 1991; "Media–Art–Critic," Munich 1993; "From Simulation to Stimulation," Graz 1993; and "Artificial Games," Munich 1993. His publications include: *Französische Philosophen im Gesprach*, Munich 1986; *Denken, das an der Zeit ist*, Frankfurt 1987; *Digitaler Schein*, Frankfurt 1990; *Kunst machen*, Munich 1990; *Strategien des Scheins*, Munich, 1991; and *Philosophen—Gesprach zur Kunst*, Munich 1992.

David Tafler

David Tafler is a member of the Media Studies faculty of Widener University near Philadelphia, Pennsylvania. He has written extensively on interactive media and new technologies. His articles include: "I remember television . . .," *From Receiver to Remote Control;* "Der Blick und der Spring" (The look and the leap), *Kunstforum;* "The Circular Text," *Journal of Film and Video;* "Autonomy/Community: Marginality and the New Interactive Cinema," *Cinematograph;* "Beyond Narrative: Notes toward a Theory of Interactive Cinema," *Millennium Film Journal;* and "The Techno-Cultural Interface: Tracking the boundaries of high-tech and traditional cultures" (co-edited with Peter d'Agostino),

Media Information Australia. He has recently completed a book co-edited with Peter d'Agostino titled *TRANSMISSION... Toward a Post-Television Culture.*

Nell Tenhaaf

Nell Tenhaaf is an artist who works with electronic media, new technologies, and drawing. In the past few years her work, both in visual art and in writing, has addressed the "hidden texts" of scientific representations and relationships between different kinds of knowledge about the body. She has exhibited her work across Canada and in Europe, published numerous articles and reviews, and currently teaches in the Visual Arts Department of the University of Ottawa. In 1991, she co-organized a seminar at the Banff Centre for the Arts. She lives in Montreal, where she is represented by Galerie Lallouz & Watterson.

Gregory Ulmer

Gregory L. Ulmer, Professor of English and Media Studies at the University of Florida, Gainesville, is the author of *Applied Grammatology* (1985), *Teletheory* (1989), and *Heuretics: The Logic of Invention* (1994). He has produced videotapes with Paper Tiger Television and the Critical Art Ensemble. He is coordinator of the Florida Research Ensemble project for a new consultancy, and is an officer in the Florida Media Arts Center (FMAC). His current project is an FMAC experiment with Gainesville as an electronic community.

McKenzie Wark

McKenzie Wark lectures in communications at Macquarie University, Australia. He writes a column for *The Australian* newspaper on new cultural phenomena. His essays on media and culture have appeared in the journals *Cultural Studies, New Formations, Impulse, Art & Text,* and *21*C: The Magazine of the Australian Commission for the Future.* His book *Logic Bombs: Living with Global Media Events* will appear in 1994.

Richard Wright

Richard Wright is an artist working in electronic media, particularly computer animation. After originally training as a painter, he received a B.A. in Fine Art from Winchester School of Art and an M.A. in Computing in Design from Middlesex University. His work explores the area between the organic and inorganic, the sensual body and "artificial life," and the living computer and dead nature. He has written articles and essays about computer imagery in science and art for books and for magazines such as *Mediamatic*, and exhibition catalogs such as the Siggraph art shows. His latest project is a computer animation about Louis XIV and the technology of the imagination, which he is producing with Jason White. He is currently Lecturer in Computer Graphics at London Guildhall University (formally City of London Polytechnic),where he is researching a book on the cultural implications of scientific visualization. He lives in London, is a semivegetarian (white meat only), and likes horror movies.

INDEX